JANE WYMAN

○ ○ ○ ○ ○ ○ ○ ○ ○ ○ ○ ○ ○ ○ ○ ○ ○ ○ ○ ○

JANE WYMAN

A BIOGRAPHY

JOE MORELLA &
EDWARD Z. EPSTEIN

DELACORTE PRESS 🆅 NEW YORK

Published by
Delacorte Press
1 Dag Hammarskjold Plaza
New York, N.Y. 10017

To Chris Kachulis

Manufactured in the United States of America

First printing

Designed by Judith Neuman

Library of Congress Cataloging in Publication Data
Morella, Joe.
   Jane Wyman.
   Includes index.
   1. Wyman, Jane, 1914–   . 2. Moving-picture actors
and actresses—United States—Biography. I. Epstein,
Edward Z. II. Title.
PN2287.W8M67 1985   791.43′028′0924 [B]
ISBN 0-385-29402-6
Library of Congress Catalog Card Number: 84-28646

BOOK ONE

○ ○ ○ ○ ○ ○ ○ ○ ○ ○ ○ ○ ○ ○ ○ ○ ○ ○

1

YES, SHE IS AN ACADEMY AWARD WINNER, A FOUR-time Academy Award nominee, and has enjoyed an unusually long and distinguished career. Few actresses have worked as hard at building a career, one now capped by enormous new-found recognition as the star of one of television's top-rated series, *Falcon Crest*. At $100,000 per episode, she reportedly is currently the highest-paid actress on television.

But Jane Wyman is more than a successful actress. While her career achievements rightfully stand on their own, there is an aspect of her life that separates her from others of her profession, making her unique.

Chances are, when television is a relic of the past, when all film has turned to dust, when all awards are forgotten, Jane Wyman will still be written about, talked about, wondered about: her place in history is assured as the first ex-wife of a President of the United States. In fact, there are people who contend that Ronald Reagan would not have become president if Jane Wyman had not left him. Even after his success at the polls, President-elect Reagan was touchy about the subject of divorce: "I was divorced in the sense that the decision was made by somebody else."

One hundred years from now there may have been many divorced presidents and history may record many ex-mates. But Jane Wyman stands as the first. And she is not a former wife who has edged into obscurity.

Since she and Ronald Reagan rose to prominence together—at one time during their marriage she was even more famous than he—since their two children are now highly visible—and since public perception has linked Wyman and Reagan for more than four decades—Jane Wyman is one of the most intriguing women in America.

Wyman had been married before she wed Reagan. And she was married twice (to the same man) after Reagan. However, it is her eight-year marriage to the President that understandably elicits enormous interest.

Through the years, Jane has been perceived as the heavy in the breakup of the Wyman-Reagan marriage—sacrificing their "storybook" union for her career; callously dropping her husband when her career was on the rise, his on the wane. The situation, of course, was not so clear-cut, so simple.

The passage of time has blurred many facts. The truth is that during the last two years of their marriage, the Reagans experienced a series of harrowing events worthy of any drama their home studio, Warner Bros., had ever filmed.

And few people realize that Ronald Reagan's career ambitions —and interest in politics—were equally to blame for the couple's estrangement.

To mainstream America of the 1940s the Reagans represented something very personal and special: togetherness. They appeared to be typical, intensely likable, nonfrivolous yet fun-loving all-Americans. They won the hearts of the public. The image makers had done their job well. During the war, "Janie and Ronnie" represented stability in a young married couple facing hardships. He served his country while she kept the home fires burning.

Therefore, the disintegration of the marriage was Hollywood's biggest story of its kind since the breakup of Douglas Fairbanks and Mary Pickford. The Reagans' split was a turning point for each of them. It affected everything that came after, and brought into focus all that had come before.

"Button Nose" and "Dutch," as Wyman and Reagan were affectionately known by close friends, had enjoyed the quintessential Hollywood romance. When they married, on January 26, 1940, the queen of the gossip columnists, Louella Parsons, was their fairy godmother and hosted their wedding reception.

Jane was a high-spirited twenty-six-year-old rising starlet marrying a handsome twenty-nine-year-old actor with a career even more promising than hers. They had a storybook courtship that culminated in a storybook wedding. But for Jane Wyman, the future had not always looked this bright. . . .

St. Joseph, Missouri, was a very provincial city in the early days of the twentieth century. It was not the kind of town that encouraged dreams of glory or flights of fancy—consequently, those of its inhabitants who longed for more dramatic or creatively fulfilling lives shared a common objective: to leave St. Joseph for greener pastures. But while many dreamed of living other lives, few actually had the means or the courage to attempt a change.

St. Joseph was Jane Wyman's childhood home. It has been generally reported that she was born there on January 4, 1914, although through the years other dates—1917, 1918—have been incorrectly mentioned. And recently, out of the blue, Jane Wyman has said that her birth date was January 5.

A published source reports that Miss Wyman, née Sarah Jane Fulks, is an adopted child. Another source even asserts she is the daughter of a turn-of-the-century French music hall singer, LeJerne Pechelle. The fact that for years Miss Wyman never cared about what misinformation was printed, and often did not even read bios circulated by the studios, may be one reason that stories such as this reached print and cloud the issue of her real background. It should be remembered that in the 1930s the vogue in Hollywood was to invent fanciful and exotic backgrounds for the starlets who were vying for precious space in the press of the day.

Information appearing in birth records on file in the Missouri Division of Health in Jefferson City can be released only to the registrant, a member of his or her family, or a legal representative. Therefore, since Miss Wyman herself has neither confirmed nor denied that she is adopted, the allegation cannot be flatly dismissed. In any event, Sarah Jane Fulk's childhood in St. Joseph was hardly carefree or filled with happy memories.

Her mother, Emma Reise, had been born in Germany and had come to America as a young girl. Sarah Jane's father, Richard D. Fulks, has been described by his daughter as chief of detectives of St. Joseph. Through the years, his occupation has been variously reported as civil servant, mayor, county collector. One thing is clear: Mr. and Mrs. Fulks had been married for many years and already had a son and daughter, both teenagers, when Sarah Jane arrived.

As an adult, she reflected on her childhood: "I was reared under such strict discipline that it was years before I could reason myself out of the bitterness that I had brought from a childhood hemmed in by rigid rules, many of which I broke without knowing it and was punished long afterward by being denied something I had joyously anticipated."

Some sources report that at one point Mrs. Fulks became obsessed with getting her young daughter into movies. It is true that in 1922, when the girl was eight, Mrs. Fulks and Sarah Jane made a trip to Los Angeles, most probably to visit Sarah Jane's older brother. But the little girl had been taking dancing lessons and would continue to do so for many years. And she has recalled, "One of my vivid childhood memories is of Hollywood. I was one of those blonde curly-headed kids and my mother thought I was destined for the movies."

Whatever reason for the trip to Los Angeles, Sarah Jane and her mother returned to Missouri. In later years Sarah Jane revealed that although she and her mother were hardly close, there was one activity they enjoyed sharing. On Saturday afternoons Mrs. Fulks would take her daughter to lunch in downtown St. Joseph and then to a play at the local theater.

However, Sarah Jane longed to be independent of her parents' control. One must realize that there was a *great* age difference between Sarah Jane and her parents, as well as between her and her siblings. As a result, there was little understanding between mother and daughter. The older children had undoubtedly found it easier to adjust to being brought up by old-world standards in the period before World War I.

But Sarah Jane grew up during the Roaring Twenties, the era of the Flapper, Flaming Youth, and "It."

In 1929, Mr. Fulks died. Sarah Jane was fifteen. Her older brother was already an M.D. and had made his permanent home in Los Angeles, as had her older sister, Elsie. Mrs. Fulks and Sarah Jane again ventured to the West Coast.

The girl attended Los Angeles High School, but her mother and brother continued the strict discipline under which Sarah Jane had been raised by her father.

"I was never allowed to see one of the football games," she has recalled of her high school days. "It wasn't malice on the part of my family. It was thoughtlessness. I was told to be home at a certain hour each day and there were to be no excuses of any sort for not being there. . . . It was a routine that they thought was good for me and believed was right. I thought and I still think that I missed something important, something that would have been good for me, in my school days. Maybe it was because there was so much difference in age between my mother and me. Perhaps it was because my sister was older and was able, somehow, to accommodate herself to Mother's standards more easily than I did."

Her sister had graduated from college. Apparently the Fulkses were upper middle class enough to have both the necessary funds and the attitude to seek higher education for women, and it was expected that Sarah Jane would attend college.

But "I loathed school as I grew older," and Sarah Jane later admitted she "goofed off" in high school and did not have the necessary marks to get into college.

It didn't matter, however, since by the time she had completed high school, the Depression had set in and, even if she could go on to college, there was little money. In her words: "My family was flat broke. I mean we lost everything, except the little roof over our heads."

To support herself, Sarah Jane worked for a brief time in a coffee shop. It was tedious and not too lucrative, however, and she soon realized that what she liked to do most—dance—might also be a means of earning money. One must assume also that the freedom and fun a dancer's life seemed to offer held a powerful attraction for the sheltered young girl. Furthermore, she held no illusions about being an Isadora Duncan: "My goal—like everyone else's at the time—was just to survive."

Back in Missouri, she had studied with choreographer LeRoy Prinz's father, and that connection now provided her with an introduction to a group of chorus kids in Hollywood, just at a time when musicals with huge dancing casts had exploded on the movie scene.

For a girl who had been raised to be wary of everyone and everything, the anything-goes milieu of Hollywood in the early thirties was surely an eye-opener for Sarah Jane Fulks. One *had* to be an extrovert to succeed. Many of the young men and women working at the studios seemed eager to gain attention at *any* cost, since that was the name of the game: *Get yourself noticed.*

"A person didn't have to be a 'nut' to succeed," quipped humorist Robert Benchley, "but it helped."

In what might be construed as a backlash to her strict upbringing, Sarah Jane bleached her chestnut-brown hair into the currently popular blond popularized by Jean Harlow, and began wearing *lots* of makeup—after all, actresses were not noted for playing down their assets. On screen, their faces, it seemed, were painted-on masks with inch-long false eyelashes and pasted-on beauty marks. Wearing heavy makeup was, it appeared, essential.

While some seemed to get themselves "noticed" overnight, for Sarah Jane Fulks and many others who drew the line at how far they would go to get themselves attention, it would be a long, hard climb to achieve recognition.

Eighteen-year-old Sarah Jane landed a job as a dancer in the chorus of Busby Berkeley's *The Kid from Spain* at the Goldwyn studios. Other aspiring chorus girls then on the lot included Lucille Ball, Betty Grable, and Paulette Goddard. The four girls were all, at the time, blondes. Lucille and Betty, like Sarah Jane, would work long and hard for many years before career results began to be achieved. Paulette, by attracting and holding the interest of such men as mogul Joseph Schenck and comedian Charlie Chaplin, took another route.

Hedda Hopper, an actress herself during this period, noted: "You had to have perseverance to sustain in this town." It was a quality Sarah Jane Fulks had in abundance.

It is amusing to note that in the interest of making Sarah Jane's background more colorful, publicity material would later state that in 1933 she returned to Missouri to study music at the University of Missouri. In fact, she never set foot in the university. The imaginative publicists would also, in later years, state that Sarah Jane changed her name to Jane Durrell and became a blues singer on radio. Again, not true.

Nineteen thirty-three was undeniably an important year professionally in Sarah Jane's life. She appeared in a Joe E. Brown comedy, *Elmer the Great,* at Warner Bros.–First National studios. Director Mervyn LeRoy, who claims to have discovered virtually everyone who passed through Hollywood, has recalled there was "a girl making her film debut . . . Jane Wyman. I found her on the lot. Although Jack Warner had signed her, he hadn't used her in anything. I saw her walking around the lot one day—I'll always remember she was wearing a yellow polo coat—and I decided she'd be right for *Elmer* and put her in it. She did a beautiful job and her career was launched."

She may have been wearing a yellow polo coat, but Jack Warner had not signed her, her name was not yet Jane Wyman, and her career was not yet "launched."

Director LeRoy did give Sarah Jane Fulks a bit in *Elmer the Great,* however, and the following year she was seen in *College Rhythm* at Paramount. At Paramount she also had bits in three other films: *All the King's Horses, Stolen Harmony,* and *Rhumba.* In the latter, a George Raft–Carole Lombard starrer, Sarah Jane was again a chorus girl.

Sarah Jane was not placed under contract to Paramount, however. She was simply an extra liked by the casting directors, a perky blond, button-nosed girl, five foot five—tall for the day—whose hair and trim figure were in style. Her high cheekbones and huge brown eyes were also photogenic assets, but in fact she was self-conscious about her appearance. She was a hard worker with no pretensions. People of the time recall Sarah Jane as seeming to be perfectly happy being a dancer.

Around this time she met William Demarest, an agent (later an actor). He was with the Small and Landau Agency, and encouraged the girl to go after acting parts rather than remain in the chorus.

"Bill, I don't know how to act," she told him.

"So you'll learn," he retorted. Via Demarest and LeRoy Prinz she was sent to a dramatic coach, who told her, "Your face doesn't go with your voice." She continued working in the chorus and the other chorus girls supposedly affectionately nicknamed her "Dog Puss" because of her unusual pug nose and high cheekbones.

At Twentieth Century-Fox she appeared in *King of Burlesque,* which starred Warner Baxter and Alice Faye. She was in the Bing Crosby–Ethel Merman Paramount version of *Anything Goes* and had a very small role in Universal's *My Man Godfrey,* starring William Powell and the glamorous Carole Lombard. In the latter film, Sarah Jane was in the scavenger hunt scene, although most of her footage ended up on the cutting room floor. "I'm still in the picture, next to the monkey and the organ grinder," she later recalled. "But you have to look fast to see me." With characteristic humor, she has also recalled: "That monkey bit me, too."

During the 1930s, Warners, more than any of the other studios, had a huge roster of low-paid contract players. The Warner studio seemed to favor people who possessed "personality" and potential acting ability as opposed to rival studios MGM and Paramount, whose casting people looked first and foremost for players with extraordinarily good looks.

William Demarest took Sarah Jane to Warners. To this date she remembers the exact day Warners signed her to a standard contract: May 6, 1936. Her name was changed to Jane Wyman.

She was immediately thrown into picture after picture—five in 1936. Although they were bits, it was a beginning, and the start of developing Jane Wyman's on-screen persona as the wisecracking tough-talking chorus girl. It was a role she convincingly and distinctively played with bite and a seemingly natural hard edge. In fact, she was so adept at it that the studio seemed content to let her play the role indefinitely.

Meanwhile, Warners began the slow, methodical studio factory "buildup." Perhaps it can be more accurately described as a merchandising process—the opportunity for the player to be presented to the public via countless photographs and special layouts placed in newspapers and planted in magazines. The purpose, of course, was to familiarize everyone with actors' and actresses' faces.

"A lot of people were given the same 'buildup,' " noted Warner Bros. player Joan Blondell. "It was still the public who picked up on certain faces, and showed no interest in others."

Jane Wyman possessed that intangible quality that somehow made an impression, although not enough so that studio executives felt they had a "Hollywood comet" under contract. And certainly not enough so that Miss Wyman felt "secure" about her future—she observed that people more good-looking and talented than she were signed and discarded overnight.

"Today's headline-maker is tomorrow's bit player," to quote one wag of the day. "An actor always has his feet firmly planted in the quicksand." It was an attitude the studios didn't discourage—always keep actors off-balance and dependent. That way, they were easier to control.

Jane, of course, cooperated completely with the publicity department and posed for countless promotional photos. In addition to the publicity buildup, there was another advantage to being under contract to a studio—the majors like Warner Bros. ran their own drama schools. On the Warners lot the school was headed by Fred Beckwith, a well-respected dramatic coach.

Before long Jane was being groomed as the "new" fast-talking blonde—the studio's third- or even fourth-string Joan Blondell/ Ginger Rogers/Glenda Farrell type.

In *Stage Struck*, Wyman had a memorable line. The star, Dick Powell, asks chorus girl Wyman: "What's your name?"

"My name is Bessie Fufnick. I swim, dive, imitate wild birds, and play the trombone."

Dick Powell, a shrewd observer of the Hollywood scene, later said he had recognized Jane Wyman as having that "something extra." In Powell's words: "Janie had something you couldn't learn—*presence*. It was something that just registered on film—it 'cut through,' so to speak, and the audience noticed you. An actor can learn how to intensify this quality—there are tricks of movement you can learn to catch the camera's eye. But 'presence'—I guess it's also a kind of concentration—is there even when you're totally still, and Janie had it."

Jane had a bit in another major film, *Cain and Mabel*. With this production, Wyman certainly had the opportunity to observe firsthand how Hollywood's "other half" lived. *Cain and Mabel* starred Marion Davies and Clark Gable. It was Davies's first picture at Warners. After an argument at MGM, William Randolph Hearst had moved Marion and her famous twelve-room-"bungalow" dressing room, to the Warners lot. Now Warner Bros. would have the advantage of massive publicity coverage in the vast Hearst chain of newspapers, and the Warner Bros. "family" had the opportunity for a bird's-eye view of the unbelievably extravagant Hearst-Davies life-style.

Wyman's brief bit in *Cain and Mabel* was followed by bits in *Polo Joe* and *Gold Diggers of 1937*—all unbilled. Then, for the first time, the name Jane Wyman appeared on screen. It was a "B" film, *Smart Blonde*, which starred Glenda Farrell as Torchy Blane, girl reporter. Miss Farrell, an extremely amiable and down-to-earth person, liked Jane Wyman, and after the picture was completed she told her: "We ran *Smart Blonde*, Janie. With you in the same studio, I'll have to watch my step!"

The film turned out to be a hit and launched a series of Torchy Blane programmers.

Jane Wyman was billed eleventh in an "A" film, *Ready Willing and Able*, which starred Ruby Keeler. One of the people credited with the screenplay was Jerry Wald, who would later become a producer instrumental in furthering Jane's career. (Wald was one of writer Budd Schulberg's prototypes for "Sammy" in his classic novel about Hollywood, *What Makes Sammy Run?*)

The King and the Chorus Girl was next on Jane's schedule.

Directed by Mervyn LeRoy, the story was obviously inspired by the current romance of British King Edward VIII and America's Mrs. Wallis Warfield Simpson. Fernand Gravet and Joan Blondell played the title characters. Wyman was again a wisecracking chorus girl. This time Gravet, a big star in Europe, was getting the big buildup and was billed above the film's title. Even Joan Blondell was billed below.

In *Slim*, with Henry Fonda and Pat O'Brien, Jane Wyman was window dressing, playing Stuart Erwin's girl friend, as usual with characteristic sarcasm and humor.

In her private life, Jane was typical of that era's young-starlet-on-the-rise. She frequented the glamorous nightclubs of the day, such as the Trocadero and Cocoanut Grove, and was always made-up and dressed to the teeth. (There is a tale, perhaps apocryphal, that Jane always wore too much makeup until one of her fellow chorines recited the old cliché "Powder is powder and paint is paint. But we like a girl that these things ain't.")

Jane was certainly overdressed on these nightclub excursions, complete with an abundance of ostentatious costume jewelry. Like many of her contemporaries, Jane had come to Hollywood brainwashed by the images of the glittering, bejeweled glamour girls of the cinema. Unable to afford real star sapphires and diamonds, Jane piled on the fabulous fakes.

Always vibrant, gregarious, and fun-loving, she was "a good egg," pleasant to be around. Photographers who covered the nightclub scene liked her—consequently, her picture appeared frequently in the papers and fan magazines.

Around this time she met Myron Futterman, an older, divorced man from New Orleans who was a successful dress manufacturer. And in early 1937, Jane traveled to New Orleans and married him in a brief ceremony. Futterman had a teenage daughter. Few people gave any real chance for a marriage between a twenty-three-year-old Hollywood starlet and a fortyish businessman to work. True to predictions, it proved to be a short-lived union. They separated, not acrimoniously, only months later.

Work kept her very busy. After another small role, this time in *The Singing Marine*, a Dick Powell starrer, Jane was given a bigger role in *Mr. Dodd Takes the Air*, directed by Mervyn Le-Roy and Alfred E. Green. Singer Kenny Baker was making his film debut in this remake of *The Crooner*.

Then Jane was given a "big break." Since she had been getting good reviews, even in small roles, she was now assigned a lead, and would get top billing, in a B film entitled *Public Wedding*. In it she co-starred with William Hopper (Hedda's son). The film was a fifty-eight-minute programmer, but Jane proved herself worthy.

The studio routine continued. One day while shooting public-ity stills, Jane met a fellow contract player, Ronald Reagan. He was known around the studio as "Dutch" or "Ronnie." He was a handsome young man in his late twenties and talk around the lot was that he'd originally been signed to replace actor Ross Alexander, a similar all-American type who'd recently committed suicide.

Reagan had already starred in *Love Is on the Air*, a B film, to be sure, but a starring role nonetheless. He'd quickly been used in many other films.

At this juncture, Jane was still officially married. And Reagan, so the grapevine said, after having had a crush on his first leading lady, June Travis, was now playing the field.

One account says that after they met, Jane was interested in dating the handsome bachelor. When she saw him in the com-missary, she invited him to sit at her table. He joined her for lunch, told her how much he had enjoyed *Mr. Dodd Takes the Air*, but did not ask her for a date.

Supposedly, Jane pursued the matter. She went to casting di-rector Max Arnow and said, "Look, you're always working on publicity for people. Sending them out to nightclubs together.

How about working it on this Reagan and me?" But Arnow told her, "No. You ought to go out with a bigger name than your own. So should he."

But Jane wanted to date Reagan. She tried another approach. She had recently moved into a new apartment, and her friend Betty (Betsy) Kaplan suggested that she ask Reagan over for drinks. Jane phoned him: "Let's have cocktails at my place." But to Jane's surprise, he innocently asked, "What for?"

Although separated, Jane was still a married woman. And unbeknown to her, the young Reagan was a very straitlaced, principled fellow—and not much of a drinker, either (his father was an alcoholic).

Jane dropped her campaign to get a date, but she would still see a lot of Ronnie—both were assigned to Bryan Foy's B-unit at the studio. During these years, Warner Bros. produced fifty-five to sixty-five movies a year, many of them B's. Reagan was earning $200 a week at the time, but Jane, in her words, was earning only "$68 a week after taxes and being scared each time my contract came up for renewal that I'd be dropped. I didn't blame anybody but myself for my slow progress. I thank Bryan Foy for keeping me busy."

Foy (the eldest of Eddie Foy's sons and one of "The Seven Little Foys") was one of Jane's (and Reagan's) biggest boosters. He liked them both and appreciated the fact that Wyman and Reagan were dependable and cooperative as well as talented. He felt both of them had what it took to be stars—it was a matter of "keeping at it, kid," until "the break" came. Foy has recalled that Janie was the nervous one—Ronnie handled everything in stride.

Other studios were interested in borrowing Jane for their B-units, and Foy loaned her to Universal for *The Spy Ring*, and to Columbia, where Joe E. Brown was making *Wide Open Faces* with Alison Skipworth.

In the spring of 1938, Jane was briefly hospitalized for a stomach ailment. Then it was back to work. Small roles at Warners in

He Couldn't Say No and *Fools for Scandal*, Mervyn LeRoy's film with Carole Lombard and Fernand Gravet. There was a loan-out for a small part in an A movie over at MGM, *The Crowd Roars*. It starred Robert Taylor and Maureen O'Sullivan.

Then Jane landed a plum role on her home lot. She was cast in *Brother Rat*. It was to be an A film and had the advantage of having been a hit play on Broadway. In addition to buying the play, Warner Bros. had also signed the hot New York actor Eddie Albert and had brought him out to the Coast to star in the film version. But, in typical Hollywood fashion, Albert would not re-create the role he'd played on stage—that part went to Wayne Morris. Although Morris and Priscilla Lane were the titular "stars" of the picture, Albert and Ronald Reagan as the other cadets, and Jane Bryan and Jane Wyman as their romantic interests, had equally large roles. In effect, all six youngsters would be highlighted. (Jane Bryan's husband-to-be, Justin Dart, was a multimillionaire businessman who would be instrumental in the political career, decades later, of Ronald Reagan.)

Before Jane went on location for *Brother Rat*, she and Myron Futterman, unofficially apart for some time, now legally separated and she filed for divorce.

The cast and crew of *Brother Rat* went to San Diego to shoot exteriors at the San Diego Military Academy. It was during this trip that Wyman and Reagan finally began dating. At first it was not romantic. They were merely friends, often taking long walks at the beach at Coronado.

Jane learned all about Ronnie. He regaled her with stories of his family, their hardships, his education, and the story of how he'd gotten to Hollywood and his easy access to a Hollywood contract.

Reagan had been born in Tampico, Illinois, a very small town, on February 6, 1911 (he was three years older than Jane). He had an older brother, John Neil. Their dad, Jack (John) Reagan, was a dark-haired Irish Catholic whose parents had emigrated from

Ireland. Jack Reagan had married Nelle Wilson, a Protestant girl of Scots-English background, and Ron had been brought up as a Protestant. But both boys had inherited much of their father's Irish charm.

Reagan revealed to Jane that Jack Reagan had a drinking problem, and as a youngster Ron had often seen his beloved dad "under the influence." The family moved around a great deal, with Jack continually seeking employment as a shoe salesman. He liked nicknames and called his elder son "Moon"; Ronnie he called "Dutch" because as an infant he looked like "a fat Dutchman."

For most of "Dutch" and "Moon's" childhood the boys moved from town to town before settling in Dixon, Illinois, when "Dutch" was about ten years old.

Dixon, a town of about 10,000, is ninety miles from Chicago. There Ronald Reagan had a "typical" American childhood. While Jane was spending unhappy hours in school in St. Joseph, Reagan was happily playing football in high school, but he was unable to play baseball because of his poor eyesight.

The Depression had hit the Reagan family hard, and at one point Nelle even had to go to work in a dress shop. "Dutch" worked as a day laborer and as a lifeguard during the summers to save for his college education. He made his way through Eureka College, a strict Disciples of Christ school in Eureka, Illinois. Reagan was only an average student, but his personality made him a campus favorite and he was also something of a rebel, organizing a brief student strike forcing the school administration to relax the ban on dancing, smoking, and drinking.

Ron told Jane that in college he was on the football team and in the dramatic club. He had taken economics and sociology courses at Eureka, but when he finally graduated with a BA degree, he was determined to break into radio.

During the filming of *Brother Rat*, Reagan entertained Jane and the other actors with stories of his days as a sports announcer at radio station WHO in Des Moines, where he had often been heard on coast-to-coast sports broadcasts covering football games and big-league baseball games, swimming meets, and track events.

It was obvious to the cast and crew of *Brother Rat* that Reagan loved to talk, so it was no surprise to learn that back in the Midwest he had gained quite a reputation as a speaker at banquets. Reagan also loved the outdoors and politics—he was at the time an ardent Democrat. He had inherited this interest from his father, who had even worked for the government's Works Progress Administration (WPA) and was a staunch supporter of Franklin D. Roosevelt.

Ronald Reagan first got the idea of coming to Hollywood and getting into the movies when a hillbilly band appearing on WHO was signed by Gene Autry to star in one of his films.

Unlike Jane Wyman, however, Ronald Reagan entered films on a fairly high level. He was in California in the winter of 1937 covering the spring training of the Chicago Cubs on Catalina Island off the coast of Los Angeles. When he got to Hollywood, the first thing Reagan did was to contact Joy Hodges, a singer-actress he had met in Des Moines.

Via Miss Hodges he was introduced to agent George Ward, who worked for the Bill Meiklejohn Agency. Mr. Ward has vividly recalled meeting Ronald Reagan: "He came into the office on a Thursday and informed me that he was on a limited expense account and was going back to Des Moines. One of my contacts was Max Arnow, the head of talent at Warner Bros. studios. I phoned Max and told him I had this attractive, promising young man in the office, and he said, 'Bring him out.' The studios, you see, were very anxious for new talent then. They sent Ron over to the talent department, where he read for them."

A screen test was scheduled, but before the test, Ward took Reagan to Paramount, where they instantly put him into a short subject they were shooting that Sunday. He was there early in the morning for makeup and assumed he'd be through in ample time to cover the exhibition baseball game he was broadcasting that afternoon. However, when Reagan learned that he probably would not be called before the cameras until the late afternoon or even evening, he walked out. After all, he reasoned, he had the upcoming screen test at Warners, so what did it matter if he didn't bother with Paramount?

The Warners test went well, and the would-be actor was told that he would be contacted in several days, after Jack Warner had taken a look at the test. But the cocky young man said, "I'm leaving tomorrow." The Cubs were scheduled to return to Chicago, and it meant that Reagan would be back in Des Moines broadcasting the game.

When he arrived in Des Moines, he received a telegram from George Ward. Amazingly, Warners was offering the young announcer $200 a week on a seven-year contract with yearly options, starting June 1, 1937.

Reagan was earning $90 a week at the radio station, not an inconsiderable sum in 1937 (the average weekly salary in the United States at that time was about $15). The $90 was enough for "Dutch" to support his mother and father, send his brother Neil $10 a week ("Moon" was now enrolled at Eureka College), and even to buy himself a new Nash convertible and pay cash for it.

But the lure of Tinseltown was obviously strong, and Reagan drove the Nash out to Hollywood. On his first day at Warner Bros., he was warned that he might not work for weeks or months. But much to his delight and surprise, he was immediately put to work.

Perc Westmore, head of the makeup department at Warner Bros., restyled Reagan's hair. Frank Westmore has recalled, "My brother cut and reshaped Reagan's heavy thatch of hair (parting it on the left side), and consoled him when all his scenes in his second movie, *Submarine D-1*, were considered so bad they were cut."

Reagan worked constantly, doing an incredible eight pictures in eleven months. He played the lead in some and bits in others, but he worked with Warners' top stars: Dick Powell, the Lane sisters, Pat O'Brien. In fact, things looked so rosy that Reagan felt secure enough to send for his parents and move them to Hollywood.

There is no doubt that being cast in *Brother Rat* was a big step in his career, as well as in the career of Jane Wyman. Reagan has candidly said, "My part was easily good enough to provide a stepping-stone for stardom." But he admits that, unhappily, he learned there was room for only one discovery per picture, and this picture's discovery was Eddie Albert.

Brother Rat concerned itself with cadets at the Virginia Military Institute, three cadets in particular. Reagan's character becomes involved with the commandant's daughter (Wyman). In the story, he is rather indifferent to her at first, but she is smart and aggressive in a likable way. It almost seems that their roles paralleled their real-life situation.

Jane had changed her hair color many times in the past two years, but it was blond again for her role in *Brother Rat*. The part was a departure for Jane, since she portrayed not a fast-talking chorus girl, but an intellectual, demure ingenue. Happily, she proved that she could handle this kind of role with ease.

One of the "shticks" in the movie is that she is a bespectacled bookworm and Reagan's character is not attracted to her until the inevitable take-your-glasses-off scene. The irony, of course, was that in real life Reagan was the one who could not see very well without glasses.

The director of *Brother Rat*, William Keighley, was a highly talented man noted for putting together fast-paced, energy-filled films, the kind for which Warner Bros. was famous. He responded to actors who were, to use his phrase "fast on the uptake."

Wyman and Reagan were both "quick studies," stated Keighley many years later. "I didn't have to 'pull' the performances out of them—they both got things right pretty fast, and I think even then they both had very distinctive screen personalities . . . I was surprised big things didn't happen for the Wyman girl a lot faster than they did. Things *were* happening in Reagan's career, as I recall—he was very well liked by Jack Warner, I remember that very clearly."

Although many sources claim that Reagan and Wyman began *seriously* dating from this time on, the point is debatable, since both were still seeing others. Of this period in her relationship with Reagan, Jane has said, "We'd sit around the set and talk. But Ronnie was always going around with his college frat brothers. He never seemed to have time for girls. They were all enthused in sports."

Reagan and Wyman did not seem to have much in common. During this period of her life Jane loved nightclubbing and socializing, while Ronnie was an outdoors-type person.

Reagan was already becoming involved in the political side of Hollywood. Character actress Helen Broderick (mother of Broderick Crawford) had recruited Reagan for the Screen Actors Guild. It was through his involvement with SAG that Ronald Reagan became friends with some of Hollywood's top stars. His winning personality and interest in the politics of the Guild soon led to the young actor's being voted onto the board of directors.

Most of the board members—Dick Powell, Cary Grant, James Cagney, Edward Arnold, Robert Montgomery, and Charles Boyer—were already stars, but in 1938 there was a drive on to have all levels of actors represented, and Reagan would represent the contract players.

In contrast, Jane seemed apolitical. Her career, and having fun, seemed all-important. Wyman has recalled, "When I first met Ronnie I was a nightclub girl. I just had to go dancing and dining at the Troc or the Grove or some night spot every night to be happy."

Jane's fan magazine buildup began to gather momentum, and she was an important enough starlet so that in December 1938 her divorce from Futterman made news. Her attorney, Harold E. Aaron, had already arranged a settlement out of court.

Jane testified at the divorce hearing that Futterman "continually compared me to his former wife and always nagged me about money matters and accused me of being extravagant." Every wife in America could identify with those laments. But there were two elements of the divorce that made more sensational news. Jane had wanted a baby and Futterman hadn't. He told her, "I have enough family." In addition, Futterman was jealous and, Jane testified, "When we went to parties, he would accuse me of flirting. If I mentioned anyone's name more than once, he would accuse me of having a new heartthrob."

Recently, Wyman talked about the marriage of nearly fifty years ago, the union that has faded from most memories. "I thought I was doing the right thing at the time. Myron was a lovely, charming man, but it just didn't work out. I guess I married too young."

At the time of the divorce, Jane's name was not linked with Reagan's publicly—nor with any man's. Having her picture in the papers certainly didn't hurt, however, as far as her career was concerned. In addition, people in the industry were very much aware of her rising status as one of Warners' contract players. Around this time Warners took out an ad in the trade papers highlighting ten of their contract players, and calling them "Ten for the Top." Jane was pictured along with Gloria Dickson, Doris Weston, Linda Perry, Virginia Dale, Willard Parker, and Jeffrey Lynn, among others, including a young New York actor who had not yet even made a film: John Garfield. (Only Jane and Garfield would reach the top predicted for them.)

Other studios continued to borrow Wyman. She went to 20th

for another wisecracking role as "Alabama," one of the female fliers in the Alice Faye–Constance Bennett starrer *Tail Spin.*

It was during this picture that another event occurred in her personal life that creates, rather than answers, questions about her early years. At this time, 20th issued a press release announcing that one Ernest Wyman, "the father of Jane Wyman," had died. In research on Jane's background, there is no mention of an Ernest Wyman, and no one who knew Jane during this period remembers him today. There would have been absolutely no reason for the studio to have issued this press release other than having been told by Jane Wyman that her father had died. One explanation is that Mrs. Fulks had at some point remarried and Jane had adopted her stepfather's last name.

After *Tail Spin,* Jane returned to her home lot, where she kept bouncing between small parts in A films and co-starring parts in B films. She did *Private Detective,* a B in which she had the lead as a female sleuth. It was obviously a lesser Torchy Blane–type role. Then she went into *The Kid from Kokomo,* which starred Pat O'Brien, Wayne Morris, and Joan Blondell. By now the studio was viewing Wyman as a replacement for Blondell and Glenda Farrell and announced that "after a three-year probationary period, Jane is being groomed for stardom."

Although there was talk of lending her for another Joe E. Brown film at Columbia, she stayed on her home lot.

Glenda Farrell had already left the Torchy Blane series, and Lola Lane had done one film as Torchy. Now the powers-that-be cast Jane as the ace girl reporter in *Torchy Plays with Dynamite,* destined to be the last of the series.

In *Kid Nightingale,* a programmer, Jane appeared opposite John Payne. "A grade-B farce but gets enough points on giggles," noted the *New York Times* reviewer.

Jane has recalled that during these early years, when she was learning the ropes, all the first-level stars at Warners, such as Kay Francis, were kind and helpful.

"I was always being invited over to her house," remembered Jane of Miss Francis. "It was like a big family rather than a studio. Jimmy Cagney was a strict disciplinarian, although I never appeared in his films. Pat O'Brien was always teaching me the tricks of the business. Even Bette Davis was kind and encouraging to 'the kids,' as we were called." According to Miss Wyman's recollections, even on days when they weren't working, many of the "kids" would lunch together in the studio commissary.

Jane's continually rising status at Warners was evident when she was chosen that spring to be part of an important junket to the premiere of the film *Dodge City*, the elaborate Errol Flynn in-color-by-Technicolor western. It was a four-day journey to Kansas aboard a special luxury train, and Jane traveled with her pal Ann Sheridan, as well as Jean Parker, Wayne Morris, John Garfield, Humphrey Bogart, and, of course, the star of *Dodge City*, the flamboyant, womanizing Flynn.

At the time, Warners seemed to be grooming Ronald Reagan as a rival to Flynn. Ron had been given a small but important part in the Bette Davis tour-de-force *Dark Victory*, and Reagan received a healthy fourth billing. He was cast as a playboy-alcoholic, "best friend" of the leading lady.

Although in his autobiography (published in 1965) Reagan skirts the issue, it seems apparent that his character was interpreted by the director, Edmund Goulding, as a young homosexual. Reagan would not play it this way. He had problems with the director but has said, "In the matter of studio standing, I was outweighed. He was a top director doing only top pictures. I was up in that class on a raincheck."

In true "jock" fashion, Reagan bristled when the director suggested he should play the part as "the kind of fellow who could sit in the girls' dressing room dishing the dirt while they went on dressing in front of me. I had no trouble seeing him in that role," Reagan has said, "but for myself, I want to think if I strolled through where the girls are short of clothes, there would be a great scurrying about and taking to cover."

Although Reagan says he was terribly disappointed in his performance in *Dark Victory* and feels that his compromise made him deliver a bad performance, that is not true. He is very effective in the film, and it was instrumental in furthering his career. But in true studio fashion, after he was given exposure in an A, it was back to the B's.

Working on the Warners lot was no different from working in a huge office complex or factory, as far as social life was concerned. There was always an awareness on the lot of who was dating, "seeing," or "lusting" after whom.

Up to this point Reagan was still playing the field, if he dated at all. Sources say Reagan spent most of his free time with his family and his college chums. There were studio-arranged dates, of course, including at least one with newcomer Susan Hayward. The striking redhead from Brooklyn had been signed and cast in *Brother Rat.* The story goes, however, that Jack Warner had seen a screening of *Four Daughters* and knew that Priscilla Lane would become a star, so he replaced Hayward with Lane. Susan was then cast in a very minor role in a quickie in the B-unit, *Girls on Probation.* That film was supposed to be the debut of newcomer John Garfield, but his part was given to Reagan. Everyone noted what a striking couple Reagan and Hayward made. But Susan's option was soon dropped and she was off the lot. However, Ronnie *and* Jane would see more of her the following year.

Jane noticed that Reagan was also paired, for publicity reasons, with seventeen-year-old sexpot Lana Turner, who had come to the studio via her mentor, Mervyn LeRoy. And Jane could not have failed to notice, as had many others on the lot, that one of Ronald Reagan's relationships was not studio-planned.

Through most of the year he dated a pretty young actress in the B-unit, Ila Rhodes. She had co-starred with him in *Secret Service of the Air.* This film was the first of four in a series in which Reagan played Brass Bancroft, an undercover agent. The series also starred Eddie Foy, Jr., as Reagan's sidekick. It was films such as these that seemed to be typecasting Reagan in programmers and gaining him the title "The Errol Flynn of the B's."

Miss Rhodes has candidly recalled: "I was twenty-one, and he was around thirty, tall and cute. Ronnie was very attractive, and I didn't take any antidote to ward off this attraction. . . . The short time we filmed together led to lunch-break trysts and weekends out together, snatched from a hectic Hollywood schedule. . . . I became engaged to him with a ring on my finger. . . . In all, the engagement lasted eight or nine months, when the studio decided romance between their stars was bad for box-office business."

However, it is very doubtful that Warner Bros. had anything to do with the breakup of Reagan and Miss Rhodes. Of all the studios, Warners had the least interest in their contract players' private lives (unlike MGM, which literally tried to program the private lives of its contractees). Certainly in 1939 Reagan wasn't a big enough star for the front office to "worry" about. He probably could have dated anyone he pleased, in or out of the business, without comment from the studio.

The facts seem to indicate that Reagan just wasn't that interested in getting serious until he and Wyman began dating again when the studio reteamed them along with all the cast members of *Brother Rat* for a sequel: *Brother Rat and a Baby*. And this time, recall those on the scene, Miss Wyman set her cap for the elusive and very eligible bachelor.

She has been quoted: "I still remember our first date. We had a dinner date and went to a Sonja Henie opening afterward. We had a wonderful time and it seemed to me we made a pretty good team off screen as well as on. Neither of us was going with anyone special at the time, so we decided on each other. Our favorite night spot was Grace Hayes Lodge. We used to go there for dinner and sit and listen to our 'theme song,' 'Deep Purple,' and hold hands under the table."

There are, of course, many versions of their courtship, but all point to the fact that Wyman did the chasing. She, who heretofore hadn't been either athletically inclined or inclined to like the outdoors, suddenly decided she could change.

"I used to be the kind of person who sat around swank nightclubs with a big hat on my head and a long cigarette holder sticking out of my face," she has recalled. "Athletics held no charm for me. First I was too lazy, and then what for? Till along came Reagan and all I heard was football and track and swimming and golf. The only way I could get to see him was out on a golf course. So where do you think I went? Out on a golf course." (Her interest in golf has sustained to the present day—she is considered a good player.)

Jane also noted, "One day the studio took Ann Sheridan, Ronnie, and me out to the ice rink to pose for some publicity pictures. I couldn't even stand up on ice skates. Ronnie held me up long enough for pictures. He kidded me so terrifically about it, that Annie and I decided to skate or die. For two months we'd go out there every morning until we could actually figure skate."

Apparently, Reagan began to view Jane in a different light. They did have their careers in common. They were both extremely bright people with drive, and although neither had become a star yet, Reagan was well on his way and both he and Jane were keen at learning their trade. They were absorbing the techniques of film acting, and each was building the foundation for a future career.

They certainly made a handsome-looking couple on the Hollywood social scene. Their names, as an "item," began to be linked in gossip columns.

The couple occasionally double-dated with Perc Westmore and his wife, actress Gloria Dickson. Perc had become a good friend to both Wyman and Reagan.

Jane even took an interest in Ron's activities in SAG and accompanied him to the union's mass meeting held in the Hollywood Legion Stadium that fall.

Jane's final divorce decree from Futterman wasn't due until December, so no public announcement could be made of the couple's plans. But years later Jane revealed that Ron had proposed to her on the set. She conceded that they had had a very romantic courtship, "but the proposal was about as unromantic as anything that ever happened." According to Wyman, "We were about to be called for a take. Ronnie simply turned to me as if the idea were brand-new and had just hit him and said, 'Jane, why don't we get married?' I couldn't think of any reason why we shouldn't. I'd been wondering for a whole year—ever since I first saw him—why he hadn't asked me. I was just about to say a definite yes when we were called before the cameras. In trying to step down off my own personal cloud, I managed to muff a few lines and toss in a whispered 'Yes' after the director said 'Cut!' "

But if the couple made the decision while in Hollywood, they kept the news to themselves. After completing *Brother Rat and a Baby*, Jane and Ron were set to embark on a special junket, and the junket would become even more special when their romance and engagement were revealed.

In 1939, although Louella Parsons wielded incredible power with her audience via both her radio program and her column, people in the newspaper industry knew that there was in-fighting among Hearst employees, and Louella had lost some of her popularity among the editors of the vast syndicate. The shrewd Miss Parsons thought up a surefire idea: She would take to the road with a vaudeville tour and show the syndicate just how popular she was.

When word got out that Louella would be taking a group of contract players on tour, each studio eagerly submitted the names on its rosters—this would be unlimited free publicity for the players over the next two months.

Mecca Graham, an actor under contract to Warners, was a good friend of both Louella's and her husband's, Dr. Harry ("Docky") Martin. Parsons signed Graham for the tour. He would be her offstage escort as well as play a part in the onstage revue. The show would consist of Miss Parsons "writing" her column onstage while various hopefuls, who were trying to plug their films, would stop by and "entertain" her.

Susan Hayward had recently scored in Paramount's *Beau Geste* and had been on the cover of *The Saturday Evening Post* that October. Louella chose her for the tour. Dancer-contortionist June Preisser, who had scored in MGM's *Babes in Arms,* was chosen because she was a seasoned in-person performer. So was singer Joy Hodges. Starlet Arleen Whelan added glamour. Louella liked the up-and-coming actor Ronald Reagan, who had the added advantage of being from Parsons's hometown, Dixon, Illinois. Jane Wyman was picked to complete the group.

Years later, Louella said, "Jane was openly and enthusiastically pleased at being invited along . . . it was obvious that she was especially pleased at being in such proximity to Ronnie, whom she considered a 'famous star.' "

In addition to the publicity and prestige of being "picked," the tour would be lucrative for the half-dozen performers. They would each earn around $700 a week, a veritable fortune in 1939 dollars.

On November 13 the troupe drove up to Santa Barbara, where they broke in the show. They continued on to San Francisco, where "Louella Parsons and Her Stars" played the Golden Gate Theater. Then the show headed east, by plane (they became "Louella Parsons's Flying Stars"), making various stopovers en route to Philadelphia. There, at the Earle Theater, they were mobbed. Then they traveled by train to Pittsburgh, where thousands of fans packed the railroad station, even at an early-morning hour.

Fan magazines and gossip columns by now had already reported to the country that Jane Wyman and Ronald Reagan were "the darling couple of Hollywood," and fans across the country had the opportunity to see the lovebirds in person. They were indeed a strikingly attractive duo—"Janie" with her blond hair, mink coat, and flashy costume jewelry; "Ronnie" in his meticulous suit-and-tie, smiling his ingratiating grin.

Louella Parsons's version of the Jane of 1939: " 'Janie, you look like a walking Christmas tree!' I told her one day when she was loaded with such 'jewels.' Janie just grinned.

" 'I know, mother,' she said, 'but it's such fun!'

"Yes, it was fun for her, and fun was the keynote of her life in those days. Gay fun, thoughtless fun. The world to her was a beautiful big party, and she was the belle of the ball."

Recalling the trip, Joy Hodges has described the Ronald Reagan of 1939: "I used to think he was a real college boy when he would sit and sing college songs as we were riding in the bus when we went on the vaudeville tour . . . but it was all his way of pulling us out of the awful boredom. We were always together then, all of us, and sometimes tempers flared, but there was never a flare-up between 'Dutch' and anybody. He was the happy catalyst. . . . There was a stage manager, but the girls all went to 'Dutch' with any problem. He and Jane were planning on getting married, but they were very discreet and he was as attentive to the rest of us as to her."

In each city, Jane and Ron would duck away from the group to have a quiet dinner together. They usually found an inexpensive little Italian restaurant for the spaghetti that Reagan loved.

In Baltimore, in Washington, D.C., at the Capitol Theater, and in New York the tour was a sellout. At each stop the troupe presented four, sometimes five, shows a day. Part of the revue included Louella holding a symposium with the audience, telling them what they *really* wanted to know about their favorite stars.

Unreported to the public was a bit of backstage drama involving Jane Wyman and Susan Hayward. As part of the show, Reagan had a comedy sketch with Hayward. Joy Hodges has recalled: "She played with incredible fervor. I can still see her—the blue velvet dress with that red hair. The spotlight on just the two of them. In the skit, she stabbed 'Dutch,' and every time he tried to sit up, she'd bop him down again. Susan played it completely straight. The audiences howled but she never faltered, and not even when 'Dutch' broke up, as he usually did. We all marveled at how she kept her composure."

Hayward might have kept her composure *onstage*, but she was angry that Jane Wyman stood in the wings every performance. "She makes me nervous, standing in the wings every night. Does she have to do that?" Hayward huffed to Parsons. Louella told Jane, "Dear, Susan is very upset. . . ." Jane was adamant: "Too bad about her. If I don't stand there and watch, she'll knock Ronnie out."

Obviously the rivalry between the two starlets, by the time the troupe reached New York, had percolated to overflowing. Jane seethed at the force with which Hayward struck Reagan. "She hits him too hard," Jane told Louella. "She just slaps him that hard because she thinks it makes me mad."

If that was indeed Miss Hayward's motive, it succeeded. Those who were there say that Jane was furious. Meanwhile, Louella kept peace among "the kids" as well as she could.

They were in Chicago, where the tour ended, in early January 1940, when an excited Jane took Louella aside. Parsons observed: "Her brown eyes were sparkling and her voice was bubbling with happiness as she told me: 'Have I got a scoop for you! Ronnie and I are engaged!' I had known that Jane worshipped Ronnie, but I hadn't realized he was falling seriously in love with her. I announced the engagement that night from the stage and in the newspapers."

This was the kind of exclusive "scoop" Louella lived for.

The tour had been an enormous success for all concerned. Parsons had personally grossed an astonishing $3,000 a week, and signed a fat new contract with the Hearst syndicate.

According to writer John Landon, the Parsons tour was important to Reagan's career as well. While the group was in Philadelphia, Reagan had trouble getting out of his hotel and to the theater without being mobbed by female fans. Although he didn't like this kind of "display," he appreciated the attention and undoubtedly both he and his agents brought the matter up to the Warners staff. It was agreed that upon Reagan's return, he was to be given the "buildup" as a romantic lead. This, too, was news on the movie pages of newspapers throughout the country.

Front pages, however, were occupied with more pressing matters occurring throughout the world. By now, the German Army had conquered Poland. Britain and France were in a war against Germany. President Roosevelt had taken to the air and asked the nation to observe "true neutrality." The Germans weren't the only aggressors. Soviet troops had also marched into Poland and by November had begun their invasion of Finland.

The world was hurtling toward catastrophe, but not even the most patriotic film fan could deny that in Hollywood the primary topic of conversation was the premiere of *Gone With the Wind.*

Thanks mainly to Louella Parsons, coverage on the Wyman-Reagan romantic relationship was kept near the top of items-for-movie-fans. Would they *really* be getting married? And if so, would it be soon? . . .

○ ○ ○ ○ ○ ○ ○ ○ ○ ○ ○ ○ ○ ○ ○ ○ ○ ○ ○

2

IT WAS NOT A LONG ENGAGEMENT. LOUELLA WAS MORE than delighted when "the youngsters" decided to tie the knot. In a burst of enthusiasm, the fifty-eight-year-old columnist announced that she would even host the wedding reception at her home—an incredible coup for these rising young players.

Louella took a proprietary interest in "Ronnie and Janie" and their careers. Like countless others, the columnist was particularly charmed by the handsome young man who was the epitome of the "family boy"—unlike Hollywood's playboys, Reagan led an exemplary life. He really *was* the "boy next door." It wasn't just a screen image; it was real. Louella and other columnists in Hollywood felt that surely Reagan and Wyman would enjoy an ideal marriage.

Ronnie and Janie were willing participants in the columnist's public relations program from the beginning. Miss Parsons and others were instrumental in "toning Jane down," advising her to be more subtle in her makeup, clothing, and attitude. Jane was a fast learner—a trait that would enable her eventually to accomplish miracles in her career.

The wedding was set for January 26, 1940, and the bride chose a floor-length high-necked, long-sleeved blue satin frock, quilted on the bodice and snugly fitted. She planned on wearing a dark fur hat and matching fur muff, an ensemble that showed off her coloring to perfection. In addition, Reagan had given her a huge (52-carat) amethyst engagement ring (it was her birthstone).

But then the groom-to-be came down with the flu and the wedding almost had to be postponed. Ronnie recovered sufficiently to obtain the marriage license, however, and went back to bed until the ceremony.

The wedding was a beautiful and formal occasion. The men wore tails, the women floor-length gowns and orchid corsages. A beaming Nelle and Jack Reagan, along with Jane's mother, Emma, were present. "Don't take 'Dutch' away from us," the elder Reagan reportedly said to Jane.

"Everything's going to be the same" was Jane's response.

Ron was, and would remain, close with his family. And it had been obvious, even before the wedding, that if Jane wanted to be close to Ronnie, she would have to be close to the entire Reagan family.

After the wedding, the couple left for a brief honeymoon in Palm Springs, but not before giving Ruth Waterbury an interview.

When had they *actually* decided on marriage? "Janie said it was about six months ago," wrote Miss Waterbury. "Ronald said it was seven. Then they sat very straight, looked at each other, wide-eyed, and whispered: 'That was September, more than a year ago.'"

Miss Waterbury noted, "It being Jane's third *[sic]* marriage, and Ronald's first, they recognized that they have certain snares to guard against." Waterbury's reference, like many others of the day, to Wyman's *two* previous marriages, never gave names or details but kept alive a rumor of Jane's teenage "mystery marriage."

On their honeymoon in Palm Springs, Reagan was surprised to

learn that Jane could not swim. He tried to teach her, but in this area she was not a very good student.

When they returned from their honeymoon, they moved into Ron's apartment, one he had heretofore shared with his parents. Now he bought the elder Reagans a small house, which they moved into in March 1940.

When Reagan and Wyman returned to Warner Bros., the studio immediately teamed them as husband and wife in a new film, *An Angel from Texas,* a reworking of George Kaufman's old Broadway play *The Butter and Egg Man.* It was about Broadway "sharpies" trying to talk a Texas yokel into backing a show. Wayne Morris and Reagan portrayed the fast-talking producers, Eddie Albert the yokel. Rosemary Lane played Albert's girl friend.

Filming was completed quickly, due in part to the fact that both Wyman and Reagan were frequently able to get scenes right on the first take, and never later than on the second or third. Wyman and Reagan were "no problem" actors; they knew their lines and listened to the director.

The picture was scheduled for a fast release to cash in on all the publicity on the Wyman-Reagan marriage. But once all the hoopla about the nuptials died down, it appeared that their careers were still mired in programmers. Jane went into a pot-boiler, *Flight Angels,* a forgettable little tale about stewardesses. And Reagan was cast in yet another of his Brass Bancroft films. The actor was so disenchanted with B films, he went to his friend Brynie Foy and begged him not to use him any longer. Foy replied, "Don't worry, nobody will see the new picture!" *Murder in the Air* was not released in the Los Angeles area.

Despite Reagan's distaste for these programmers, they served him well. They set up and reinforced in the public mind his character of the honest, straightforward, heroic young man.

On the home front the Reagans were experiencing the same problems that faced all newlyweds. Unlike other newlyweds,

however, the Reagans shared their innermost thoughts with
their growing following of fans. Wyman told columnists that Ronnie had changed her life. She made very revealing statements
about herself and the marriage in these days when the honeymoon with the press was still on. She admitted that before knowing Reagan she was a person who generally did not trust people.
"This was a terrible thing for me, all this distrust. I was so afraid
that I should make a wrong move or jeopardize my opportunity
in some way! I guarded my budding career so fiercely and with
such terrible suspicion of everyone that I made it extremely
difficult for anyone to help me. . . . Then, of course, Ronnie
really came into my life. It was *his* easy friendliness which attracted me to him first. Everyone liked him and it seemed to me
that he liked nearly everyone. I began to try to analyze what it
was in *me* that he liked . . . and to try to have more of it! I began
to analyze whatever there was in me that anyone else could like,
too, and to wonder what traits I could acquire which would
attract people."

People who know Jane Wyman attest to the fact that she is, to
this day, a *very* private person, guarded, and might even be
described as introverted when it comes to dealing with strangers.
But they agree that statements like these did capture the essence
of her feelings about the early part of her marriage.

One area in which the couple did share problems common to
other newlyweds was the matter of finances. Reagan and Wyman
had different attitudes about money and budgeting. It has been
reported that when she married Ronnie, Jane was up to her neck
in debt. But knowing the way he felt about debts, she had striven
to pay all her bills before their marriage. "Ronnie has a phobia
about bills. If a bill is ten days old he starts having a fit. As a result,
every bill is paid and out of the way by the tenth of each month."
And she noted that "Ronnie and I are a good balance for each
other." They had both come through the Depression, but obviously it had affected Reagan in a different way. Their salaries at

this time were reported at $500 a week each, but it is more likely that Jane was earning only about $250 (or less).

The image makers had done their job, and the fan mail poured in for more details on this "perfect marriage." To the ladies in the audience who yearned to capture handsome bachelors of their own, reporters were eager to point out that Janie had been the aggressor in the relationship: "Long before Ronald was aware of Janie's existence, she knew *he was there*. He didn't look Janie's way for a long time. When he did, it was all over but the wedding."

The courtship, the wedding, and the attendent publicity had not, however, catapulted either Jane or Ron into starring roles at the studio. Jane was relatively complacent, but Reagan wanted top roles in top films right away and was willing to fight for them. Through the years a mistaken impression has evolved—Ronald Reagan is perceived as a grade-B actor working in grade-B films and "not knowing any better." Quite the contrary, Reagan was totally aware of how the Hollywood system was set up, where he was on the ladder, and where he wanted to be.

Reagan was determined to land a role in an A film then in preparation at the studio, *Knute Rockne, All American*. The role Reagan wanted was a small but pivotal one, that of George Gipp. Almost a dozen actors had been tested for the part. Reagan's pal Pat O'Brien was to play Knute Rockne, the Notre Dame football coach. Hal Wallis was producing the picture, and Lloyd Bacon was to direct.

Brynie Foy suggested to Reagan that he show his Eureka College football pictures to producer Wallis, but Ron cleverly went to O'Brien instead. Reagan was extremely popular with fellow actors. He was the kind of man who inspired instant camaraderie, and older, more experienced actors like Jimmy Cagney, O'Brien, and Dick Powell took "the kid" under their wing and helped show him the ropes.

Years later, Pat O'Brien recalled what happened. O'Brien was excited about *Knute Rockne* because he was a sports buff. But to Jack Warner, it was just another film.

"Who's going to play 'The Gipper'?" O'Brien asked Warner.

"Who's 'The Gipper'?" Warner retorted.

"It's a hell of an important role, Jack," O'Brien told him. "A lot of the guys you have up for it don't know a football from a watermelon. Reagan does. Tell you what I'll do—I'll make a test with him."

"All right," Warner said. "If you're that excited, make a test."

Needless to say, the test was successful and Reagan got the part. It would breathe new life into his career.

Meanwhile, director Curtis Bernhardt gave Jane a small but meaty part in an Olivia de Havilland starrer, *My Love Came Back*. Wyman and Olivia were cast as violin students, and Jane swiftly learned how to "fake" the finger movements of a professional violinist, while Olivia had trouble with it. Again, Jane was playing the likable friend, but this time the script had more dimension and it was definitely an A production.

Angel from Texas had opened to nice reviews. *The New York Times* called it "a bright little farce" and noted that it was "smartly acted by Eddie Albert, Wayne Morris, Ronald Reagan, and Jane Wyman." It did not prove to be a box office bonanza, however.

The powers-that-be at Warners decided to give the Reagan-Wyman on-screen teaming one more chance. Ironically, except for *Brother Rat*, they hadn't really "clicked" as an on-screen duo. But in all fairness, their subsequent two films together after *Rat* had hardly been of top-drawer caliber. Unfortunately the new vehicle, *Tugboat Annie Sails Again*, turned out to be no exception. "And those lovable sweethearts played by Ronald Reagan and Jane Wyman"—that is how the couple were featured in the ads—couldn't save it. Jane and Ron were the young couple/love interest in this disappointing sequel to the classic Marie Dressler–Wallace Beery *Tugboat Annie* made years ago at MGM. Marjorie

Rambeau now played the title role, opposite Alan Hale, and the hope was that a new series might be launched. It wasn't.

Tugboat Annie Sails Again is memorable today only because it features Reagan, Wyman, and, in a bit role, Neil Reagan. "Dutch" had tried to launch his brother as an actor and had convinced Bryan Foy to sign "Moon" for the B-unit. Neil was also cast in a small role in another film, this one of A caliber, *Destroyer*, starring Edward G. Robinson. But Neil Reagan soon realized his film career would be negligible and turned to radio. (He would later become a director of radio programs and for years directed the CBS favorite *Calling Dr. Christian.)*

Tugboat Annie's reviews mentioned that "Ronald Reagan and Jane Wyman made a pleasant pair of lovebirds," but it proved to be the last film the couple would make together.

The studio did try to launch the picture with some fanfare, by having the premiere in Tacoma, Washington, and sending Rambeau, Hale, Ronnie, Jane, and columnist Hedda Hopper for the festivities. Although Louella and Hedda were arch rivals, and disagreed on many issues and personalities, they agreed on the Reagans as "Hollywood's ideal couple." Hedda was a fierce moralist, and the upright Ronnie and Jane were her kind of people.

Even at this early point the Reagans were on the "A" list of the Hollywood social scene. Their friends were top stars, and one of Jane's closest pals was Mary Livingstone, Jack Benny's wife. The Bennys were leading party givers, and Jane and Ron were their welcomed guests and valued friends. The Reagans were also friends with George Burns and Gracie Allen, and with the young couple David "Sonny" Werblin, a rising agent, and his wife, singer Leah Ray.

Ron and Jane were still avid nightclubbers—Jane adored the ambience and Ron simply loved to dance. (One magazine referred to Wyman and Ronald Reagan by stating, "The Mocambo's their home.")

These were the days when all the stars, on one or two nights a week, would gather and socialize at the various "in" night spots like "the Troc" or Mocambo. These would be evenings when there were no early morning calls the next day, and in one night the photographers would take all the photographs they needed to keep the newspapers and magazines supplied for many weeks —sometimes months.

Jane and Reagan were often photographed out on the town with their friends, and these photos were cropped and reused many times, depending on the particular needs of a magazine or newspaper and the popularity of the player the month the magazine was going to press. The Reagans were snapped with Eddie Albert; Jane was photographed with James Stewart; Reagan, with Claudette Colbert and Barbara Stanwyck; Jane, with Stanwyck's then husband, Robert Taylor.

Jane was fortunate to have her spot in the public's mind as "the perfect wife," because she could hardly compete (not via the roles the studio was giving her) with the actresses making the news as glamour girls that season. Vivien Leigh was *the* actress of the year, thanks to *Gone With the Wind.* Jane's Warner Bros. confreres, Priscilla Lane and Olivia de Havilland, were getting lots of attention. The public was showing enormous interest in Linda Darnell, Judy Garland, Paulette Goddard, and Merle Oberon. Beautiful young Gene Tierney was on the rise and had made headlines that year when she eloped with young designer Oleg Cassini.

But unlike most other stars, who were only seen nightclubbing, Wyman and Reagan were often involved in sports activities together, such as playing golf. It is amazing that during this period the couple even had enough free time for an occasional golf game. Warners seemed to be working them constantly—in 1940, Reagan made five movies, Jane made six, and moviemaking was a grueling task. Sometimes actors were working on more than two movies at the same time—while they were shooting one, costume fittings for the next were in progress, as well as inserts, retakes, and dubbing for the last. The work was taxing, draining, and often frustrating.

Jane rounded out the year by doing yet another silly B, *Gambling on the High Seas*, with Wayne Morris, Roger Pryor, and Gilbert Roland. Then she bounced to best-friend-of-the-lead in an A, *Honeymoon for Three*. Ann Sheridan and George Brent (soon to be married in real life) were the stars.

Ann Sheridan was, and would remain, one of Jane's best friends. There was no rivalry between the women, although the gorgeous Texas-born redhead was enjoying the kind of career that Jane Wyman could only dream about.

While Jane's current on-screen "image" was still basically that of wisecracking chorus girl, Sheridan, after being on the Warners lot approximately the same time as Jane, was an undisputed glamour queen being cast in top pictures. She had clicked in the public mind as "The Oomph Girl," an appelation dreamed up by Warner Bros.'s publicity ace, Bob Taplinger. It was a label Sheridan despised, but it had done its job. It was obvious Jane's "perfect wife" label, however, wasn't launching Wyman into enviable screen roles.

But Jane was ecstatically happy on another level—she learned she was pregnant. Reagan later said, "I think Jane started talking about a baby the day after we were married. I wanted one, too, but I used all my male logic to persuade her that every young couple ought to wait a year. She agreed I was right as usual and she was wrong. So we had a baby." In fact, Reagan was even happier than Jane about the pregnancy. Both eagerly awaited the birth of their first child.

Reagan's career was certainly on the rise. He was getting the personalized publicity buildup with major fan magazine stories such as "Call Me Dutch." After *Knute Rockne*, Hal Wallis had cast Ron in *Santa Fe Trail*, starring Errol Flynn and Olivia de Havilland. Reagan would play the second male lead, the best friend of the hero, and fight for Olivia. He would lose her, of course, to Flynn, but Susan Peters would provide consolation.

While Reagan would get fourth (and below-the-title) billing, Flynn was not unaware that the studio was grooming Reagan for roles that he now played. And though in later years Reagan spoke glowingly of virtually everyone he worked with, Flynn was the one exception. Reagan has remembered Errol Flynn as petty and jealous. Flynn even tried to have fellow actors "block" Reagan from the camera's view!

Reagan, however, had learned a few camera tricks of his own. He made sure he was seen to best advantage. His role was large, and in *Santa Fe Trail* he was as handsome as Flynn. In fact, the film was filled with handsome men, including William Lundigan, William Marshall, David Bruce, and Van Heflin. Although the picture presented a muddled account of abolitionist John Brown's hanging (Brown was played by Raymond Massey), it was a highly effective Warner Bros. Technicolor adventure, directed by Michael Curtiz, and was destined to be a very big hit.

MGM asked to borrow Reagan for a role in *The Bad Man,* a western starring Wallace Beery, Lionel Barrymore, and Laraine Day. Meantime, *Knute Rockne, All American* was set for a huge premiere in South Bend, Indiana, at the University of Notre Dame, and the studio was sending a special train with the cast of the picture and Bob Hope and his radio show, to the opening.

Nelle Reagan told her son that his father was dreaming of making the trip too. Reagan made a call to the front office to ask permission for his dad to accompany them. In Reagan's words: "You could battle about a lot of things but you traveled first cabin with them—the studio said yes before I got the question out of my mouth."

Jane was awaiting the birth of their baby. It had been a problem-free pregnancy. She had made no secret that she wanted a boy. He was to be named Ronald.

Writer Helen Ware reported that when Pat O'Brien asked

Reagan whether he wanted a boy or a girl, Reagan said, "A girl. I wouldn't want any son of mine to go through what I'm going through, waiting for the baby to arrive!"

Ware noted that the expectant Reagans were different from the usual couple. "Ronnie is scared! Jane Wyman isn't. She's still the flip, wisecracking young modern." Miss Ware went on to say that it wasn't that Jane wasn't excited about the baby, but that she "has whipped the old-fashioned fears and bugaboos that usually herald the approach of the first baby."

On January 4, 1941, Jane gave birth to a girl, whom the Reagans named Maureen. At the hospital, after Jane found out it was a girl, she supposedly wailed: "Oh, don't talk about it. . . . Oh, Ronnie, it took so long, and it's *still* only a girl." Later, said friends, Jane "argued Ronnie" into believing she had wanted a girl all along.

It made good press that the baby had been born on almost the same day as Jane's birthday (which was January 5). This was an unbelievable "hook" for publicists to plant the story. It may be the reason that Jane's own birthday—that is, whether it is January 4 or 5—has been in question ever since. Although Jane has never denied the year of her birth, 1914, or that she was twenty-seven when Maureen was born, she has taken exception to the statement that her own birthday was January 4.

Reagan shared details about Maureen's birth with the Reagan-Wyman fans. He explained that the experience "made all this cartoon stuff about prospective fathers seem cheap." He had followed a strict schedule from the time Jane was hospitalized. He would go directly from the studio to Jane's hospital room. He was glad he was busy because "it kept my mind off things."

But he was happy to report that when Jane went into labor, "She threw aside the nurse's hand and the doctor's hand and grabbed mine and hung on to it for dear life . . . that gave me such a thrill as I can't believe."

On their first wedding anniversary, only two and a half weeks after Maureen's birth, it was reported that Reagan gave Jane an amethyst clip to match the engagement ring and other jewelry he had given her. Over the years he would add to this collection. Reagan was obviously a thoughtful husband as well as a sentimentalist. He always remembered Jane's birthday, their anniversary, and other special occasions. On Valentine's Day each year, Jane would receive a bouquet of red and white roses.

Now that they were parents, the Reagans, of course, had new interests. "Instead of nightclubbing, we spent most of our free time looking for a lot, looking at model homes," recalled Jane. At a screening one night they saw Rosalind Russell's new picture, *This Thing Called Love.* Jane has remembered, "As soon as her house flashed on the screen, both Ronnie and I said at once, 'That's it.' Next morning we dashed over to Columbia and got the plans. We had a miniature house made—it became a regular plaything, with us deciding little changes here and there, and how we'd arrange our furniture to fit."

Shortly after Maureen's birth, the Reagans found a piece of property that they liked in the Hollywood hills. Reagan's father, Jack, was in failing health, but he took great pride in his new granddaughter and in the fact that "Dutch" was successful and had been able to buy him and Nelle a house of their own. He also took great joy in the fact that "Dutch" had bought this new piece of property and was planning to build a house for himself and his new family. Jack often drove up to the lot Jane and Ron had bought, just to visualize the house they would someday erect. And Jack Reagan had even confided to his wife, after the fabulous trip to Notre Dame for the *Knute Rockne* premiere, that now he was ready to "go."

Ron had been picked that year, by Quigley Publications, as one of the film industry's "Stars of Tomorrow." His salary was up to $1,000 a week.

In April, Ron and Jane were making a publicity trip to the East

Coast and they stopped by Jack and Nelle's house to say good-bye. While the Reagans were in the east, Jack Reagan died, and a grief-stricken Ron and Jane returned for the funeral.

Jane was soon back at work. She shot a short subject with her husband, *How to Improve Your Golf.* Then came a Dennis Morgan–Wayne Morris western, *Bad Men of Missouri,* in which she had only a small role. Although her part was brief, Wyman was noticed. One critic observed, "The love scenes go by in a blur of speed. Jane Wyman, apparently, is a very pretty girl but she has what must be one of the shortest romantic roles in the history of horse opera."

The Body Disappears cast Wyman with Jeffrey Lynn and Edward Everett Horton. Then came *You're in the Army Now,* a comedy with Jimmy Durante and Phil Silvers. The draft had been reinstated in anticipation that America might enter the ever-enlarging war, and comedies about the draft were big box office: *Buck Privates* and *Caught in the Draft* had been huge hits in early 1941, and Warners was jumping on the bandwagon.

You're in the Army Now had one scene that has gone into the record books: it contains what is reported to be the longest kiss in screen history. The kiss, between Jane and Regis Toomey, lasts three minutes and five seconds (or about 4 percent of the film's total running time).

Reagan was on the set the day the scene was shot. "Ronnie was on the sidelines," recalled Toomey. After the scene, Reagan went over to Toomey and asked: "How did you get her to sit still that long?"

Reagan, too, was very busy that year. The studio had thrown him into two more programmers, *Million Dollar Baby* and *Nine Lives Are Not Enough.* Then he got the lead and top billing in *International Squadron.* The ads proclaimed: "It's the role that zooms Ronnie to the heights of stardom!" It was another story of a

Yank in the RAF. America had not yet entered the war, but sympathies were obviously with the British.

Now that he had finally proven himself, the studio rewarded Ronald Reagan with a lead in an A picture: *King's Row*. Ann Sheridan and Robert Cummings were to be top-billed, but Reagan's role was more than equal. The film was to be top director Sam Wood's version of the classic Henry Bellamann novel, a provocative and powerful tale of small-town life.

The role in *King's Row* had not been an easy one for Reagan to land. He was up against stiff competition: Eddie Albert, Jeffrey Lynn, Franchot Tone, Robert Preston, and even Dennis Morgan and Jack Carson were in the running.

In addition to the leads, the cast, which included Betty Field and Nancy Coleman, featured a superb group of character actors: Claude Rains, Charles Coburn, Judith Anderson, Maria Ouspenskaya, Harry Davenport, Ludwig Stossel. It was a top-notch crew as well: James Wong Howe was cinematographer, William Cameron Menzies (of *Gone With the Wind* fame) designed the sets, and Erich Wolfgang Korngold composed the musical score.

Frank Westmore has recalled, "For *King's Row*, Perc himself made up all the stars, but he categorically refused to apply any makeup at all to Ronald's visage. And he had a battle royal over it with director Sam Wood. Perc said, 'I am directing the makeup on this picture, and for the Reagan character to be believable, he cannot go around looking like a department store dummy.' Perc won. And Ronald Reagan never forgot that his makeup artist friend, by not making him up, helped him stand out in one of his few memorable performances."

Bob Cummings has recalled that the picture "was shot in about seven weeks, incredible for a film of this scope, for only around $760,000. But with all the talent and ingenuity involved, it looked like millions."

As soon as shooting on *King's Row* was finished, Reagan and Ann Sheridan were quickly teamed again in *Juke Girl*, a melodrama of migrant workers in Florida. California's San Joaquin Valley substituted for Florida. Reagan has recalled this film vividly because "I discovered how nervous fatigue can creep up on you. On the night shift, going to work at 6 PM, we shot night exteriors 'til sunup for thirty-eight nights."

In the meanwhile, Bill Meiklejohn, Reagan's agent, had sold his talent agency to MCA, including the contracts of all his clients. MCA was already a famous organization founded and headed by Dr. Jules Stein. It was not yet in a league with the Myron Selznick or William Morris agencies, but it would eventually be in a league all its own. Reagan was to be handled by the bright young MCA agent, Lew Wasserman.

After a rough cut of *King's Row* was ready, expectations were high and the studio wanted to renegotiate Reagan's contract even before the picture was released.

Reagan, always aware of the financial aspect of show business, wanted to wait and hold out for a better deal. Lew Wasserman reminded Reagan that as a member of the army reserve Ron had already been called in for a physical and might soon be called up. Reagan told Wasserman that the opinion of the medics at that time was that because of his poor eyesight he would never be called. Still, Wasserman pointed out to him, there was no sense taking chances. Others were joining up. Some actors had already been drafted. "We don't know how much time you have" was Wasserman's advice. "Let's get what we can while we can."

And so, while *Juke Girl* was still shooting, Reagan signed a new contract for a hefty $3,000 a week. With Reagan's climb to star salary and Jane still in the minor financial leagues, the usual questions arose about two-career families. Was there professional jealousy? Reagan said no: "I think the trouble usually comes from people resenting each other's success. This is especially true of actors. As for us, I can honestly say we share in one another's success, and we have fun talking about our work to each other."

The Reagans were enjoying their daughter and busy with

building their dream house. Fans were told, "The Reagans are sensible folk. They live on an allowance, and what they don't actually need goes smack into the bank every week and no nonsense. It makes it a little easier that Jane and Ronnie both work and they admit it. Those weeks when one or the other is on layoff, why, there's just that much less money to go into the bank."

But the fans were also given ridiculous accounts as to Reagan's behavior as a father. According to one fanciful report, in a meeting Reagan had with Jack Warner, "All [Ron] kept watching was a clock on the boss's desk, eyeing it with increasing dismay as each minute passed. Finally he could stand it no longer. He stood up in the midst of one of Mr. Warner's sentences and said, 'You'll have to excuse me, sir, but I can't stay a minute longer—I've got to go. You see, if I don't get home in fifteen minutes I don't get to bathe the baby, and that's my job. So long—I'm very late.'"

But, despite these silly exaggerations, it was true that Reagan enjoyed his new role of father. And in a beautiful tribute to Jane, he noted, "You know, the nice thing about having a girl is that you have a sort of picture of the girl you married, the girl you're in love with as a child and a young girl—you kind of watch her grow up. I know it's silly, but it gives you a kick."

Around this time it seemed as if Reagan's career was about to go into orbit. The studio announced that Ann Sheridan and Reagan would be teamed yet again, in a film tentatively titled *Casablanca*, and that Dennis Morgan would have the third lead. But there were many casting changes before *Casablanca* started production. (It is always interesting to speculate how certain films would have turned out with the casts initially intended by the studio.)

There was no doubt that Reagan was now traveling professionally on a different level than his wife. No longer, like Jane, did he *have* to do pictures that were assigned. Even he has admitted his surprise when Hal Wallis phoned him and said, "I'm sending over two scripts. Take your choice."

Reagan liked one of the scripts, but it would be a co-starring part with Errol Flynn. He told Wallis he couldn't decide between the two stories and he would do whichever Wallis suggested. Wallis was surprised—rarely did a star on Reagan's salary level leave such decisions to a producer. Wallis advised Reagan to take the co-starring role in the Flynn picture, *Desperate Journey,* rather than a starring role in a lesser script. Reagan conceded he also thought that the wisest choice but expressed his reservations on working with Flynn again.

"Will my part on the screen be as good as it is in the script?" Wallis promised the script would be shot as written.

In addition to Flynn, not everyone on the Warners lot at the time was charmed by Ronald Reagan. Marguerite Chapman, a popular player during these years, has remembered an encounter with him. "He was a big shot at Warners then," Miss Chapman has recalled. According to her, they were sitting at the same table in the commissary one day when Reagan embarrassed her. He wanted to know why she was a Catholic. "I was born one," she answered. "That doesn't mean you have to stay one," Reagan countered.

Miss Chapman has said that she has never liked him since. The actress appeared that year with Jane Wyman in two films: *The Body Disappears* and *You're in the Army Now,* which was due for release in early December.

You're in the Army Now, however, would soon be more than just a film title in the lives of Jane and Ronald Reagan.

○ ○ ○ ○ ○ ○ ○ ○ ○ ○ ○ ○ ○ ○ ○ ○ ○ ○

3

COUNTLESS AMERICAN LIVES WERE CHANGED BY THE
Japanese attack on Pearl Harbor on December 7, 1941, and by
the subsequent United States entry into World War II. Some lives
were altered in tragic ways. Most were touched in definite
though more subtle ways. Many millions of young men and
women found themselves transplanted to other parts of the
country and the world, often meeting and marrying people they
would never have encountered in peacetime conditions. At the
same time, a great many prewar marriages that might have survived a lifetime could not endure the strain of a long separation
and the changing moral and social attitudes the war would
evoke.

For the Reagans, as with millions of other couples, the war
meant change. In their case, their interests, and ultimately their
careers, would begin to veer in totally different directions.

At this point Ron was being groomed for stardom. Wyman,
although she had made great strides, was still a second-stringer.
Typical of her personality, she was honest about just where she
stood: "I'm queen of the sub-plots. I'm the girl who's the second
romantic lead. I always get a man, too, but the customers worry

about the star first, then about me. For years I've been the leading lady's confidante, adviser, pal, sister, severest critic."

Later, of these Warner Bros. years, she observed: "While Bette and Cagney were battling the studio, I went on working. I was a team player."

One of the amusing stories on the Warners lot during these years, when Davis and de Havilland would take suspensions rather than do what they considered inferior scripts, was that Jane had on more than one occasion said: "Give it to me—I'll do it!"

Years later, Reagan conceded, "True, Jane wasn't satisfied with the way her own career was going along." According to him, she would say, " 'I have so much of everything I won't be unhappy because I'm not getting the pictures I want.' " But sources indicate that this was not necessarily Jane's own philosophy—it was Reagan and others who had to point out to her that she had a great deal to be thankful for, and that she should not allow the frustrations about her career to spoil her happiness.

As the year 1941 drew to a close, the Reagans' seven-room dream house was almost complete. Although not a mansion by Hollywood standards, by the standards of the rest of America it was a palace. Its final cost was around $15,000, and Reagan had taken a twenty-year FHA mortgage to pay for it. Their monthly mortgage payment, including taxes and interest, was $125. They could have afforded a much larger dwelling, but the always practical Reagan was aware that the days of the big salaries could end instantly. This was a house they could afford even if he were working at a job outside the movies.

It was reported that the Reagans pooled their money. It was conceded the system worked only because Ron's ego was not at stake. At this time he made considerably more than his wife. In fact, the couple revealed that all of Jane's salary, and part of Ron's, had to go to pay income tax. Of course, their agents took out their 10 percent, and a big chunk went into their savings account for income tax. Ron and Jane lived on only about 25 to 30 percent of their earnings. Each had a car, and each reportedly took a cash allowance of $25 a week.

Their house, though costing $15,000—not a lot of money in movie star terms—was still out of the reach of 98 percent of Americans. It must be recalled that an average home in an average community at that time was priced at about $3,000. So although the Reagan place was not a fantastic, opulent estate along the lines of Pickfair, nor even a grand mansion like Jack Benny's $60,000 home or Bob Hope's $80,000 home, it was nonetheless relatively lavish.

The most extravagant feature of the house was its three bathrooms, two of them combination bathroom–dressing rooms—one for Jane, one for Ron. This was a necessity, since both had early-morning calls and needed space to prepare for work without interfering with the other.

Both actors owned extensive wardrobes, but again this had to do with their profession. Although he preferred sports clothes offscreen—tweedy jackets and slacks—Reagan did maintain a wardrobe of about ten suits, since he often provided his own clothing in modern-dress pictures. Jane provided her own shoes and stockings for her pictures.

There was a nursery, of course, and a porch, a huge yard, and gardens. And there was space, and plans, for a swimming pool. Although there was a kitchen and dining area, most of the downstairs of the house was a combination living room–den with pine-paneled walls and a brick fireplace. Jane was quoted as saying: "Paint and paper make a house. Brick and wood make a home."

Supposedly, Jane and Ron had changed the design of the house many times while it was being built, and Reagan himself had a great deal of in-put in the design and decoration. The walls were stained instead of painted; bookshelves were built in; and the house had an eclectic look—part English farmhouse, part southern plantation.

It was located high in the Hollywood hills and had a magnificent view. Shortly after the first of the year the Reagans moved in, even though the house was only partially furnished. What should have been the happiest moment of their lives was of course clouded because of the war situation. Everyone in America, during those first few months of 1942, was frightened and confused as to what course the war might take. People in California were especially concerned because there was a great fear that the Japanese would invade the mainland, and the West Coast seemed the most vulnerable.

However, Hollywood had already rallied to the call, and for the time being it was thought that the best course for the movie industry was to continue business as usual.

On the Warners lot, Reagan was making *Desperate Journey* with top-billed Errol Flynn, a tale of the RAF on a bombing mission to Germany. Every nationality of the British Commonwealth was represented, and then some: Flynn, the Australian; Arthur Kennedy, the Canadian; Alan Hale, the Scotsman; Ronald Sinclair, the Englishman. And, of course, Reagan as the American volunteer. It was another Yank-in-the-RAF, *International Squadron*-type story and typical of Hollywood's contribution to the war effort.

Jane, too, was busy with film assignments. Director Lloyd Bacon had used her in *Larceny, Inc.*, an Edward G. Robinson starrer (Jane played his daughter). Jack Carson was also in the cast, finally coming into his own after having been around Hollywood for years.

Comedian-actor-producer Harold Lloyd asked for Jane to be lent to RKO for his comedy-thriller musical, *My Favorite Spy*, which starred bandleader Kay Kyser. Jane's old pal William Demarest and Ellen Drew were in the cast. Tay Garnett was the director.

At Warners, Wyman was used in another programmer, *Crime by Night*. Then Jane went to 20th for the backstage musical

Footlight Serenade, a Betty Grable–Victor Mature vehicle with Gregory Ratoff as director.

Lucille Ball had originally been cast in the role that went to Wyman. But Lucy, under contract to RKO, was fearful that she would lose the lead in her home studio's upcoming *The Big Street* if she accepted the *Footlight Serenade* loan-out, so Ball took a suspension rather than do the Grable film.

Earl Luick was costume designer on *Footlight Serenade.* He recalls that Betty Grable was difficult to get along with, and was "convinced that everyone was against her." Grable nixed one of Luick's designs, "So I erased her name on the sketch and gave it to Jane Wyman. And Jane got all the wolf calls, much to Betty's displeasure." But Grable was still the star and Jane was once again the best friend, and while Grable and Wyman had both been dancing in the chorus line together eight years earlier, now Grable was the one rocketing toward the number-one spot as the top box office draw in the nation.

Wyman managed to maintain her status in the realm of movie stars, certainly in part because she was half of Hollywood's "most popular married couple." (Now, some seven years into her film career, she was selected a Quigley "Star of Tomorrow.") She was twenty-eight, however, and at best her career was at a standstill. Unfortunately, there was little Jane could do at the moment to improve her professional situation, other than spreading the word via columnists and friends and letting key executives at Warners know that she was eager and willing for bigger and better roles.

The Reagans' happy marriage and contented parental state had continued long enough so that it was no longer news. Naturally, it would be newsworthy if they *weren't* as happily married as the public had been led to believe. . . .

Gossip is what the name "gossip column" is all about, and there were always those who were out to speculate and predict discord in Hollywood's "ideal marriage."

One day Jane had a lunch date with Joy Hodges. Miss Hodges had to cancel at the last moment, and since Jane was already at the restaurant she lunched with one of the Warner Bros. directors who happened to be there. The next day a column item appeared: "Wonder if the Reagans are breaking up?"

Although the Reagans said they laughed at such nonsense, the lesson—that the press could be dangerous—was not lost on either of them. Ron was very astute about the workings of the Hollywood press corps. He would never allow photographers to place him in a position where the resulting "candid" photos would make it appear he was "alone" with another woman. And even when asked to pose with studio starlets for publicity, he made sure that the shots were *obviously* for publicity.

Despite the beginning of the inevitable press speculation of discord in the Reagan marriage, this was in fact a time of great personal happiness and togetherness for Jane and Ron.

Then, while shooting *Desperate Journey*, Reagan received the envelope so many young men in America were anticipating. It contained the call to duty; Reagan was expected to report to Fort Mason in San Francisco in fourteen days.

Before Ron left for Fort Mason, Jane threw a small farewell party for him. Guests included Jack Benny and Mary Livingstone, Robert Taylor and Barbara Stanwyck, Pat and Eloise O'Brien, and Ann Sheridan and George Brent.

King's Row hadn't yet been released, but thanks to Lew Wasserman's foresight, Reagan's new contract was in force. The actor had already collected his $3,000 weekly salary for ten weeks— $30,000. But now the Reagans faced a problem that confronted all couples caught in the draft situation: He would have to take a *drastic* cut in salary when he entered the army—from $12,000 a month, Reagan's income would now drop to between $250 and $300 per month.

But as far as his career was concerned, a fascinating situation was about to occur, one that not only would keep Reagan in the public eye for the entire time he was serving his country but would dramatically elevate Jane's visibility as well. As Wyman and Reagan had symbolized the ideal Hollywood couple in publicity up to this point, they would soon find themselves representing something far more lofty and pertinent. They would epitomize "The All-American Soldier and His Wife," starring Jane as the woman left behind, but with a job of her own, to support herself, raise their family, and contribute to the war effort.

Beginning now and continuing through the war years, the Reagans would receive coverage in the all-important fan magazines unmatched by virtually any other couple in film history.

Reagan's departure for San Francisco in April 1942 was the start. Everything that had previously been written about the duo was prologue for setting them up now as Hollywood's "Mr. and Mrs. America Fighting the War." And the Reagans seemed tailor-made for their roles. "So long, Button Nose," he may have said to Jane personally, but he also said it to millions of fans. Jane was left at home with Maureen—to wait, pray, and, of course, to survive.

Magazine stories accentuated Jane's involvement in the war. "It's Jane's war now. She read about it, she worked for the Red Cross, and had been wakened by anti-aircraft fire and entertained the boys at army camps. She'd seen Ronnie's sick face bent over a picture of the small, swollen bodies of children starved to death in Poland. 'This,' said the war-hating Reagan, between set lips, 'would make it a pleasure to kill.' After he had been called up," the article continued, "Jane realized 'Now it's real. Now it's Ronnie's war and mine.' "

The death of Carole Lombard in a plane crash—the star was on a bond-selling tour—brought Hollywood its first wartime casualty. From this point on, the town quickly assumed a toned-down facade. Diamonds were discreetly discarded for less ostentatious adornment. Jane's own glamour garb was discarded for "at home" photo layouts in which an apron replaced her mink coat. Baby daughter Maureen assumed a starring role in publicity—

"The All-American Baby," so to speak, waiting for Daddy to come home on leave.

Although fan magazines and columns gave the impression that soldier Reagan was far away from home for a long time, in reality he was only in San Francisco for eight weeks before returning to Hollywood, where he was eventually reassigned from the cavalry Reserve to the Army Air Corps and given a position with the special services unit headquartered at the Hal Roach Studios in Culver City.

"We were thirteen hundred men and officers, very few of whom had had any military training, and trapped by an Air Force regulation that said only flying officers could command a post," Reagan has recalled. "Our only flying officer was the stunt pilot, Paul Mantz. Paul had been commissioned a major because of his background as a great motion picture stunt pilot and his vast knowledge of aerial photography." (Mantz was better known in Hollywood as "The Honeymoon Pilot." He had flown virtually all of Tinseltown's celebrities who eloped to Las Vegas or Yuma.)

The stars and industry people stationed at "Fort Roach" were referred to as the "Culver City Commandos." At one time or another during the war Clark Gable, Alan Ladd, George Montgomery, Van Heflin, Arthur Kennedy, and Craig Stevens were stationed there. The First Motion Picture Unit actually had, at one time, six production units working simultaneously. There were a lot of shenanigans going on and Lt. Reagan, of course, participated in many of them.

Reagan was post personnel officer, and when he wasn't busy narrating or acting in training films, he had to assume clerical duties. They were often dull, and to pass the tedious hours on the base, Lieutenant Reagan would let his imagination roam. On one report to post commander Paul Mantz, Reagan noted under "Observations": "Very poor place to make pictures. Recommend entire post be transferred as near as possible to 42nd Street and

Broadway, New York City. Also suggest several westerns to be made to round out the program."

In another report to Mantz the future Commander in Chief, who would make worldwide headlines for his off-microphone flip jokes, showed that even this early he was capable of kidding the existing situation. In a report listing "Irregularities and Disturbances," Lieutenant Reagan joked: "3 A.M.—Post attacked by three regiments of Japanese Infantry. Led Cavalry charge and repulsed enemy. Quiet resumed."

King's Row was now in general release and was proving to be the sensational hit everyone knew it would be. Although screenwriter Casey Robinson had had to alter some of the novel's plot points—such as changing incest to insanity, and skirting completely the issues of homosexuality and euthanasia—it was still a powerful story that the American Medical Association was not very happy about, since it presented doctors in a generally poor light.

However, the picture had given Ronald Reagan *the* role of his career—a young playboy whose legs are amputated by a sadistic and moralistic surgeon (played by Charles Coburn) in retaliation for the boy's philandering ways. In the film, when Reagan's character discovers his legs have been amputated, he cries out: "Where's the rest of me?" It was a shattering moment and Ronald Reagan played it to perfection. (Reagan would later use the line as the title for his autobiography.)

With a picture and a performance like this under his belt, Reagan had every right to expect a career on the level of his contemporaries James Stewart and Robert Taylor. And if the war hadn't erupted at this time, there is every reason to believe that such would have been the case.

Undoubtedly the Warner Bros. hierarchy thought so as well, since while Reagan was still in the service, Lew Wasserman once again renegotiated the actor's contract so that when released,

Reagan would be receiving $3,500 per week, forty-three weeks per year, instead of $3,000 per week forty weeks per year.

By June 1942 there were rumblings that Jane had developed the clown's traditional yearning to play *Hamlet*. Ron had proven that he could, via *King's Row*, make the transition from light comedy to drama, and Jane was more than ready to do the same, ready to add another "role" to those she was presently playing. She was, after all, three distinct personalities: Mrs. Ronald Reagan; the mother of Maureen; and Warner Bros.' on-screen "dumb bunny." Jane would never be at a loss for screen work as long as she continued to take the roles of wisecracking sidekick. But as soon as she moved to broaden her horizons, roles became fewer and farther between.

And something else now occurred in the industry that affected Jane's career. All studios had cut production of B pictures. Raw film footage was, like many items during the war years, suddenly rationed. And because of the war, with servicemen concentrated in certain areas and factories working swing shifts, movie houses were now filled day and night. Films that ordinarily would have played three days to a week were now held over for three and sometimes four weeks. The motion picture industry found it had its largest audience ever, and was making its most money, while having to produce fewer pictures! The major studios, which had each brought out more than sixty films a year in the late thirties, were now producing only half that amount.

So Jane no longer had the option of being able to fall back on B's for leading-lady roles. And by moving into the ranks of A films, the competition for parts became much keener.

Jane realized there were hazards in pursuing career ambitions as far as her marriage was concerned. She was quoted as saying: "Maybe two serious careers would be too much in a single family. Perhaps it's better to let Ronnie play drama and let me work at having fun. It keeps a balance in our family."

Perhaps, she reasoned, the studio should make use of her other abilities. She was a better than average singer. In Hollywood, for fun, Jane would often sing at parties for friends and they would all encourage her to use this talent on screen.

Finally, it was the entry of the United States into the war that provided Wyman with an opportunity to utilize her singing talent. Hollywood had instantly mobilized to aid in the war effort by providing entertainment for servicemen. (Bob Hope and Dorothy Lamour had begun entertaining the troops even before America's entry into the war.) Now almost everyone in Hollywood was involved in one way or another. There was always a problem, however, when sending certain stars to entertain: What could most of the stars *do?* Crosby and Lamour could sing; Hope, Jack Carson, and Joe E. Brown and other stand-up comedians could tell jokes. Orson Welles could perform magic tricks. Astaire could dance. But most stars were ill-equipped for in-person performing. Other than standing there and looking good, what could beauties like Linda Darnell, Veronica Lake, and Hedy Lamarr contribute?

The Victory Committee learned that Wyman could sing, and this made her a valuable asset for camp shows. Singing at these shows not only gave Wyman an opportunity to stretch her talent, it exposed this side of her abilities to the Hollywood community. And this acceptance of her talent undoubtedly increased her desire to convince Warners to utilize her as a singer.

Jane had returned to the home lot for another "friend" role, this time in *Princess O'Rourke*, an Olivia de Havilland–Robert Cummings starrer. Wyman was paired again with Jack Carson. The film was written and directed by Norman Krasna.

De Havilland was unhappy at the studio and fighting with her bosses, so it was a tense set that summer of 1942. In addition, Cummings was making another picture at Universal at the same time. However, in *Princess O'Rourke* there was an interesting scene for Jane in which the flip character she played also displayed a serious side. The scene was with Jack Carson and took place while the couple were dining in a Chinese restaurant. Although at the time it hardly changed her life, this particular dramatic scene would later prove to have a significant effect on Jane Wyman's career.

The Warners' point of view, however, was to keep her "funny." They felt they had finally found the perfect partner for her in wisecracking Jack Carson, and the front office planned to team the duo again.

Bob Cummings has recalled working with Jane on *Princess O'Rourke,* and noted, "She could be a lot of fun." Regarding Reagan and Jane, Cummings later observed, "I never heard him say one bad word about her, but I've personally heard her say plenty about him. I don't know why she did that. I remember she told me, '. . . all he talks about morning, noon and night is world affairs.'"

Jane was scheduled to leave on a bond tour September 9. On Saturday the 6th, just as she was finishing her last scene for *Princess O'Rourke* she got a call from the Victory Committee. Rita Hayworth was ill, and Jane was asked to take over Hayworth's tour to Kentucky.

For four weeks Wyman toured southern towns. There were luncheons, speeches, meetings with dignitaries, and the constant chore of selling bonds. For most of the trip she subsisted on tea, toast, and fruit juices, since solid food upset her stomach in the rush of travel. It was reported that Jane lost fourteen pounds on the tour.

She and John Payne worked the tour together. They had known each other for years and helped keep up each other's morale on this grueling trip. Jane would auction off songs from John: "How much will you lend Uncle Sam to hear John sing?" And often fans bought bonds to hear Jane sing. Once, having sung the first two lines of a tune, she slid to a halt. "If somebody's got a thousand bucks," she said sweetly, "I'll start this over again in the right key."

Sometimes, in the spirit of the moment, she'd sell her earrings, compact, or cigarette case. Payne would auction off his necktie. The auctions were a hit with the fans and sold many bonds.

At one of the rallies, one man astonished even Jane. Wyman has unique powers of description and she said the man "looked like a businessman who walks from one place to another and eats lunch." The man asked if she had a $15,000 bond. She blanched, recovered, and said: "If you can find the fifteen thousand, I guess we can find the bond."

It turned out the man was a big-time gambler. But characteristically Jane asked, "If he'd been a doctor, you'd say so, and people would feel good about doctors. Why shouldn't gamblers get credit?"

At the end of the tour Jane was off to Dixon, Illinois, where she joined her husband, Bob Hope, Ann Rutherford, Bebe Daniels, Ben Lyon, and Jerry Colonna. Reagan's home town was sponsoring Louella Parsons Day. To end the madcap month Jane returned to Hollywood, and, accompanied by her soldier husband, attended the premiere of Warner Bros.' James Cagney blockbuster *Yankee Doodle Dandy*.

Although the columns and fan magazines continued to indicate that Wyman and Reagan were undergoing the same deprivations that every young military couple were enduring, this was not quite the case. Although they never outright lied, all articles implied that from the beginning Reagan and Wyman continued to be separated by the war—this was not true. While working at the Hal Roach Studios, where the First Motion Picture unit of the Army Air Corps was stationed, Lieutenant Reagan often lived at home and commuted to work. Also unlike most American families at this time, the Reagans had a great deal of household help. Maureen had a nanny, and there was a couple who helped keep house.

Meanwhile, Lieutenant Reagan was not idle at Fort Roach. The Air Corps did utilize his talents as an actor, casting him in three training films—*Mr. Gardenia Jones, Rear Gunner,* and *For God and Country.* In the last he played a Catholic priest.

When the Reagans made the social circuit together, he was, of course, always seen in uniform.

In early 1943, Lieutenant Reagan returned to the Warners soundstage. He had been cast in Irving Berlin's all-star propaganda musical for Warners, *This Is the Army,* a re-creation of the hit Broadway stage production. According to Reagan, "This was a military assignment and we drew our military pay. I was a First Lieutenant at the time, so my gross was about $250 a month."

Joan Leslie, who had scored big in *Yankee Doodle Dandy,* was Reagan's love interest in the picture. (Both she and George Murphy were billed over Reagan in the final release.) Miss Leslie has recently recalled, "Ron and I enjoyed working together. We had the same kind of opinions about our studio. . . . It was known as 'the factory,' you know. People who were under contract were expected to do what they were told. We had little to say about the films we were put into or loaned out for. If you wanted to go higher, you had to gather your forces—your talents, your agents, whatever—to take stands."

Referring to Jane Wyman during these years, Miss Leslie recalls, "She was under contract . . . and not much was happening. She was determined, though, to move out of the light parts she was getting."

Much of *This Is the Army* was filmed at Camp Pendleton near San Diego, and Joan Leslie has recalled that Reagan "seemed to have more knowledge of the overall problems of production than the average actor, and wasn't only concerned with his own motivation and part."

But Reagan has noted, "It was a thrill for me to get away from the desk and feel once again that I was part of the picture business. There were old friends to work with: George Murphy played my father and I've never let him forget it."

Murphy and his wife, Julie, were quite friendly with Wyman

and Reagan and would often attend the same parties. Actually, Murphy and Reagan had a great deal more than partygoing in common. As Tom Lewis, the founder and then head of Armed Forces Radio, says today: "George Murphy and Ronald Reagan were never really actors. They were always politicians. They knew more of what was going on behind the scenes."

There is no doubt that Reagan and Murphy's friendship was based primarily on their mutual interest in what was happening in the Screen Actors Guild—a subject about which Wyman felt little enthusiasm. She did, however, always seem interested when an activity or discussion was all about movies. The 1943 Academy Awards ceremonies were held at Grauman's Chinese Theater, and a radiant Jane, accompanied by her very handsome soldier husband, attended the ceremonies.

During these war years, Reagan, free of hectic moviemaking schedules, had time to get more involved in the inner workings of the Guild and to observe firsthand what was happening behind the scenes in all the various unions associated with the motion picture industry. Now that he was virtually removed from the world of moviemaking, he was able to devote energy and thought to other matters. Like many others, he was concerned about what the world, and especially the industry he was returning to, would be like after the war.

On the home front, people who knew them at the time recall that when Reagan's brother, Neil, visited their home, Jane was not too happy. It was not because she disliked "Moon," but because she knew the kind of evening she was in for. "Argument is meat and drink to Ron and Neil," one source stated, and apparently "they'd rather argue than do anything else."

When "Dutch" and "Moon" were together, Jane didn't stand a chance of getting an opportunity to talk. Jane even spoke to the press about her dislike of the Reagan brothers' get-togethers. One scenario quoted Jane as telling her deep-in-discussion husband and brother-in-law one evening, "Okay, gentlemen. I'm going to bed."

But their loud voices rose to the bedroom, where she was trying to read. She was angry and took action. She rang for one of the servants.

"Will you please ask Mr. Reagan to come up?"

"Which one?"

"Both of them."

When they arrived, Jane was adamant. "Moon," she said, "you've got to go home."

"Why, what did I do?"

"First, you won't let me get a word in edgewise, and now I can't even read."

The men stared at her.

"Don't *look* at me that way."

Ronnie, the tale concluded, cajoled her out of her anger, and "Moon," or so the story goes, went home.

It became painfully obvious during this period that Jane and Ron had little in common when it came to "issues of the day." Jane was interested in her family and her career and, of course, the end of the war. But she was apolitical and bored with "talk, talk, talk."

Although Reagan had little to do with the actual war, magazines continued to accent his involvement: "Acting is something he did in another life. His mind has no room for it now. Morning or noon, midnight or five o'clock, he's buried deep in the war."

Jane continued to entertain the troops. She reportedly loved these activities and downplayed both her and her husband's film careers when pressed to comment on what a dual-career household was like. "Ronnie and I look on our careers as business propositions and not as anything glamorous or out of the ordinary," she said. "Our Maureen has given us a new perspective and certainly she has given us both the inspiration to be doubly successful in our business and to plan for the future. . . . And

the beginning: a starlet
liating personality-plus,
en in "bit" roles.

With William Hopper (Hedda's son) on the set of *Public Wedding* (1937), a programmer in which Jane played her first leading lady part.

Metamorphosis: Wyman in her sultry-platinum-blond-siren phase.

Jane had such a fondness for elaborate, glitzy jewelry (mostly costume), that Louella Parsons once told her she looked like a walking Christmas tree.

Ronald Reagan, unlike Wyman, was considered star material from the very beginning of his film career.

Above: Wyman and Reagan in *Brother Rat* (1938), their first picture together. At the time Jane was still married to her first husband; Reagan had never been married and was playing the field.

Below: Jane and Warners heartthrob Wayne Morris, in a scene from *Brother Rat.*

Portent of things to come: Jane adjusting a light in the studio photo gallery. She was, in much later years, to become a lady famous for calling *all* the shots in her career.

Never-before-published candid of Jane Wyman and Ronald Reagan—by 1939 the couple was "a serious romantic item."

Above: Wyman, on Reagan's lap, holds on to her hat as they are driven to a film preview in a vintage car. Garnering publicity was the order of the day for all contract actors.

Below: January 26, 1940: Jane becomes Mrs. Ronald Reagan. In-laws Nelle and Jack Reagan flank the bride and groom.

In *Tugboat Annie Sails Again,* made after their marriage, Wyman and Reagan were playing lovebirds. The picture wasn't a big success.

Jane learned to fake playing the violin for *My Love Came Back* (1940). The star of the picture, however, was Olivia de Havilland.

Reagan hit the big time with *King's Row* (1941). Leading lady Ann Sheridan was one of Jane's best friends.

America's "perfect couple" frequently made the nightclub circuit. Reagan loved to dance; Jane loved to nightclub. By now America was at war. Reagan was a lieutenant in the Army Air Force.

Presenting Maureen Elizabeth Reagan—"the all-American baby."

Below: "The perfect family": Ron, Maureen, Jane. This was typical of the image presented of the Reagans for years.

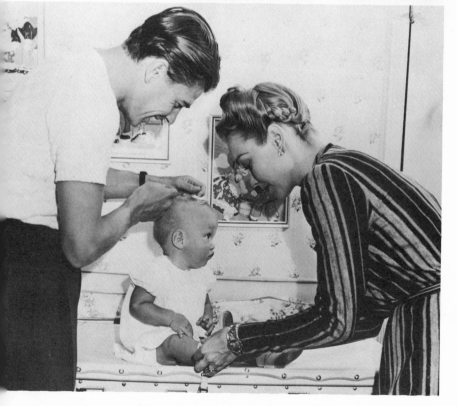

Mother and daughter.

Husband and wife: the epitome of wholesome sex appeal.

"The perfect wife," ostensibly doing all the housework. (In fact, there were two servants.)

Wyman doing her bit for the war effort. She models "the latest in welding outfits for lady factory workers."

MODERN SCREEN

JANUARY

10 CENTS

E WYMAN
LD REAGAN

"MY SOLDIER" BY JANE WYMAN

"The ideal couple" adorn the cover of *Modern Screen* (January 1943).

Captain Ron, daughter Maureen, and Mama Jane. In 1944, as World War II raged on, Wyman and Reagan were still "Hollywood's constant honeymooners."

Three-year-old Maureen helps Mommy gather newspapers to be used as salvage material to aid in the war effort.

Jane poses in front of war posters: "Keep working to *keep* him winning," says one; *"United* we win!" says the other.

The "typical American wife" and her "typical American daughter" enjoying "a typical day" at home.

Although Ann Sheridan *(center)* and Alexis Smith *(right)* were the stars of *The Doughgirls* (1944), Jane received the best reviews.

what marriage can go on the rocks when plans are always being made for tomorrow and next year and the years after that?"

The Reagans' staying happily married during the war years was seemingly an inspiration to millions of other couples who might have difficulty with their relationships during this tense time of separation and uncertainty.

Jane entertained at the Hollywood Canteen and continued to travel on tours to sell bonds. Wyman is credited with an unusual contribution to the war effort. "Boys in the British Army can thank Miss Wyman for a contribution to morale and romance. Last fall, military censors started blacking out the x's in letters from sweethearts. They claimed the kiss symbols might be code. Jane suggested the girls press their well-lipsticked lips to the paper, a more graphic symbol of affection than x's."

After completing *This Is the Army*, Reagan spent the remainder of the war at Fort Roach.

Although *This Is the Army* was released in 1943, and Reagan had had three very successful movies released the previous year —*King's Row, Juke Girl,* and *Desperate Journey*—the actor felt that whatever progress he had made was fast slipping away.

Reagan had also undoubtedly been disconcerted when, after production of *This Is the Army* was completed, Irving Berlin took him aside and said, "You really should give this business some serious consideration when the war is over. It's possible that you could have a career in show business." Reagan has recalled, "I thanked him very much and began to wonder if he just hadn't seen any movies or if the war had been going on so long I'd been forgotten."

Reagan was hardly forgotten; 1943 brought him publicity coverage on a par with the superstars of the business. He and Jane, posed together, were on the covers of major magazines, garnering as much space during the year as Rita Hayworth, Ingrid

Bergman, Errol Flynn, Judy Garland, and new heartthrob Alan Ladd, all big box office favorites.

The image of the Reagans as the perfect couple continued to get a big buildup. "My Soldier—by Jane Wyman" was a typical movie magazine piece. "Guess who's the best-looking, all-round nicest officer in Uncle Sam's Army: Yes—Ronnie Reagan!"

Early in the year there were rumors Jane was pregnant again, but she denied them. Reagan squired her to various Hollywood social functions, and they were frequently mentioned in the columns. But fans wanted more articles on the Reagans. After all, as one reporter noted, "Their name might be Smith or Jones, they're such a typical American family; Dad wearing wings, Mom war-working and even baby saying prayers!"

This was a lot to live up to.

In June 1943, Jane appeared on the network radio program *Hollywood Theater of the Air*, playing the lead in "Bachelor Mother" (originally a Ginger Rogers movie). Radio was a chance to let producers know you could play all kinds of roles, something Jane was anxious to do. That same year Jane hosted a couple of Jack Benny's radio programs when Benny was ill.

In September, *Princess O'Rourke* opened. It was Jane's only film in release for 1943 (unusual, since previously Jane had been popping up in at least four to five films per year). It was, of course, de Havilland's vehicle, but Wyman received excellent reviews. "Jack Carson and Jane Wyman draw rich humor and honest sentiment from the roles of two friends," wrote *New York Times* critic Bosley Crowther. The film generally received good to great reviews, and Mr. Crowther was not the only one to notice that Wyman could play both comedy and drama in the same character.

More significantly, two very important people in the industry liked and responded to Jane's performance in the film. They were producer Charles Brackett and director Billy Wilder.

During the year Jane had been reteamed with Jack Carson in a remake of *The Animal Kingdom*. The leads were Ann Sheridan and Dennis Morgan, but the film, although it received a lot of in-production publicity, was so bad, it was held from release by the studio for several years. Ironically, the film Jane had made the previous year, *Crime by Night*, was also sitting on the shelf.

Wyman's friend Louella Parsons revealed Jane's feelings during this period of her career: "Time after time she would come to me in frustration and despair, asking why, why wouldn't someone give her a real chance.

" 'Hold on and keep working,' I would tell her. 'Your chance must come.' "

Around this time Jane and Ron started referring to Jane's "ulcer." Although they told people it was a nonexistent ulcer, just a gag, the tag line around the house had become, "Don't annoy me. Remember my ulcer."

Indirectly, Jane got a career boost at this time through Bob Hope. The Reagans went to a party one night attended by Hope, his wife, Dolores, and others, including Judy Garland. Garland sang, and then Wyman sang—indicating no reluctance to be compared to the girl considered by her peers to be the most talented pop singer of her era. Judy had been a regular on Hope's radio program; when Hope heard Wyman sing, he invited her to do the program as well.

Jane sang a novelty song on the Hope show—"Fuddy Duddy Watchmaker"—and did a comedy routine with Hope. Radio offers started coming in, and as a result of the attention radio garnered for her, Warner Bros. realized Jane might have a career in that medium or—even more threatening—a lucrative contract offer from a rival studio.

The events placed Jane in a good bargaining position when her seven-year contract expired, and Warners, of course, was anxious to renew. She re-signed; the studio was "home," and at last she'd made the leap to the point where they said they considered her a "leading lady."

The fan magazines continued their extensive coverage of "Those Reagans" with many spreads about "Ronnie and Janie at Home" and "Bringing Up Baby." Some articles pictured Jane "writing" to her soldier husband, and keeping him up-to-date on the baby's progress. At the time, one could not pick up a major movie magazine without reading a story about "The Reagans."

In all fairness, it must be noted that in exploiting this kind of "ideal couple" situation (the wife a successful actress and her actor husband in the service), the magazine editors had discovered that Wyman and Reagan were just about the only game in town. No other leading Hollywood couple could be perceived as Mr. and Mrs. America—Robert Taylor and Barbara Stanwyck were not exactly "typical," Tyrone Power and Annabella even less so. In retrospect, it is evident that it was publicity coverage on "The Reagans" that was the balloon that kept Jane Wyman highly visible in a very fast-moving and highly competitive business.

Producer Alex Gottlieb sent Jane a script for a new film. Warners wanted to team Jane again with Jack Carson in something called *Make Your Own Bed*. Carson was now being given the big buildup, but with this film Jane would at least achieve the rank of co-star billing—above the title. Despite the good intentions, however, the script for *Make Your Own Bed* was weak, and the players couldn't save it from being merely another programmer.

Jane had set her sights on an ambitious project owned by Warners—the life story of torch singer Helen Morgan. In her campaign to land the role, Jane even posed for stills in the studio gallery, gowned and coiffed as a chanteuse, complete with long silk handkerchief in hand. But in typical Warners fashion the property about Morgan languished for years, until 1957, when Ann Blyth got the role.

Although Wyman was obviously being led to believe big things were in store, after *Make Your Own Bed* the studio wanted her for another supporting role, this time in *The Doughgirls*. Mark

Hellinger was producing this film version of the hit Broadway play, a comedy about the housing shortage in wartime Washington. It was an A film, of course, but Jane would be fourth-billed under Ann Sheridan, "new" star Alexis Smith, *and* Jack Carson. It hardly seemed the kind of film or situation that would further her career.

She was pressured to do *Doughgirls*. She did, after all, have a new contract with a healthy salary hike. But for the first time the young actress, who'd always played the "game" and had never made waves, may have contemplated risking the studio's ultimate weapon—suspension—and that meant loss of income. Sources indicate that Jane's pal Ann Sheridan finally convinced her to join the cast of *Doughgirls*.

"Ah, do it!" said Sheridan, pointing out they'd be together, it would be fun, and besides, "What can you lose, a lousy fortune?"

"Annie" Sheridan, as she was known to her friends, remained a close pal of both Wyman's and Reagan's and often saw them socially. Miss Sheridan once told a story about an evening she spent at the Reagan home. "I'd go there because Jane was such a good cook. On one occasion Ronnie, a baseball nut, had heard a game on radio and he gave us a play-by-play account. After the fourth inning, Jane said, 'Ronnie, please stop, Annie doesn't care about baseball.' But he went on for all nine innings."

Jane used to tell Sheridan and other friends that Ronnie was such a talker, he made speeches in his sleep!

The government utilized Reagan's speechmaking abilities by sending him on a bond-selling tour in 1944 with a number of other stars including John Garfield. Leo Guild, who was a publicist with Warners at the time, has recalled that on tour, "when Garfield and I were out chasing women, Reagan was in the hotel room studying scripts. He was a very serious man."

Back in Hollywood, working on *Doughgirls* proved to be fun for Jane. It became evident that Wyman, and Eve Arden were stealing the picture.

The studio had promised Jane that after *Doughgirls* they would give her an opportunity to sing on-screen. *Hollywood Canteen* was in preproduction. It was one of Warner Bros.' all-star Hollywood tributes, loosely based on the founding of the Hollywood Canteen by Bette Davis, John Garfield, and others. Davis and Garfield would be in the picture along with practically every star on the Warners lot. Billing would be alphabetical, so Jane would still, ironically, be at the very bottom of the list. Her old friend LeRoy Prinz would create and direct the musical numbers. In the picture, Jane and Jack Carson would sing a duet, a song titled "What Are You Doing the Rest of Your Life?"

Make Your Own Bed was released in early 1944; and Warners, two months later, brought out the shelved *Crime by Night. The Doughgirls* was released that summer, and Jane received very good reviews. *The New York Times* said: "She played a priceless nitwit who is a great admirer of President Roosevelt's because of his fine acting in 'Yankee Doodle Dandy.' "

And even though Wyman received fourth billing, many newspaper reviews of the picture included a photo of her rather than the other women, indicating her growing popularity.

Everyone knew her career was gaining momentum. Jane was quoted as writing to her husband: "Don't look now, hon, but that little speck miles down the road behind you is me. Took me two and a half years, while you were in the service, to get even that close."

About this time it appeared that Ron and Jane were having a few real problems in their relationship, mainly because Ron's interests simply were no longer the same as Jane's. One account stated that although "she's poured her time and strength into war work, in Hollywood and out, like most of us she needs occasional surcease from the subject. Ronnie doesn't." Reagan's growing interest in world affairs superseded any interest he had in his wife's career. When Jane wanted him to share her enthusiasm about her new status at Warners, he said, "That's swell, Janie. It's about time." But then he quickly changed the subject to what was happening in politics and the war.

During these publicity-filled years, Jane did not succeed in charming all columnists. Hy Gardner, Hedda Hopper's former legman now writing a column of his own, was one whom Jane undoubtedly, if unknowingly, snubbed. Gardner subsequently wrote: "The Wyman woman, unlike the genuine cream of the cinema crop whose names are boxoffice magic, seems to consider the approach of a reporter as an irksome intrusion upon the privacy of a high-priced public goldfish."

Jane devoted a lot of time to working at the Hollywood Canteen. Reagan had been promoted from lieutenant to captain, and publicity continued to mislead the public into thinking that Reagan was stationed far from home. Some column items, such as "After Ronnie left Jane and Hollywood for the Army, his fan mail swelled to second place at Warners," furthered this misconception.

Cracks in the facade of the Wyman-Reagan idyll were filled in and covered over by the continuing tide of family-oriented publicity. "Mur-mur," as Maureen Reagan was then known to Wyman-Reagan fans, was the most photographed and publicized child of Hollywood. (Supposedly, Maureen had had trouble with her r's and dubbed herself "Mur-mur.")

The Reagans were obviously willing participants in the constant publicity about Maureen's upbringing. A typical story: "They play with the baby till bedtime. She rides the length of the room on Ronnie's back, clutching neck or collar or hair, whichever comes handiest, and thinks he's a bucking bronco. They watch Nanny bathe her and feed her and put her to bed. Sometimes Ronnie takes over all three jobs. . . ."

Furthermore, although they had a three-year-old much publicized daughter, the Reagans were still referred to as "the constant honeymooners." However, by late 1944, with Jane's career starting to make progress at last, Reagan was being talked about good-naturedly in some stories as "Mr. Wyman."

However, these snide references to Reagan as a has-been were simply not rooted in fact. Throughout 1944 he continued, via publicity, to be on a par with the silver screen's elite—Reagan and Van Johnson were the two male stars most featured on magazine covers. Van represented the young men at home; Ron represented the young men in uniform.

One of the Reagans' close friends was Dick Powell. In 1944, Powell married June Allyson. Miss Allyson has said that Ron and Jane "were two of the most interesting new friends" she made. The Reagans, and George and Julie Murphy, were among the newly married Powells' first dinner guests at their Bel-Air mansion.

"Dick Powell, George Murphy and Ronnie Reagan were all very involved with the Screen Actors Guild," recalled Miss Allyson, "and this also formed a bond between us three couples."

June Allyson has described Reagan and Powell as "close buddies—a love of arguing politics drew them together just as a distaste for the same subject brought me and Jane Wyman together in a fortuitous blending of couples. . . . Richard was also old friends with Jane Wyman . . . Richard had earned the right to call her 'Button Nose' and she loved it."

"Button Nose" went to New York City in the summer of 1944 to do publicity for *The Doughgirls*. While in Gotham, Jane got a call from Billy Wilder. He wanted her to read a currently popular book, *The Lost Weekend*. She bought the book, and, in Wyman's words: "I couldn't for the life of me find any part for me to play; I was so conditioned to think of myself as a comedienne, I was completely floored when Billy Wilder said he wanted me for the part of the girlfriend to the hero."

Charles Brackett, producer and co-writer of the film's screenplay, would later explain, "We wanted to get away from the suffering type. We wanted a girl with a gift for life. We needed some gusto in the picture."

When the press got word that Jane was up for the part, they deluged her with questions. She told them bluntly: "There's no use my trying to talk about the girl's part. I don't know a thing about it. You see, they've had to write it in. The girl in the book is just a bit. The picture will make her part equal with the man's. Barbara Stanwyck was first reported to have the part. But, I don't know why, now they've got me for it. All I'm sure about is that the girl is not a drunkard."

Wilder's film of the previous year, *Double Indemnity,* starring Fred MacMurray and Barbara Stanwyck as murderers, had been an incredible success both critically and commercially. But even with this big hit under his belt, Wilder still had difficulty convincing Paramount executives to do *Lost Weekend.* Though the novel was a best seller, its theme, alcoholism, was so downbeat that the studio did not want to proceed.

In an effort to make the script palatable, Brackett and Wilder had written in a love interest. The collaborators were famous for their "meet cute" scenes—that is, the one where the hero and heroine first encounter each other. As usual, they managed to work this scene into the screenplay. In addition, they changed the cause of the male character's alcoholism from latent homosexuality to writer's block and gave the story a hopeful ending.

They cast Ray Milland in the lead. He was one of Paramount's top leading men, and his matinee idol stature would give *Lost Weekend* an immediate cachet with theater exhibitors and the public. Most importantly, Milland was a necessary choice because the character he was to portray was one the audience ultimately had to feel sympathy for. "Don Birnam" engages in several despicable actions—lying, cheating, manipulating those around him. The studio calculated that people would more readily accept these defects from the attractive Ray Milland, whereas they would almost certainly reject a more obvious character-actor choice for the role. And not to be overlooked was the excitement of seeing a star—known only for a certain kind of role—suddenly light up the screen with an unsuspected talent. It was the opportunity for a star to become a superstar.

Wyman was undoubtedly chosen in part for her likability factor. The role of Helen St. James called for no wall-climbing histrionics, but rather for someone who represented a sympathetic, "average" young American woman—not unlike the "average" Mrs. Young America she represented on all those magazine covers—who had fallen in love with a man with a drinking problem. She had to be strong but not aggressive, and above all *likable*.

Although the film today is perceived as a tour de force for Milland, Jane did have a large part and was given co-star billing above the title with Milland, an important career boost. Making the film was a high point for Jane. A major director had personally chosen her, and the role was challenging, calling for many subtle touches. Brackett and Wilder were convinced she could deliver the goods and they had been right.

Shooting on *Lost Weekend* was scheduled to begin on October 1, 1944. Although Milland and Wilder had done location shooting in New York, all of Jane's scenes would be shot at Paramount studios back in Hollywood.

By December 1944, the film was in the can, but it appeared, once again, that the fates were against Jane. Talk was that Paramount was not going to release *The Lost Weekend*! Although Brackett and Wilder had given the story an upbeat, positive ending, it was still considered too downbeat a subject. And what most people don't know is that the liquor industry lobby did not want the film released and was offering Paramount millions for the negative. *Lost Weekend* went on the shelf.

Warners had nothing for Jane—it appeared they were still not taking her dramatic acting talent seriously. After all, they had Bette Davis, Joan Crawford, Ida Lupino, and others for dramatic roles. The studio also had commitments with Barbara Stanwyck.

As well-liked as Jane Wyman was, she was still just considered a reliable well-paid contract actress.

During the war years women stars had assumed new importance. A few—Lana Turner, Betty Grable, and Rita Hayworth—had gone from featured player to superstar status. Jane's studio had developed Joan Leslie and Alexis Smith into stars and was giving Eleanor Parker leading roles. And a new twenty-year-old siren on the lot named Lauren Bacall had exploded on the scene co-starring in her first picture, *To Have and Have Not*, with husband-to-be Humphrey Bogart.

Although Jane had been on the scene for almost ten years, newcomers Gene Tierney, Jennifer Jones, Betty Hutton, and June Allyson had been in the business for only a brief while and had far outdistanced Jane. It is a tribute to Wyman's perseverance that she emerged from these years with her ambition intact.

However, in publicity coverage, "Jane and Ronnie" were on the same level as the box office giants. It was a peculiar situation, since Wyman's movies up to this point certainly did not merit this attention.

The studio finally came up with an assignment for Jane. But incredibly, even after she had worked with Brackett and Wilder, Jane found that all Warners had for her was a minor supporting role in their upcoming lavish Technicolor musical *Night and Day*.

Before the start of the picture Jane made a trip out of town without her husband, and it caused much speculation. But a week later Reagan and Jane were happy to reveal the reason for Jane's mysterious journey; they had adopted an infant boy, just days old, and named him Michael Edward Reagan. Reports conflict as to why the Reagans adopted. One source says that Jane was too busy with her career and it was much simpler to adopt. Another source reports that they were trying to have more children but were unable to, so they decided to adopt. It's possible that Reagan's salary (although he had been promoted to captain) was only a few hundred dollars a month and they needed Jane's income to keep up their life-style. She couldn't take the time out to have a baby.

And there was yet another opinion—that precocious four-year-old Maureen wanted a baby brother and kept badgering her parents to get her one.

Grown-up Maureen has recalled, "I wanted a baby so badly that I went to the toy department at Saks Fifth Avenue and asked if they had baby brothers—to the surprise and chagrin of my poor father, who had to stand there and listen to this." Maureen had "wanted two things in this world—a baby brother and a red scooter. And they kept telling me that if I wanted a baby brother, I would have to save up. And one day they said I was going to get what I wanted that night. I was sort of looking for a red scooter. But sure enough, it was a baby brother, a four-day-old baby brother. And my father said, 'Where is it?' And I went up the stairs. I had ninety-seven cents. So I gave the lady from the adoption agency my piggy bank."

After the adoption the Reagans allowed it to be reported that finding "the right baby" was a serious and difficult matter, and the reason they had decided to adopt was that in a world where there were so many children in need of care and love, and a real home life, they felt it was important for people like them "to add from the outside to our family" and then regard the newcomer as their "real" child.

Years later Wyman said bluntly: "Michael was only twelve hours old when Ronnie and I got him. I've never thought of him as an adopted child, and he's never thought of me as an adoptive mother. As far as we're concerned, we're blood. What else can I say? He's my baby boy."

Interestingly, it was Captain Reagan, not Jane, who was featured in magazine color layouts as the new Reagan baby took his place center stage. Adopting a baby further solidified the Reagans' public image as "the perfect couple." While others were getting divorced, the Reagans were adding to their family. It is obvious that Ron and Jane were perfectly happy to submit themselves, and their family, to this kind of publicity. Of course, like it or not, it had snowballed to a point where, even if they had wanted to, there was nothing they could have done to alter the situation. And, in a way, it had been part of their contribution to the war effort.

In 1945 it was pointed out that despite the high divorce rate in Hollywood, there were many couples in addition to Jane Wyman and Ronald Reagan who had lasting marriages. People such as the Ray Millands, the Fred MacMurrays, the Nelson Eddys, the Fred Astaires. But there were few like Reagan and Wyman where *both* parties were active in the industry (other than professional "teams" such as George and Gracie, Benny and Livingstone, Ozzie Nelson and Harriet Hilliard).

The Reagans were constantly visible on the burgeoning Hollywood social scene, and there were portents of things to come when Hedda Hopper observed, "At parties, Ronnie Reagan talks politics while Jane perches atop the piano and makes like Helen Morgan."

Reagan's official reentry into the film colony was imminent. By late 1945, many of the Hollywood stars in the army would be discharged and return to the Hollywood scene—Tyrone Power, Henry Fonda, Robert Sterling, Gene Kelly, Victor Mature, Wayne Morris, Robert Montgomery.

However, during the war, new faces had made an impact on screen: Gregory Peck, Robert Walker, Robert Mitchum, Cornel Wilde. Others, like John Wayne (who had been a western star), became romantic leading men during the war years.

The major question: Would Ronald Reagan regain the popularity he had finally achieved three years earlier with *King's Row*? It was a question he was asking himself as well.

And Jane had to be wondering what was going to happen with her career. True, in *Night and Day* she would have the opportunity to sing a couple of Cole Porter's best songs. But after nine years in the business, she was still playing a chorus girl!

4

MEANWHILE, THERE WAS AN INTERESTING DEVELOP-
ment at Paramount Pictures. For some reason, unknown to this
day, Barney Balaban, head of Paramount's New York office, made
an executive decision overriding Y. Frank Freeman (head of West
Coast production) and all other Paramount executives. He ordered that *The Lost Weekend* be released.

At Warner Bros. filming had begun on *Night and Day*. Jane's
role was not only small but nonessential to the plot. However,
this film was an ultra A production, with Cary Grant starring and
the top director on the lot, Michael Curtiz, at the helm. Alexis
Smith was playing the role of Cole Porter's wife, and Mary Martin would portray herself singing the Porter song that had made
her famous: "My Heart Belongs to Daddy."

Although Jane had been brunette for several years and had
told friends it was too much trouble to go back to being a blonde,
the role of Gracie Harris in *Night and Day* required her old
persona, so it was back to the bleach bottle.

While Jane was filming *Night and Day*, Warners' production
chief, Steve Trilling, called her into his office one day. "Did you
know you were up for *The Yearling*? Benny Thau wants to see

you." There had been rumors that she was being considered for this film, but Jane had not allowed herself to take them seriously. Even though *Lost Weekend* was as yet unreleased, directors and executives in town had seen the film and were impressed with her performance.

An appointment was set up for Wyman to see Thau, then head of talent at MGM and one of the most powerful men in Hollywood. At the meeting Thau did most of the talking.

"I saw you in *Lost Weekend.*"

Jane waited.

He continued. "We're doing a picture here called *The Yearling.* There's a good part in it, which you might be right for. It's something like Rainer's part in *The Good Earth.*"

Wyman continued to sit quietly.

"I'd like you to meet Sidney Franklin and Clarence Brown." Thau buzzed his secretary and the producer and director of the film were sent in. Franklin was surprised at Jane's appearance and blurted out, "I thought you were a brunette."

"I am," Jane quickly explained. Of course, her blond hair could be changed back.

"We want Ma Baxter dark-haired. I don't know. You'd have to work on both pictures at the same time. It might not work out."

But director Clarence Brown disagreed. "Look, Peck's so dark," said Brown. "Maybe it would be good to make the mother a blonde. After all, where would the blond kid come from?"

The three men agreed that Jane could test for the part.

The Yearling, considered to be a troubled production, was already before the cameras and months of location work in Florida had been shot with actor Gregory Peck playing the male lead and the young Claude Jarman as his son.

Back in Hollywood, Brown called Peck one day. "Greg, will you make a test tomorrow?"

"Sure. What's it for? Who is it?"

"Jane Wyman. For Ma Baxter."

Peck's look of surprise was unmistakable. "Jane Wyman?"

Brown said, "Did you see *The Lost Weekend*?"

"Not yet."

Later, Peck revealed, "I wondered if Brown had been touched by the sun. Jane Wyman for Ma Baxter!" Like others in Hollywood, Peck thought of Jane only in terms of light comedy.

The Yearling was the highly acclaimed Pulitzer prize–winning novel by Marjorie Kinnan Rawlings that had been a best seller in 1938 and 1939. The story was about a boy and his love for a young deer—ostensibly simple enough, but as a film it seemed a jinxed project. It had been in and out of production for four years. MGM had begun it in 1941, with Spencer Tracy playing Pa Baxter and Anne Revere cast as Ma Baxter. A young actor named Gene Eckman played their son, Jody. Sidney Franklin was the producer, and Victor Fleming, of *Gone With the Wind* fame, was the initial director.

Location shooting had begun in Florida when all sorts of problems arose. There was trouble with the animals and the weather, and major disagreements arose between the producer and director. Fleming was taken off the picture and King Vidor was brought in to replace him. In the meantime, MGM was very unhappy. The film had already cost half a million dollars (equivalent to over five million in 1980s dollars) with very little usable film.

Roddy MacDowall was then tested for the role of Jody, and there was talk of revitalizing the project in 1942. But the war intervened and war pictures, not animal pictures, were in demand.

Then in 1944 MGM decided to revive the project by launching a national search for "Jody." The new director, Clarence Brown, personally interviewed thousands of youngsters. There was a great deal of publicity, culminating when Brown finally signed a young boy from Tennessee, a nonprofessional, Claude Jarman,

Jr., to play the role. One of the key problems in making the film was that the faun, Flag, would constantly outgrow his part, so for this production, director Brown and his crew rounded up more than a dozen fauns during the nine-and-a-half-month shooting schedule.

By casting Gregory Peck, the hottest young actor in films at the time, the decision had obviously been made to go "younger" with the parents. Major actresses had been tested for the role, but none seemed right playing opposite Peck. Peck had met Jane socially years before, and they liked each other. After making the test with Jane, he could not contain his surprise.

"You were wonderful," he beamed.

"Good God," she said, "don't act so surprised!"

Clarence Brown had directed the test himself. Brown was one of Hollywood's most distinguished directors, a veteran of the silent screen days. He had started in the film business in the early twenties as an assistant to the famed Maurice Tourneur. Later, Brown had directed Valentino in *The Eagle;* then he had made two classic silents with Garbo, *Flesh and the Devil* and *A Woman of Affairs,* and was chosen to direct Garbo's first talkie, *Anna Christie.* In the thirties he had scored with *Anna Karenina* and *Conquest,* then in the forties with the decidedly non-Garbo film *National Velvet.*

Because the script of *The Yearling* did not give the Ma Baxter character dialogue in which to fully express motivations and feelings, the part called for an actress who could express herself fully with her eyes and her face, much as the silent screen stars had. Ma was a tough backwoods young woman who was reticent, perhaps incapable, of expressing herself in words.

Brown had undoubtedly seen in *Lost Weekend* and now in the test for *The Yearling* what Jane could do silently to express emotion. She had the unlearnable talent of being able to act via subtle reactions.

It was decided—they wanted her. She was signed for the part

and would receive co-star billing with Gregory Peck. She would report to the MGM lot in mid-August, after she finished *Night and Day* at Warners. It was as simple as that.

As it does for many, success for Jane Wyman seemed to come overnight. Clarence Brown wanted *her!* MGM, the Tiffany's of the movie business, wanted *her! The Yearling* was the kind of prestige project that came along only infrequently.

The icing on the cake was that when *Lost Weekend* was released, a few weeks after Jane's signing for *Yearling,* it was an immediate sensation both with critics and at the box office. The film's hard-hitting view of alcoholism intrigued the public. Milland, of course, received incredible praise, but the critics and public alike joined film executives and directors in suddenly recognizing that Jane Wyman was more than a screen "cutie"—she was indeed *an actress.*

Typical of the praise for her performance was Bosley Crowther's comment in his review for *The New York Times:* "Jane Wyman assumes with great authority a different role." The *World-Telegram* stated that she displayed "unsuspected talent." And the *Herald Tribune* noted that Jane was "properly restrained as the fiancée."

That same month, when Reagan was discharged from the army and Jane was completing one film and preparing for another, Ron found that he had lots of time on his hands. He read books, worked in the garden, even built a sidewalk and a wall, and began laying flagstones for a patio around their home. Concerning his free time during this period, in Reagan's words: "What did I do with my newfound freedom? I built two model boats—the U.S.S. America and a freighter. They were about two feet long, took two months to construct, and cost me a total of $105.25. I drove people like Dick Powell nuts, trying to convince them life wasn't complete until you built a model boat. I suppose this was proper therapy."

While Ron was whiling away the time, Jane was absorbed in

studying the script of *The Yearling*. The role of Ma Baxter was a challenge unlike any other she had faced. Even in *The Lost Weekend* she had played a young woman not so different from herself, but in *The Yearling* she was playing a distinctly character role in a period piece. She had to learn how to milk cows, chop wood, weed the garden, and feed the animals—not only that, but she would be playing a woman who had to cook, sew, and scrub. It was more than a great departure from the "cocktail party" parts that had constituted her repertoire for the past ten years—it was a wonderful challenge for a thirty-two-year-old actress.

Meanwhile, there were many delays in the filming of the over-produced *Night and Day*. For one thing, it was an unusually hot summer, and the lights necessary for Technicolor filming were intense, especially so on soundstages that had primitive methods of air-cooling. In Wyman's words: "They had tried putting blocks of ice on the roof to stifle the heat, and it didn't work. We were doing a big production number when the roof of the soundstage caved in. The sets had to be reconstructed."

In later years Wyman used this story to explain why at one point she was working simultaneously on both *The Yearling* and *Night and Day*. Research proves, however, that this was not the case. Although *Night and Day* was way behind schedule, Wyman's few scenes had been completed early and she had gone on the MGM payroll August 15. But because of *Lost Weekend*'s success and the publicity surrounding her signing for *The Yearling*, Jane's stature had risen suddenly and dramatically. Warners and Jane's agents knew it would be wise to beef up her role in *Night and Day*. Studio executives were told to borrow Wyman back from MGM and write her into the end of the picture. Thus, one week that fall, Jane toiled on both lots. However, she had psychologically worked herself into the character role of Ma Baxter, and she told friends that "rushing back and forth between the sets unnerved me."

For three days Warners put her back into the hairdo, clothes, and persona of the chorus girl "Gracie Harris" to film closeups that would be intercut into the final print of *Night and Day*. Jane would be edited into the big production number, "Just One of Those Things," and the illusion would be created that her character was important throughout the film.

Then she had to quickly transform herself back into the simple, stern Ma Baxter. The part called for subtle yet powerful acting. In *The Yearling*, the turn-of-the-century story of a backwoods Florida family, she is the loving but severe mother to a young boy who must learn the realities of rural life—no matter how cruel they seem. It is the mother who must kill her son's beloved faun because the faun is eating their crops.

One day on the set Peck came up to Jane and said, "I've finally seen *Lost Weekend*. You deserve all the acclaim you're getting." She accepted his praise with typical gracious humor.

Peck was impressed with Jane's lack of vanity in playing Ma Baxter. He recalled that she never looked in a mirror in order to "improve" or "glamorize" herself. She remained totally in character. He was also impressed with her offscreen non-star behavior, and like many who have worked with her, he noted that she was great fun to be with.

When *Yearling* filming on the soundstages was finally completed, the cast, crew, and their families transferred to Lake Arrowhead, an alpine-like mountain village one hundred miles from Los Angeles, where the final location shooting would be done.

Ron accompanied Jane and their children up to Lake Arrowhead. During the weeks there both the Reagan family and the Peck family had cabins on the lake and speedboats that took them to and from the set. The Reagans and Pecks would often spend the evenings together eating with their kids, family style.

At first, like all former soldiers, Reagan reveled in his postservice freedom. But unlike most others he was now back to collecting an astronomical salary, $3,500 per week. Still, the years in service had changed Reagan. His political attitudes had been heightened and, in his words, "I was blindly and busily joining every organization I could find that would guarantee to save the world."

He was also, at this point, critically interested in resuming his film career, and he was happy that Warners was thinking in the right direction. They were prepping a prestigious project for Reagan's "comeback." He would co-star with Humphrey Bogart and Lauren Bacall in *Stallion Road*, a big-budget Technicolor production about one of Reagan's favorite subjects, horses. Reagan couldn't have been more pleased. He liked the script, a great outdoors adventure about a veterinarian who breeds stallions. Astute as always about the business side of his career, the actor knew it was best to co-star with proven draws rather than head-line, solo, a lesser film. The studio was relaunching his career properly, in the company of the biggest box office duo of the year. It seemed Reagan and Jane were both finally finding the success they had worked so hard to achieve.

However, now that the war was over, there was a fascinating change in attitude concerning two-career marriages and toward women in the job market in general. For the past four years women had stood right beside men in the work force. They had toiled in factories, offices—wherever manpower was needed. But now the men were returning from the war, and a massive gov-ernment-directed campaign was launched to bring women out of the workplace and back into the home to be wives and mothers. After all, wasn't that the way of life they had fought for?

Consequently the Reagans were now questioned by the fan magazines about the pitfalls of a dual-career marriage. Jane de-fended their status. "Thousands of nice young couples all over this country have two jobs in one family, and they do all right. They adjust to it and one another because they want to get along. There's no reason why two actors can't do the same if they're in love and don't start taking themselves big. Even if Ronnie and I ever started getting that way I think the kids would stop us, because I assure you that both of us combined can't top our Maureen for pure hamming."

She also said at the time, "Every family is different, I know. Perhaps the way in which my husband and I have arranged our lives couldn't be copied by others, but it *has* worked well, and *is* working well for us."

Jane declared that she and Reagan had married with the understanding that both would continue their careers. "We wanted children, but that was to be an incident in the over-all development of our lives together." It was not, according to Jane, a reason for her to give up her work.

Being a *good parent* was nonetheless paramount in Wyman's scheme of things. Jane was delighted when she was named the "Ideal Working Mother" by the North Hollywood Women's Professional Club: "And *that* was a surprise," Jane noted years later, emphatically stating: "The publicity department didn't have anything to do with it."

When *The Yearling* was finished shooting in February 1946, and the Reagans moved back to Hollywood, Ron was scheduled to start work in *Stallion Road*. He discovered, however, that there had been some drastic changes in the production—Bogart and Bacall had dropped out, supposedly because they didn't see themselves as an "outdoors" couple, but perceived themselves on screen as quintessential urbanites.

The budget on the picture was cut in half, and to Reagan's further dismay, plans to film in color were also abandoned. Zachary Scott and Alexis Smith were cast in the Bogart-Bacall roles as the novelist and the love interest. While Reagan recognized that these were talented co-stars, they certainly did not bring the prestige to the endeavor that "Bogie" and "Betty" would have.

Although everything had fallen into place so easily for Ronald

Reagan when he first entered films back in 1937—from now on it seemed that nothing would go right. And while Jane Wyman's career had been such a long, uphill journey, from now on for her *all* would go right.

The Lost Weekend received a bevy of Oscar nominations and went on to win the Academy Award as best picture of the year. Wilder and Brackett won an Oscar for best screenplay and Wilder was named best director. Ray Milland was voted best actor. *Lost Weekend* was recognized as, and remains to this day, a classic film. Although Jane was not nominated, her contribution to the film was certainly noted; she had co-starred in the best picture of the year.

Over at MGM, Clarence Brown and Sidney Franklin had scheduled a private screening of *The Yearling*. Peck and his wife, Claude Jarman, Jr., and his mother, and Ron and Jane were in attendance. Obviously all were greatly impressed with the final product, indicated by the audience's silence when the film ended. Clarence Brown finally asked, "Will someone say something?"

Reagan said: "I don't know if I should go to church, or if I've just been there."

It was obvious to all that the film was destined to be a success. Everything about it was just right—the sentiment rang true, the production values were superb, and the acting was flawless. Not only was *The Yearling* a great picture, but Jane and Ron recognized it was a great MGM picture—this meant it would receive the kind of distribution and attention it deserved. Equally important, it would warrant the kind of predistribution publicity that heralds a unique screen achievement.

Hollywood was soon abuzz with the word of *The Yearling*'s impending success.

Taking advantage of Jane's new status, Warners now released *The Animal Kingdom*, retitled *One More Tomorrow*, which had been on the shelf for years. Although Dennis Morgan and Ann Sheridan were the stars, it was Wyman and Carson who were the "hot" properties at the moment, and it was their names on the marquees of theaters in small towns of America.

This was a time of major change in Jane Wyman's life and career, and she knew it. "By nature I have always been a very serious-minded person. There were many times when I felt I was ready to do serious roles. But invariably, when a dumb-bunny role came along, I was elected. I realize now, if they had given me a chance at serious drama, I wouldn't have been ready. But, of course, then I could think of only one thing—they'll *never* accept this turned-up nose for anything but comedy."

This "change" in Jane's thinking had begun when she was cast in *The Yearling*. Wyman immediately knew that acceptance of her "new" self—*her* new way of perceiving herself—would be met in some Hollywood circles by cynicism and mockery. She didn't care.

"There are many who will understand my great feeling of release. There are those who won't understand and who can't understand. For the first time in my life, I was no longer shy, or afraid of being ridiculed about my ambition. From that moment my turned-up nose became something that nature placed in the center of my face. Period."

For Reagan, too, this was a time of change and readjustment. Returning to filmmaking was not easy. Even though he hadn't left American shores during the war, the actor had lost touch with the day-to-day intricacies of filmmaking. He was insecure and touchy about being taken advantage of—he wanted the studio to realize they could not make him work long hours, telling production people he wouldn't work past six o'clock.

"You're going to be pretty lonesome that last hour," Reagan was told. It seems that quitting time was now five o'clock! And he saw at once that because the government got much of the profits the studios made via an excess-profits tax, production practices had loosened considerably. Moviemaking was, in subtle ways, an entirely new ball game.

However, the "moral code" regarding what went on screen was as strict as ever. *Stallion Road* co-star Alexis Smith has recalled one amusing scene in the picture with Reagan: "We get off a horse and kiss under a tree. I was lying down in the grass and Ronnie lay down beside me and the director immediately yelled to him to get up on one elbow. 'You both can't be in a prone position at the same time,' he said, so Ronnie had to play the whole love scene on one elbow."

Nelle Reagan visited her son on the set during the shooting of this picture, and at those times Ron seemed "a happy, carefree individual." As far as Nelle was concerned, if her son was in a picture, then that film was the equivalent of *Gone With the Wind*, no matter how the script read or how many compromises had been made since the initial concept.

During the making of *Stallion Road*, Reagan became friendly with the film's technical advisor, Nino Pepitone, who was an expert on horses. The men shared an intense interest in the animals and eventually became partners in a breeding enterprise. Reagan even bought the black Thoroughbred mare he rode in *Stallion Road*. He named her "Baby," and would later use the horse again in other films.

Reagan and Jane bought a ranch in the Northridge section of the San Fernando Valley (they dubbed it "Yearling Row," after their respective movies). To Pepitone's surprise, Ronald Reagan was not a man who hired outsiders to do work around the ranch —Reagan *liked* to do it himself. It was relaxing, tension-releasing fun for him.

Although Jane had never really shared these bucolic interests with her husband, she had heretofore at least appeared to appreciate them. The situation was changing, however. Jane Wilkie observed, "I was interviewing Jane when 'Ronnie' hove to and, as he polished his riding boots, held forth without a pause on a political diatribe. It struck me that Jane was faintly bored by the lecturer." The fans, of course, continued to be told how happy the Reagans were.

Over at MGM, Clark Gable's first postwar film, *Adventure*, co-starring Greer Garson, was in release. It was a mediocre effort and would quickly fade from memory, but the ad line for it— "Gable's Back and Garson's Got Him!"—was a slogan that was sweeping the nation. Warners publicists borrowed the slogan for the Reagans and planted such stories as: "Peace, it's wonderful. God's in His Heaven, all's right with the world—'cause Reagan's back and Wyman's got him!"

But contractually, Warners had them both, and after completing *Stallion Road*, Reagan was thrown into a heavy melodrama, *Night Unto Night*, in which newcomer Viveca Lindfors, a Swede whom Warner Bros. was hoping to build into "a new Ingrid Bergman," was being introduced.

Everybody was unhappy on this picture. Lindfors's agent had told her that Reagan was not a big enough star to launch her career. And Reagan was unhappy to be in another picture that obviously did not contain the necessary ingredients for success.

Night Unto Night was a muddled story of an epileptic bio-chemist (played by Reagan) who meets a widow when both retreat to the Gulf Coast in Florida. The film's director was young Don Siegel; it was his second film, and Warners had great hopes for him. Soon into production, however, it was obvious that the script was not going to translate well to the screen.

Stallion Road was concurrently undergoing extensive post-production and would not be released for some time, so in 1946 Reagan had no films in release. He did appear on radio, however, and with his wife starred in the *Screen Guild Theater* radio version of "Christmas in Connecticut," which had been a Barbara Stanwyck–Dennis Morgan film.

Jane had two pictures in theaters: *One More Tomorrow* and *Night and Day* (in which she was billed sixth). Wyman was later vocal about disliking her work in the big-budgeted *Night and Day*. "I don't like that addle-pated type of comedy role. It's mostly a fill-in, contributing nothing but a few vaudeville laughs."

But in 1946 the upcoming *Yearling* continued to be talked about as a milestone in Wyman's career.

The Reagans were kept busy, since in addition to their work there was Ron's deepening involvement with the Screen Actors Guild. And it seemed, for the moment at least, that Jane was actually sharing her husband's political interests, all of which placed her in an awkward position because the management at Warner Bros. was not happy with Reagan's political activities on behalf of SAG.

It seemed to the people at the studio that Ron interrupted his schedule of union activities to work rather than interrupting his work for union activities. But they agreed to holding up production on *Night Unto Night* while Reagan, Jane, and others went to Chicago, where Reagan was leading a SAG delegation to the American Federation of Labor convention. (Others who joined Reagan and Jane on the trip were Gene Kelly, Robert Taylor, George Murphy, Walter Pidgeon, Dick Powell, and Alexis Smith.)

This was a turbulent time in the motion picture industry. That September another of the now familiar strikes by various motion picture industry unions had been threatened against the studios. On September 12 the Conference of Studio Unions called a strike and picket lines suddenly appeared outside MGM and Warner Bros.

After an emergency meeting in which, as one report says, "Reagan did most of the talking," SAG decided to intervene and try to sort out the situation. But when the SAG delegates went to the AFL convention, they soon learned that although they were being tolerated and humored by the union men, they were not being taken seriously. Later reports suggested that Reagan cut through this interference by confronting the AFL's president,

William Green, with a startling suggestion: SAG would send stars to major cities in America to denounce the labor violence unless Green agreed to pass a resolution calling for binding arbitration in the Hollywood labor dispute.

This was an early indication of Reagan's true political savvy. The AFL president soon agreed and a meeting was set up between SAG and the carpenters' union president, William Hutchinson. Hutchinson would meet with no one but SAG president Robert Montgomery, who had to fly in from New York.

Although the AFL convention unanimously passed the resolution for binding arbitration, it was not enforced (a fact that Ronald Reagan, in the mid-1960s, by then a Republican, was always quick to point out).

There had been several strikes in Hollywood in the period since the war ended, and a number of these disputes had ended in violence. Now an incident erupted in front of the Warner Bros. studio in which the police, who were escorting members of one union across the picket lines of another union, suddenly clashed with the strikers. The police and fire departments of Los Angeles actually had to bring in fire hoses and tear gas to get the situation under control.

Actress Rosemary DeCamp, who was in *Night Unto Night*, remembers that Reagan "worked eighteen to twenty hours a day —at night, trying to resolve an ugly industry strike—then all day on that baffling film about a man with epilepsy. But he remained cheerful and loquacious with three or four hours of sleep a night. This went on for months."

Then came a truly jarring incident. According to Reagan's recollections, "I was back at work on *Night Unto Night*, doing location shots at the beach. I was called to a phone at an oil station nearby.

" 'There's a group being formed to deal with you,' the unidentified voice said. 'They're going to fix you so you won't ever act again.'

"I took it as a joke. I told it with chuckles to the gang; I was surprised that they took it very seriously. The police were waiting with a license to carry a gun. I was fitted with a shoulder holster and a loaded .32 Smith & Wesson. To me it was still ten-cent melodrama and I couldn't believe it enough to put on the harness. What got me to slip it on was the arrival that night of a policeman to guard our house. Somehow I didn't think the department tossed policemen around as part of a practical joke."

Her husband having to carry a gun for protection against threats to his life could not have made Jane Wyman too comfortable. This was not a film script, and if Reagan's life could be threatened, certainly hers and their children's lives might be in danger as well.

Reagan later revealed that through "the Hollywood grapevine" he heard words to the effect: "If we had wanted to throw acid in Reagan's face, we would have done it, not talked about it." And he has said: "I thought that was strange. No one had mentioned acid-throwing up to that revealing moment."

The volatile situation did not confine itself to the workplace. Even at home the Reagans had a few anxious moments. "One rainy Sunday afternoon, I answered the doorbell to see a small shrunken man, who identified himself as one of the strikers," Reagan has recalled. "I thought: 'Here it is at last, and me without that gun.'"

It turned out that all the man wanted was some straight information on what was really going on in the unions, and Reagan talked to him for hours. But incidents like this one revealed the pressures Ron's involvement in politics were subjecting Jane to, even in her own home. The stress of living with danger soon took its toll.

Very revealingly, years later Reagan stated: "I mounted the holstered gun religiously every morning and took it off the last thing at night. I learned how much a person gets to lean on hardware like that. After nine months of wearing it, it took a real effort of will to discard it. I kept thinking: 'The very night you take it off may be the night when you need it most.' "

Others have corroborated that the situation was indeed explosive and the studio was concerned. In later years, Viveca Lindfors recalled, "There was a strike going on, and we had to pass the picket lines every morning to and from the studio." She has noted that Reagan, "although openly on the side of the strikers and actors union, did not join the strike. He, being in a target position, was not safe. Some violence had occurred and on the fourth day of shooting I heard one studio patrolman tell another, 'Take Reagan home and stay on patrol all night. He is established in the picture now and we don't want to take any chances.' "

Adding to this already tense situation were problems on the set of *Night Unto Night.* Viveca Lindfors and Don Siegel had fallen in love, and this naturally disturbed the other actors, many of whom felt Lindfors was now getting preferential treatment. In addition, Reagan and the actress were not seeing eye-to-eye either creatively or personally.

Miss Lindfors's personal opinion of Reagan was not terribly high. "I don't remember a single conversation with him of any substance," she said. "I do remember some chitchat about sex, which was up my alley. 'It's best in the afternoon, after coming out of the shower,' he said, and then he laughed." Miss Lindfors has described it as a "slightly embarrassed laugh." She has also remembered Reagan as being "distant."

While Reagan toiled in *Night Unto Night,* Wyman was still sailing on choppy seas regarding her own professional life. The studio didn't really know what to do with her. Although talking about finding proper vehicles for her, Warners was obviously foot-dragging while still using her in their formula programmers, such as the western *Cheyenne,* a picture top-billing Dennis Morgan.

Wyman was delighted when RKO asked to borrow her for what surely would be a blockbuster project. She would star with

James Stewart in the Capraesque *Magic Town*. The script was by Robert Riskin, a longtime Frank Capra collaborator. For this picture, however, Riskin was going it alone. He had written and would produce the film, and had lined up veteran William Wellman to direct.

Jane's hair was dark again, worn in a soft upsweep style. As Jane was shooting *Magic Town,* Reagan was finally completing the beleaguered *Night Unto Night*. There were rumors that the film would be shelved—perhaps permanently. *Stallion Road* was still not in release and Reagan was distraught about his career. It must be kept in mind that in the Hollywood of these years, there was an accepted adage: Three flops and you're through. This would be strike number two for Ronald Reagan, after his having been away from bat for a long time.

The relationship between Jack Warner and Ronald Reagan was strained in these postwar years. Part of it had to do with the actor's involvement in the politics of SAG, but a great deal of it had to do with the parts Warner continued to offer Reagan. He had been most anxious to play a role in his pal John Huston's *The Treasure of the Sierra Madre,* a venture that Reagan's instincts told him was *sure* to be a hit. It not only had Huston directing but had Bogart as star and Walter Huston, John Huston's father, as co-star.

From Jack Warner's point of view Reagan was "nuts" to want to take a "character part" (which eventually went to Bruce Bennett) instead of a lead in another picture. Warner flatly refused to permit Reagan to do *Treasure*.

Reagan always regretted not working with John Huston. Off-screen, Ron and Jane were friendly with Huston and his then wife, Evelyn Keyes, and the two men shared a common interest in breeding horses.

The Hustons had a slambang party on their first wedding anniversary. The Jean Negulescos and the Lewis Milestones were their co-hosts. Jane and Ron were among the more than two hundred guests invited. According to Evelyn Keyes, she had convinced Fred Karger, a musician from Columbia with whom she had worked on *The Jolson Story,* to put together a group of musicians to form a band to play at the party. "It was such a smash success that night, that he formed a permanent band," Miss Keyes later recalled.

Several years in the future Fred Karger would prove to be a very important man in Jane Wyman's life.

Miss Keyes has also remembered one Sunday when the Reagans came over for a visit and all but Ron proceeded to down quite a few cocktails. "Bloody Marys seemed to be in order," recalled Miss Keyes. Later, "the four of us piled in a car and took off for the Mexican quarter."

Keyes recalled that her husband and Jane were drinking beer, but that she and Reagan had had enough, "if indeed he had much of anything at all." According to Miss Keyes's account, Reagan took charge and told Jane and Huston, who were, in Keyes's words, "giggling and clearly anything but sober," to get into the backseat. " 'Evelyn and I will sit up front. We'll be the policemen, and I'll drive.' "

Various other friends from the past, including actors Dana Andrews and Robert Mitchum, have recalled Reagan's strait-laced attitudes toward drinking. Mitchum has said that it was "always like we were being monitored by an eagle scout" and that "you always felt a little constricted with 'Dutch.' "

People who knew Jane and Ron during this period say that although Reagan had inherited his father's sense of humor and adventure, he'd also acquired his mother's puritanical outlook. Reagan obviously frowned on certain types of behavior, and this may have made him difficult to live with, but it did not stop him from having close friendships with people who were heavy drinkers, such as William Holden and John Huston.

According to Reagan, Huston never forgave him for not appearing in *Treasure.* The director felt that if the actor had *really* wanted to do it, he could have stood his ground and convinced Warner. But according to Reagan, Warner was not convincible. The mogul told Reagan he had bought the huge Broadway hit *The Voice of the Turtle* expressly for Reagan. This choice would have been fine from Reagan's point of view if Warner had intended to star him with a top box office ingenue, but the studio was planning to use Eleanor Parker. Reagan argued that the film needed someone like his friend June Allyson, currently a top-ten attraction. Couldn't Warners borrow June and make *Turtle* a first-rate production? Again, Warner refused. They would use Eleanor Parker, who, the studio felt, was going to be a big star.

Meanwhile, Reagan's involvement in politics had deepened. He had become a member of the American Veterans Committee and the Hollywood Independent Citizens Committee of Arts, Sciences and Professions (HICCASP). Ron soon decided, however, that both these organizations were connected with people known to have Communist affiliations; he subsequently resigned from both groups.

June Allyson and her husband, Dick Powell, saw a lot of the Reagans during this period. Miss Allyson has observed, "Jane Wyman seemed more upset with her husband's obsession with politics than I. I tried to make her laugh. 'He'll outgrow it,' I told her. To her, it wasn't funny."

Miss Wyman also confided to June that she found it very annoying that Reagan took forever to make up his mind about anything. " 'But, Jane,' " Miss Allyson said, " 'that's Ronnie. He always wants to be sure of what he says and simply doesn't give snap opinions.' I thought it was wonderful that Ronnie was so vitally interested in everything and was always studying a new subject."

Allyson has remembered how Reagan would respond to questions. "He answered me carefully, methodically. When Ronnie got through explaining something to me, Jane Wyman leaned over and said, 'Don't ask Ronnie what time it is because he will tell you how a watch is made.' "

Miss Allyson has also recalled, "It was a riot to listen to Ronnie, a staunch Democrat, trying to convert Richard while Richard argued just as hard to turn Ronnie into a Republican."

There were reports that the Democratic party wanted Reagan to run for Congress in 1946. Former actress Helen Gahagan Douglas was currently a Congresswoman from California, and other famous actors, such as Orson Welles, were involved in politics and were talked about for public office. But Reagan felt it was necessary for him to get back into his career, and besides, he was too involved with SAG to find time for more outside activities.

Even during these years, Reagan and Jane knew many powerful people in both political parties including Holmes P. Tuttle, a force in California politics who later would be an important man in Reagan's future.

For months MGM had been touting: "This Is the Year of *The Yearling* . . . and it's worth waiting for!" The film had been booked into New York's Radio City Music Hall and was scheduled to open there on January 23, 1947. At the request of Music Hall officials, however, there had been considerable editing of the final print, including the deletion of sequences they deemed too violent (one wherein Slewfoot, the killer bear, mauls and kills one of the Baxter family's hogs), as well as some fight scenes. The film was tightened generally so that the focus was on the interplay of emotions within the family rather than on extraneous plot points.

MGM decided that in order to qualify for the 1946 Academy Awards, they would open *The Yearling* in Los Angeles before the end of the year. The premiere would be in grand MGM style at the Cathay Circle Theater, and there would be a lavish party at Ciro's afterward.

This was the first big black-tie, klieg-lights premiere of any of Jane Wyman's films, and it was an exciting time for her. On the day of the premiere she quit work early on the set of *Magic Town* to rush home and prepare for the evening's festivities.

Friends joined the Reagans for dinner. Betsy and Irving Kaplan had brought Jane a gift, a gold locket. Inside were two pictures: one of Jane out of makeup, and one of Jane as Ma Baxter. After dinner the couples headed for the Cathay Circle.

The premiere was a grand success. The next morning Wyman was back on the *Magic Town* set, where someone had tacked a sign on her dressing room door: "To The Queen—Merry Christmas and Happy Yearling."

An interesting sidelight is that in the film, Jane is perceived as the villain who kills the deer. Even *Magic Town* director Wellman would, from this point on, humorously snap at Jane when she blew a line or spoiled a take: "You stinking deer killer!"

Five-year-old Maureen Reagan had seen *The Yearling* and, according to Wyman, would not speak to her mother for days afterward because she killed the deer.

But in the film, Jane's character is merely following instructions. Jody has been told by his father to shoot the deer that continually eats their crops, thereby threatening their survival. The boy cannot do it, Pa is confined to bed and can't do it himself, so he instructs Ma to do it. The audience hears the shot and then along with Jody finds Jane with the rifle in her hand. She has wounded the deer but not killed it.

"You know I didn't mean the critter no harm—I'm just a bad shot—"

It is Jody who must then "put the animal out of its misery."

The powerful emotions that this sequence evoked left indelible impressions in the minds of many.

Within weeks *The Yearling* opened in New York and nationwide and was instantly hailed as a triumph for all concerned: "Family entertainment" on a spectacular scale.

Claude Jarman, Jr.'s portrayal of the boy who discovers faith and courage in the midst of harrowing hardship was deeply moving. Peck's characterization of the father was unanimously praised. And Jane's Ma Baxter was acknowledged as brilliantly effective. *Life* magazine called her acting "beyond reproach." *The New York Times* noted that "Jane Wyman, while she does not have the physical characteristics of the original Ma, compels credulity and sympathy for a woman of stern and spartan stripe."

It was amazing to think that this Jane Wyman was the same woman who for so many years had portrayed all those slick, hard-edged, wisecracking girls. With *The Yearling* the public and the critics saw that Jane Wyman's dramatic performance in *The Lost Weekend* was not a one-time fluke. Wyman had now become a full-fledged *star*.

The Reagan household soon received startling but happy news: Jane had been nominated for an Academy Award as best actress for her performance in *The Yearling*. The film had received nominations in almost every major category; along with *The Best Years of Our Lives* and *It's a Wonderful Life*, it had swept the nominations. It was up for best picture. Brown had been nominated for best director. Gregory Peck won a nomination for best actor (his second nomination in this, only his fifth picture). And the film also received nominations in the cinematography, art direction, and film-editing categories.

The nominations were particularly significant this year because the Academy had changed its voting rules. Prior to this, almost 10,000 people employed by the studios nominated and then voted on the Oscar winners. But this year the rules were altered so that only Academy members could vote (Academy membership instantly rose from about 700 to almost 1,700). It was gratifying to the performers and craftsmen to know that the voting was now in the hands of the men and women who actually made pictures.

In the case of Wyman, some claim the age-old adage of "Being nominated is enough" actually applied. Others say that Jane, with her husband her biggest booster, eagerly sought to win. In any event, "Button Nose," formerly the screen's leading "dumb bunny," had finally won recognition from her peers and was put in the same league with Olivia de Havilland (nominated for *To Each His Own*); Jennifer Jones (up for *Duel in the Sun* and a previous best-actress winner for *The Song of Bernadette*); Rosalind Russell *(Sister Kenny)*; and Celia Johnson (for the British classic-to-be *Brief Encounter*). Jane told reporters that her choice was "Livvie"—Jane "knew" Olivia was going to win, and felt she deserved it.

The Yearling continued to pack in audiences across the country. Since it had been a very expensive movie, it would not initially show a huge profit, but from the exhibitors' point of view it was a bonanza hit, and it brought in over $5.2 million in rentals. It was to be the top money-maker of 1947.

That March, *Stallion Road* was finally released. It received the mediocre reception Reagan had anticipated, but the disappointment was deflected. His career had taken a different direction: He had been elected to finish out Robert Montgomery's unexpired term as president of SAG. (Montgomery and several other vice-presidents of the Guild had resigned because they had all become producers as well as actors, and this was considered a conflict of interest.)

When Hedda Hopper first heard from Robert Montgomery that Reagan was going to succeed him as president, she gasped: "He's as green as grass! What does he know?"

"Have you ever heard him talk?" Montgomery asked.

After watching Reagan chair a meeting, Hopper later had to admit that she had never heard a "clearer speechmaker." According to Hedda, she saw him "interrupt the rantings of windy orators by saying 'Pardon me, but you're mistaken about that. Here are the facts.' And then he reeled them off with shattering logic." In Hopper's opinion, Reagan was "the best-informed star in town."

Robert Stack's recollections of the time: "I'll never forget the day he was named president of the union. It was hairy. People were marching atop the roof of the American Legion Stadium. It was a time when hoods were trying to take over the union, and there were threats on Ronnie's life." Stack added: "I saw him act well under pressure."

The Communist infiltration of certain Hollywood unions was receiving a great deal of publicity. The House Un-American Activities Committee had begun its investigations of Hollywood. As a result, Reagan's passion was more than ever directed toward the inner workings of the Screen Actors Guild.

In March, Ron was working on *The Voice of the Turtle*. Jane's agents were in the midst of renegotiating her contract with Warners. The Reagans eagerly anticipated the Academy Awards ceremonies to be held on March 13. But they had something even more exciting to look forward to: Jane was finally pregnant again and they told friends they wanted a boy. Jane wanted a Ronald Reagan, Jr.

○ ○ ○ ○ ○ ○ ○ ○ ○ ○ ○ ○ ○ ○ ○ ○ ○ ○ ○

5

IT WAS ONE OF THE MOST GLITTERING NIGHTS IN THE history of the Academy of Motion Picture Arts and Sciences. As if in a scene from *A Star Is Born*, thousands of fans gathered outside the Shrine Auditorium to view the arrival of the stars. This was the first year the awards were being held at the massive Shrine; inside the vast hall—larger than Radio City Music Hall—6,700 people had seats for the gala event, a lavish show produced by Mervyn LeRoy and emceed by Jack Benny.

Mary Livingstone, Benny's wife, attended the ceremonies with Jane. Wyman later noted, "I was pregnant but was cool as a cucumber. Mary got so excited that by the time it was over she was close to hysterics. It took her days to recover."

In the course of the evening Jane watched and listened as her old pal William Demarest, nominee for best supporting actor for *The Jolson Story*, lost to Harold Russell, the nonprofessional actor and disabled veteran who co-starred in *The Best Years of Our Lives*. It appeared that *Best Years* and *Yearling* were going to split the awards. *Yearling* won for best cinematography of a color film, and for best set decoration. And Jane and all concerned with the film were thrilled when Claude Jarman, Jr., was presented the outstanding child actor award of 1946—a noncompetitive category.

When William Wyler won for direction of *Best Years*, the handwriting was on the wall. And though it must have been disappointing to *The Yearling* group, who were rooting for Peck, few were surprised when Fredric March won for *Best Years*.

Jane, however, still had a chance—none of the actresses from *Best Years* had been nominated. When the envelope was opened, the winner, as expected, was the favorite—Olivia de Havilland.

Best Years was voted best picture.

Though she hadn't won, Jane's new status was assured and her renegotiated Warners contract would finally give her the pick of good roles. Unlike her husband, she had no problems in dealing with Jack Warner. She sat down with him and they talked for several hours. Insiders say it was not a question of whether Jane would do drama or comedy. She and Warner discussed general principles of her career direction. Wyman herself later said, concerning Jack Warner, "We have a mutual respect. If one of us says 'It's raining,' the other doesn't bother looking out the window to see."

The new contract was set, but of course Jane would wait until after the birth of her baby before resuming work. Years later, recalling her second pregnancy, Jane said, "I was just delighted. I had had such a lovely pregnancy with Maureen. There were no problems."

The Reagans were happy being parents and spent more time with their children than did most working parents.

"Dad was the great psychologist," recalled Maureen. "When he enrolled me in kindergarten, I threw a fit because I wanted to go to acting school."

" 'Fine, but actresses need to learn to read and write.' "

" 'Why?' "

" 'So they can read scripts and sign contracts,' " her father told her.

Although as an adult Michael Reagan would say he did not know his parents until he was grown, it should be remembered that during this time, when the Reagans were close, Michael was still a toddler. Maureen, certainly, had close relationships with both parents for the first seven years of her life.

In a magazine interview at the time, Jane explained: "Ronnie and I have always arranged our picture schedules, whenever it was physically possible, so as to be at home with the children an hour before dinner, and they are allowed to remain up for an hour after dinner.

"When Michael was small, his feeding schedule was originally set in the afternoon at two, six, and ten. The six o'clock feeding was inconvenient for Ronnie and me, so we simply rearranged the schedule to read three, seven, and eleven. In that way, Michael slept later in the morning, of course, so was able to romp with us when we came home from the studio."

The Reagans had decided on a major change concerning raising their children. Jane stated flatly, "No interviews about them. It's a tough enough job for Hollywoodites to raise kids without their reading about themselves and getting an idea they're important."

With Michael and the upcoming baby, there would be no publicity such as Maureen had received. The children were already experiencing the dark side of fame. "I think the biggest problem was that we couldn't go anyplace together without being accosted by autograph hunters," Maureen said as an adult. "Wherever we went I'd end up standing there while Mom and Dad signed autographs, and I resented that terribly.

"Because they were mobbed everyplace they went, Mom and Dad began to depend more and more on other parents to take my brother and me along when they went places. We resented that, too, because we wanted to do things with our own parents."

Temporarily, Ron's and Jane's professional roles were reversed. Now Wyman was somewhat idle, reading scripts and waiting for the right part, while Reagan went from one picture to another.

But a subtle switch had taken place in publicity on the couple. Reagan was now covered via Jane's publicity; otherwise there wasn't much written about him at all. Frank Sinatra was the new number-one man in films, and Clark Gable, Cornel Wilde, and Tyrone Power were the actors the public was, for the moment, most interested in. Jane was still not top ten—June Allyson, Ingrid Bergman, the adult Shirley Temple, June Haver, Esther Williams, and Lana Turner held the popularity edge among female stars.

After *The Voice of the Turtle*, Reagan went right into *That Hagen Girl*. Warners had a commitment with Shirley Temple, and they were eager to complete a film with her quickly because she was currently a box office draw. But *Hagen Girl* had a muddled script that had been through many revisions. Reagan said he ultimately agreed to do the film as "a favor" to Warner. And there seems to be ample evidence that at this juncture the studio head convinced Reagan by talking about buying better scripts for him, perhaps even teaming Reagan and Wyman in a major production. The studio was buying the hit Broadway play *John Loves Mary*, and it seemed ideal for the couple.

Reagan was totally correct in his misgivings about *That Hagen Girl*. The film represents a nadir in Ronald Reagan's acting career. Although Shirley Temple ranks this as the favorite of her films as an adult, Reagan was astute enough to realize that not only did it have a silly story—about a man in his thirties in love with a girl of eighteen who had maliciously been labeled his illegitimate daughter—but that he would look foolish as well, and that the audience wouldn't accept him as a love interest to the popular former child star. How right he was.

However, the studio was getting fed up with Reagan's attempts to tell them how to run his career and they were most unhappy about his union activities. While shooting *That Hagen*

Girl, Reagan spent every possible moment not before the cameras with SAG matters, and, in addition, Reagan gave testimony at hearings held in Los Angeles by the House Un-American Activities Committee.

Toward the end of shooting *Hagen Girl,* Reagan became ill. At first the studio thought he was "sick" because he did not want to finish the film, but it soon became obvious Reagan was genuinely ill—he had viral pneumonia. Jane was five months into her pregnancy when Reagan was rushed to Cedars of Lebanon Hospital.

"My next of kin were notified the hospital might be my last address," Reagan has remembered. The pneumonia had progressed to a life-threatening stage. While Reagan was fighting for his life, Jane went into premature labor and was rushed to Queen of Angels Hospital. Although Reagan later said they had lost the child "by miscarriage," this is not the case. Jane gave birth to a girl on June 26, 1947.

The press reported the infant's birth and said the girl was given "a good chance of survival." But Jane's doctor, Robert L. Blackmun, undoubtedly knew the infant, woefully underweight, had little chance for survival, although everyone was praying for the best.

The infant died within several hours of birth.

Louella Parsons later said, "When Jane was stricken, it was Ronald's turn to worry, and he was almost desperate. He was so miserable because he was unable to be with her during her ordeal. He tossed and fretted in his hospital bed, telling how magnificent Jane had been, how fearful he was of her health."

The death of their second child affected Jane deeply. No one but the woman involved could comprehend what a tremendous physical and emotional shock such an ordeal can be. Almost all people who knew her at this period say that Jane was very depressed. Even after her physical recovery and return home, it was not easy for Jane to shake her despondency.

When Reagan had sufficiently recovered from his bout with

pneumonia, he returned to Warners to complete *Hagen Girl.* After that, he threw himself once again into union activities. He did make some attempt to spend extra time with Jane. "Reagan tried to coax Jane out to dance her nerves away," Hedda Hopper reported. Jane and Ron had always enjoyed nightclubbing and especially dancing. "But she was often sullen, rude and jittery, even to Ronnie. Usually, he took her home early," related Hedda.

Close friends knew the only prescription for a woman in Jane's state of mind would be a return to work.

There are many conflicting stories on how Wyman came to be involved with her next project, *Johnny Belinda.* Once any film becomes a classic, it is surrounded by a mythology concerning its genesis and evolution; *Johnny Belinda* is no exception.

There are many versions relating how long Wyman participated in the venture before it reached the cameras. At times she has implied that playing the role was her idea from the beginning, that she saw the play in New York and urged Warners to do it: "I just wouldn't give up." This is doubtful. The play had been on Broadway in 1940, long before Wyman was in a position to dictate properties or was thought of for dramatic roles.

Other accounts say that producer Jerry Wald wanted her for the part from the beginning, even though she was fifteen years too old for the role.

Still other accounts say Wyman knew there was a good part available in an upcoming project at the studio and vied for it. At all the studios there was fierce competition among women stars for the best stories. The stars who survived longest were those who knew the value of a great story.

Another contention states that Wald, a pal of the Reagans', offered Wyman the role *after* the death of her premature baby to help her get over her depression.

In any event, the film had gone into preproduction in late 1946 and the first mention of Wyman in the project, according to studio documents, was not until the summer of 1947. At that point, Wald had been putting the package together for over a year.

Jerry Wald was Warners' fair-haired boy. He had convinced aging star Joan Crawford to play the mother of a teenage daughter, and the role had brought Crawford an Oscar and made *Mildred Pierce* one of the biggest box office draws of 1945. But he couldn't work with Crawford again on *Johnny Belinda*. She was certainly wrong for the part, as were the other leading Warners ladies: Bette Davis, Alexis Smith, Ann Sheridan. Eleanor Parker was a possibility, but not a big enough name. Sam Goldwyn's contract star and Oscar winner, Teresa Wright, was perfect—but Warners would have to pay a huge loan-out fee for her services. All things considered, Jane Wyman, in her new actress/star persona, was the likely choice.

Getting *Johnny Belinda* produced had in fact been an uphill battle for writer-turned-producer Wald. The play had been lying around unbought by the major studios until Wald convinced Jack Warner and Steve Trilling, head of production, to purchase it. In a confidential memo dated June 1946, Wald appealed to Trilling and Warner from a commercial point of view. *To Each His Own* was then racking up huge grosses at the box office, and Wald said the film was "cleaning up at the box office because it is an out-and-out woman's story. The basic story of *Johnny Belinda* is a thousand times more commercial than *To Each His Own*. Why nobody has purchased this property before this is something beyond my powers of comprehension. In a very slick fashion, you are dealing with the most primitive emotional subject in the world—an unwed mother who is having her child taken away. The mother, in order to defend her child, kills the man who is attempting to do this." In addition, Wald noted, *Belinda* had the value of "the sensational characterization of a deaf and dumb girl."

It is incredible but endemic in the movie industry that a producer such as Wald, with a great track record, still had to convince the studio powers that he knew what he was doing. Wald told Trilling, "At least give me ten points by acknowledging that I do know something about stories. I hate to continue to harp on this property; but, if you recall, I went through the same thing on *Mildred Pierce, Serenade,* and countless other stories. Don't you think it's high time that you guys acknowledged that I do have a good mind for stories?"

And, with a sense of humor, he added, "You know, frankly, what I should do is take the notes I wrote you on *Mildred Pierce* and *Serenade* and just substitute *Johnny Belinda,* because they all run down the same road, primitive stories told in a slick, new fashion."

Warners bought the property, and by December 1946 Wald had a completed screenplay by Irmgard von Cube and Allen Vincent.

Director Jean Negulesco, under contract to the studio, had been assigned to *The Adventures of Don Juan.* But the film's star, Errol Flynn, made it clear that he did not want Negulesco. Wald knew of the conflict, so he sent Negulesco the *Belinda* script, and the director quickly flashed back a memo: "I'd love to do it."

Johnny Belinda is the story of a teenage deaf-mute who lives with her father and aunt in a fishing village in Nova Scotia. The townspeople and her own family call her "the dummy." Then a young doctor comes to town, and he is the first person to treat the girl with compassion. He understands that, while deaf, she is not stupid; he teaches her sign language and how to read lips.

Negulesco and Wald were determined to have an impressive cast. Lew Ayres, famous for his doctor characterizations, had made a postwar comeback in *The Dark Mirror,* again playing a sympathetic doctor. He seemed the natural choice.

Rory Calhoun was tested for the villain, Locky, who rapes Belinda and later attempts to take her baby away. But a young actor, Horace Stephen McNally, who had originally played the doctor in the stage version, was now in Hollywood playing "heavies." He had played the villain in the Judy Garland starrer *The Harvey Girls,* so he was cast as the villain in *Belinda.*

Contract player Janis Paige was tested for the small but pivotal role of Stella, Locky's wife—it eventually went to newcomer Jan Sterling.

Wald and Negulesco also signed an impressive cast of character actors, including Agnes Moorehead and Charles Bickford. Bickford had just scored a big hit in *The Farmer's Daughter* and was being talked about for an Academy Award nomination. He was signed for an astounding $5,000 a week for his services on *Belinda,* an indication that this was a top-drawer project from the beginning, and that no expense was being spared.

Reports said that Lew Ayres was displeased when he heard that Jane Wyman was under consideration for *Belinda.* He wanted Teresa Wright. Even Wyman herself said, years later, "It's all in the breaks. I have to thank Jerry Wald for *Johnny Belinda.* When he was casting the picture, he insisted I do the part. I wasn't so sure, but he won out and I'm really grateful."

There is evidence that before she joined the *Belinda* cast, Jane was involved in several other Warner Bros. projects that never made it to the screen. All were dropped when Wald convinced Wyman to do *Belinda.*

Jane could not have been unaware that playing this part was going to be an intense emotional experience. How could a script about a mother who almost loses her child not have tremendous impact on Jane Wyman at this juncture in her life?

The elements were in place. Jane's friend Milo Anderson was doing the costumes and, of course, Perc Westmore the makeup. It was going to be a tight-knit, supportive crew—people Jane had worked with for years.

For several weeks Jane thoroughly researched the role, studying deaf people. She later called her *Belinda* role her most creative part, although not her most arduous one. She learned sign language and years later claimed to still remember it.

A woman named Elizabeth Gessner was hired (for $35 a day) to be technical advisor, which included teaching Wyman and Ayres sign language and lip-reading. Gessner introduced Jane to a young Mexican girl who had been born deaf.

"The girl was brought to my home and to the studio often so that I could study her," recalled Jane. "And we made innumerable tests of her in sixteen- and thirty-five-millimeter film. I spent many hours with the cheerful youngster, watching her every reaction."

At the time Wyman noted that what she was "trying hardest to get into my characterization is a certain quality that I saw in her eyes. I can describe it only as an 'anticipation light,' the look of one who wants so eagerly to share in things. All deaf people have that inquiring, interested, alive look. They must be keener, more alert than the rest of us. But even after weeks of tests, my tests, something was missing. Suddenly I realized what was wrong. I could hear. I could act deaf but it lacked a realistic feeling and that showed in my face."

Wyman and the director came up with the idea of sealing Jane's ears with wax to blot out every noise except percussion sounds.

In August, while Jane was preparing to begin production on *Johnny Belinda, Magic Town* was released to mixed reviews. One person who hated it was the director, William Wellman, who was quoted as saying, "I was in on that thing from the beginning, and I wish I never started it. It stunk! Frank [Capra] and Bob [Riskin] had a big argument about the picture and Riskin asked me to do it. I told him this is the kind of picture only Capra could do. It's not my kind of film."

But despite Wellman's opinion, *Magic Town* was an entertaining picture that has stood the test of time. It was a pleasant comedy about a pollster who finds a little town where opinions totally represent those of the population of the entire country. Jane played an idealistic newspaperwoman who falls in love with the pollster (James Stewart). The picture was important in Jane's career in that it provided her an opportunity to combine her gifts for both comedy and drama. In this picture she is very much the "Jane Wyman" that fans of the late forties and early fifties would come to know. *The Yearling* and *The Lost Weekend* had stretched her abilities. In *Magic Town* she was more refined in her comic delivery than before, more subtle; the rough edges and hard bite were attractively diffused. She seemed more like a young Claudette Colbert or Irene Dunne or Jean Arthur.

But the role of Belinda would offer Jane few light moments; instead there were many highly emotional scenes. With films such as *The Lost Weekend, The Yearling*, and now *Johnny Belinda*, Wyman was no longer just acting by reading lines—she had to delve into her inner self, to call on personal emotions to convey properly the depth these characters required. In the old days it was never a question of taking a character "home" with her—she could act the part in front of the camera and leave it at that. With these new, many-faceted dramatic roles, however, it was impossible not to take some aspect of the characters—and the pressures of playing them—home with her. And often Reagan was not home when Jane got there, but was traveling on SAG business and attending numerous union meetings, at all hours of the evening.

Again there was talk of an impending breakup between Reagan and Wyman, but it was premature. For the time being, Jane's involvement in *Belinda* was all-consuming.

She did answer old friend Louella's questions about trouble in the marriage. "I swore I was not even going to deny this silly talk, but you're different. . . . Ronnie and I haven't had even a good old-fashioned family argument. Of course, I have a hot temper . . . but Ronnie, who has the disposition of an angel, just lets me blow off steam until I get my mad out of my system. He never fights back."

Insiders, however, knew that despite this whitewash, Jane and Ron were in the midst of a rocky period in their relationship.

As makeup and wardrobe tests on *Belinda* were being conducted at the studio, and Jane was studying her script and developing her characterization, the production team made the decision that instead of motoring up to Mendocino and Fort Bragg (small towns about two hundred miles north of San Francisco, by car an eighteen-hour trip in those days), where location shots would be filmed, the studio would charter a DC-4. Ayres, Bickford, and many of the others decided to fly to Mendocino on the Warners plane. But Jane decided to drive, and Ron accompanied her. After a short while, he returned home.

It was a long location schedule, and it served to draw all the actors closer together and deeper into their characterizations. Local people were recruited as extras. Even in the mid-1980s, Mendocino has a population of only a few thousand. In 1947, "The population consisted of the innkeeper and the postmaster, who served the people in outlying areas," recalled Jane. "In the evenings we made our own fun, formed a community sing among our company—hymns and folk-songs. We felt so isolated, yet oddly at peace, that no one wanted to play cards or dance. It was as though the spirit of the simple people of Belinda's remote world hung over and around us."

Jean Negulesco, who was a well-known painter as well as an art collector, was inspired by the incredible landscapes, and he encouraged others in the group to try their hand at painting. Today, Jane Wyman is an accomplished and recognized painter herself, and she credits Negulesco with being the man who initiated her into the art.

Many in the group tried to follow Negulesco's lead, and Wyman later said, "Just sitting there painting away with Aggie and Lew gave me a warm feeling."

There was soon talk that Jane and Lew Ayres had been drawn very close together. Ayres was a sympathetic, intellectual man of great compassion, and Jane was still recovering from the emotional traumas she had suffered earlier in the year with the loss of her baby.

Ayres, then thirty-nine, had a fascinating and unusual background. He had been one of the screen's most popular young leading men back in the late silent and early sound era. He had starred with Garbo in *The Kiss* and was the star of Lewis Milestone's classic 1930 film of Erich Maria Remarque's *All Quiet on the Western Front.* He married Lola Lane in 1932 and was divorced in 1934. That same year he married Ginger Rogers; they divorced in 1940. While his career had not fulfilled its early promise, he had directed several movies and made a niche for himself in films in the late 1930s when he starred in MGM's highly popular *Dr. Kildare* series.

There had been tremendous adverse publicity about Ayres during World War II when the actor, a conscientious objector, refused to fight and was sent to a labor camp. "I'll praise the Lord but not pass the ammunition," he was quoted as saying. He was vilified by ultrapatriots of the era, but he stood by his convictions. Distributors boycotted his films and MGM dropped his contract. But during the war Ayres volunteered for noncombatant duty— first he was a chaplain's aide and later he became an orderly in the Army Medical Corps, where for almost two years he distinguished himself under battle conditions.

When he returned to Hollywood in 1945, there was lingering resentment toward him. Although some thought he would enter the ministry, Ayres resumed his acting career. At first no major studio would sign him, but word of his wartime heroism soon changed the attitude of many.

Universal gave him the opportunity to play opposite Olivia de Havilland in *The Dark Mirror.* It was a comeback vehicle, of sorts, for both of them: it was her first film after breaking with Warners and being off the screen for a couple of years, and his first film after the war. The public accepted Ayres, and Warners offered him a contract. Prior to the *Belinda* assignment, he had starred with Ann Sheridan in *The Unfaithful* (a remake of *The Letter*).

Ayres had actually studied to be a doctor when he was in college, and his interest in helping people in a spiritual way was common knowledge. He was known throughout Hollywood as someone with a deep, genuine interest in religion and philosophy. *Belinda* took full advantage of the qualities he projected both on and off screen: intelligence, compassion, sensitivity.

Despite the beauty and quality of the daily rushes from the Mendocino location, one who did not appreciate the footage was Jack Warner: "They're up there shooting fog and a bunch of damned sea gulls!" he exclaimed. Warner kept having his doubts about the commercial prospects for *Belinda:* "Who," Jack Warner wanted to know, "wants to see a picture where the leading lady doesn't say a word?"

Because she had no dialogue perhaps Jane had to call on even deeper emotions to convey, visually, the anguish and hurt her character experiences. Consequently, if she had turned to work as an escape to forget recent tragedy and current problems, the role of Belinda was of no solace. Conversely, perhaps the recent tragic events were what enabled her to play the role so effectively.

Several scenes called for Jane to cry, and Negulesco said that those scenes went well—"The trouble was getting Janie to stop crying."

Throughout actual shooting, the earplugs that Jane wore—sometimes plastic and sometimes wax and cotton—prevented her from hearing the dialogue of the other actors, but they gave her the "necessary faltering indecision" to play Belinda. Everything was working very well, and the company was aware that in this film they were creating something special.

When they returned to the studio for interiors, the picture was only one or two days behind schedule. Shooting promptly slowed down, however, and soon production was running ten days behind schedule, although it was still well under budget.

Reagan frequently visited Jane on the *Belinda* set, often bringing the children. (Hedda Hopper would later dramatically report: "He haunted the set.") Perhaps this was Ron's attempt to quell rumors of discord between him and Jane. Nonetheless, they persisted. One of their former agents revealed, "I could see the handwriting on the wall where their marriage was concerned. Ron was always on his soapbox about some political issue." And an actress who worked with Reagan during these years confirms that it was a lonely time for Jane; she had two young children and her own career to contend with and didn't see much of Reagan— he was home at night only to catch a few hours sleep.

As always, the gossip columnists and fan magazines, ever eager to concoct Hollywood's perfect marriage, were just as eager to report "trouble in paradise." In all fairness, however, it must be noted that the town's two leading ladies of gossip, Louella and Hedda, both liked the Reagans and were anxious for their marriage to work and to prove to the American public that some stars were *not* the "fickle, self-absorbed people they are painted to be."

Marital problems aside, Reagan seemed more embroiled than ever in the business of SAG, even flying to Washington to testify before the House Un-American Activities Committee.

Filming on *Johnny Belinda* was nearing completion that November, and by then Jane was finally making no secret of the fact that she and Ronnie were indeed having major difficulties in their relationship. They had even had a few fights in public—one outside a Beverly Hills restaurant while waiting for their car, where she was heard to yell at him angrily, "I got along without you before and I certainly can get along without you now."

She made no effort to disguise her distaste for his deepening involvement in politics. Herman D. Hover, owner of Ciro's, has recalled, "One night California's Lieutenant Governor at the time, Goodwin Knight, came in while Ronnie and Jane were dining, and Knight made a beeline for Ronnie. They talked and talked politics, and you could see Jane was bored. She kept sighing and yawning and making no effort to hide the fact that she thought politics was all very, very dull."

On her last day of shooting *Belinda,* Jane told friends that she was going off for a long rest.

"With Ronnie and the kids?" someone asked.

"No," she replied, "just me."

○ ○ ○ ○ ○ ○ ○ ○ ○ ○ ○ ○ ○ ○ ○ ○ ○ ○

6

RONALD REAGAN WAS BESIEGED BY REPORTERS ONE afternoon in December 1947. He was stunned by the quote that Jane had given the press to pass on to the public: "There is no use in lying. I am not the happiest girl in the world. It's nothing that has happened recently, it's an accumulation of things that have been coming on for a long time. . . . We will talk things over and I hope and believe that we will solve our problems and avoid a separation."

Up to this point neither Reagan nor Jane had ever discussed any of the intimate private feelings between the two of them with the press. At least, they hadn't been quoted for the record. To do so was out of character for both of them.

It was generally known at the time that Jane had gone to New York. But why? People at the studio said she had gone to visit a girl friend who had just had a baby. Others said she went and checked into a hotel and wanted to be alone.

She was, in fact, not interested in socializing and tried to avoid reporters. But one dogged journalist who caught up with her in Gotham was Harrison Carroll, the Hollywood reporter for *The Herald-Express* (later *The Herald-Examiner*). It was he who printed Jane's quote, the item that opened up the Pandora's box of her private life.

One can guess that either Carroll must have caught Wyman off guard, or that perhaps Jane knew this dramatic move was the only way she could get Ronald Reagan's full attention and pull him out of his union and political involvements long enough to take a look at his personal life.

Subsequently Gladys Hall, a very reliable writer on the Hollywood scene (she was the only movie reporter publicity-shy Spencer Tracy would speak to), quoted Jane as having said in New York: "We're through. We're finished. And it's all my fault."

"It caught him so pathetically by surprise," says one who knew the couple. Reagan was deluged by the press for a statement. He spoke to Hedda Hopper, and confirmed: "We had a tiff. That's right. But we've had tiffs before, as what couple married eight years hasn't. But I expect when Jane gets back from New York we'll get back together all right. . . . The bad part of Hollywood is that you have to live your life in a goldfish bowl—and what you see in a goldfish bowl is too often distorted."

He added: "I love Jane and I know she loves me. I don't know what this is all about and I don't know why Jane has done it." Always the optimist, Reagan declared, "For my part, I hope to live with her the rest of my life."

And to the columnist in whose home his wedding reception had been held, Reagan said: "Right now, Louella, Jane needs very much to have a fling and I intend to let her have it. She is sick and nervous and not herself. . . . Jane says she loves me, but is no longer 'in love' with me, and points out that this is a fine distinction. That, I don't believe. I think she is nervous, despondent, and because of this she feels our life together has become humdrum."

And to Gladys Hall, Reagan admitted: "It's a strange character I'm married to, but—I love her. . . . Please remember that Jane went through a very bad time when, after the strain of waiting for another baby, she lost it. Then, perhaps, before she was strong enough, she went into *Johnny Belinda*. It was a taxing, difficult role. Perhaps, too," he conceded, in classic understatement, "my seriousness about public affairs has bored Jane."

Never before—and never again—would Ronald Reagan "bare his soul" about his private life in such a fashion.

Jane, too, was now wary of the press. Back in Hollywood, she and Reagan attended a party at Agnes Moorehead's house. Friends saw it as a possible reconciliation, but a few days later the studio confirmed that Jane would not be appearing in *John Loves Mary*, Reagan's next picture. Newcomer Patricia Neal would debut in the film.

On December 14, Jane announced that she was separating from her husband. Reagan was crushed. He vehemently denied, however, that any other man was involved. "If I've had any competition it's been only in the roles she played on screen," he was quoted as saying.

Reagan was telling friends that despite their separation, he and Jane would still be together in fifty years. Their fairy godmother Louella Parsons noted, "I wish I could believe that in fifty years they will be together. But after talking with Jane, I'm not so sure."

Miss Parsons conceded, "Some of their trouble is undoubtedly based on two careers in one family." And Parsons, who had known the Hollywood marriage scene for more than a quarter of a century, couldn't help but reveal, "If Jane and Ronnie do separate, I'm going to have much less faith in human beings."

In an attempt to keep up appearances, Reagan went to a New Year's Eve party. Another guest at the party was Patricia Neal. Miss Neal has recalled, "It was sad, because he did not want a divorce. I remember he went outside. An older woman went with him. He cried."

Friends of Reagan's have said that during this period he was "despondent" in a way they had never seen him before. On some evenings he was actually seen sitting in his car outside Jane's house.

In the meantime, Ron had started *John Loves Mary*, and on his thirty-seventh birthday, February 6, 1948, he was surprised when he was called from the set—waiting for him outside the soundstage was a new Cadillac convertible. Jane had ordered it months before as a special surprise; now she gave it to him in the names of Maureen and Michael.

Reagan was having dinner at her house that night so they could be together with the kids. But he knew she was leaving for Las Vegas in less than ten days, and the hope of a reconciliation seemed slim.

By February 17 their lawyers had worked out a property settlement. Hollywood was aghast that the Reagans were actually going through with it.

Jane went to Vegas, ostensibly to set up residence for the divorce, and checked into the Flamingo. But just a few days later she checked out.

Back in Hollywood there was talk of a reconciliation and Louella phoned Ron. He denied it: "I have not talked with Jane since she went to Las Vegas, and we did not reconcile over the phone in spite of what certain people said." Reagan lamented, "I only wish Jane would come back of her own volition and not because she has been hounded into returning to me."

Louella said that Reagan was bitter against people who reported conversations that were not true.

After Jane left the Flamingo, no one knew where she was. Reagan said, "Nevada's a big state. Maybe she's on a ranch somewhere." A spokesman for the Flamingo, however, declared that Wyman had headed back to Los Angeles.

In fact, Jane had reconsidered. She and Ron would "try again." Reagan subsequently moved back in with her and the kids. Their reunion proved to be short-lived, however, and by May 6 he had moved out again. To this day, Wyman has never publicly discussed their split, and Reagan, in his memoirs, gives no details of their breakup, but instead capsules all these months of reconciliation attempts into one sentence: "I was notified I was going to be a bachelor again, and this, I thought, only happened to other people and you read about it in the papers."

Friends like June Allyson and Dick Powell were not surprised. Allyson has said, "Richard and I were heartsick over Ronnie and Jane, but as Richard put it: 'They just seemed to pass each other going in different directions.'"

The Reagans' breakup and reconciliation attempts were beginning to make the couple topics for ridicule. "We have more hot-and-cold marriages this season," wrote Hedda Hopper in a pointed article, "Why Can't They Stay Married?" Among others mentioned, she listed Ron and Jane: "A model marriage of solid citizens like Ronald Reagan and Jane Wyman teeter-tottering throughout suspenseful months, with tickets to Las Vegas and return tickets back, confusing everyone, including themselves and their bewildered children, until Jane decided to call it quits for keeps." Hedda asked, "Has Hollywood rewritten the vows to read, 'until we change our minds'?"

The estranged couple deeply resented the picture of them that was emerging in the press. After all, neither Wyman nor Reagan was an empty-headed playgirl/playboy so typical of many of the headline makers in the Hollywood community.

Later, Jane declared, "At the time of my divorce, I used to read the trash written about how I felt and Ronnie felt and I just couldn't believe it. We were grown-up people with a serious problem and we were painted as a couple of moony adolescents with absolutely no sense of responsibility."

At the time, everyone was giving the Reagans advice, in and out of print. Everyone was trying to save their "ideal marriage." Supposedly friends even convinced the couple to see a counselor to help "straighten things out."

Sympathy generally seemed to be with Reagan. He was constantly quoted as having nothing but kind words about Jane. "Please remember Jane went through a very bad time," he pleaded. "Less than six weeks before Jane left for New York, we were happy enough for her to tell me, 'I hope it can always be like this between us.' I do too. We belong together."

Louella was, of course, the most emotionally involved—and the most shaken—of all the couple's friends: "No marital separation since I broke the story that Mary Pickford, America's sweetheart, was leaving Douglas Fairbanks has had the effect of the parting of the Reagans. Just as Mary and Doug stood for all that is best in this town, so have Ronnie and Jane. . . . To those of us who are close friends, they were an ideal Mr. and Mrs."

Louella reminded her readers that Jane and Ronnie's emotional states were deeply affected by recent tragedy. According to Miss Parsons, "Jane was so distraught that she gave birth prematurely."

But others were not so kind in their reportage. "Hollywood sympathy in this case is one hundred percent with Ronnie, who is a prince," declared an editorial in *Silver Screen* magazine. "Jane is a moody person, temperamental, ambitious, restless, and seeking, and furthermore, she is not now and hasn't been well for some time. It is to be hoped that, as her health improves, Jane's other problems will vanish, and two of the town's favorite people will resume their marriage."

It was Jane, not Ron, who moved out of their dream house, and finally, in May 1948, Jane filed for divorce.

Maureen, then seven, vividly recalled as an adult the point at which the children were told of the breakup. "I remember sitting in the car crying hysterically, with my father trying to explain it. He said the same things that parents always do at a time like that. They're still my parents and you're still their kid. We'll all learn to adjust to this."

Ironically, Reagan's career was just now coming out of the doldrums. *The Voice of the Turtle* was a success, and it appeared, for the moment at least, that Warners knew what they were doing. *Newsweek*'s review was typical: "Ronald Reagan turns in a pleasantly sensitive performance as the marine sergeant."

Professionally, Jane was dealt an unexpected blow. Jack Warner was not enthusiastic about *Johnny Belinda*. In later years Wyman said that after Warner had seen the film, "he hated it so much he stuck it in cans and nobody knew what happened to it. . . . Jean Negulesco, the director, wasn't even allowed to do his own editing. He has never to this day set foot in the Warner Bros. studio again."

Although the future of *Belinda* seemed unsure, Jane was working under her new ten-year contract at Warners, and the studio was scouting around for an acceptable vehicle for her. The new contract was a milestone to the former contract player. She was finally in the big leagues salary-wise (although her $3,500 per week was considerably less than the $5,000-plus per week Warners was paying Errol Flynn and Bette Davis). The contract gave Wyman the right to make one outside picture per year and permission to appear on the "troublesome" new medium, television.

There was talk of reviving *Ethan Frome* as a vehicle for Jane, but the property the studio finally decided on for her was a light comedy, *A Kiss in the Dark*, to co-star David Niven (who would be top-billed), on loan from Sam Goldwyn.

Meanwhile, in June, Jane received her interlocutory decree. On the summer day in 1948, when Jane appeared in court for her decree, Reagan was not in attendance. Instead his lawyer, William Berger, represented him. Jane's attorney, Charles Millikan, had filed for the divorce on the grounds of "extreme mental cruelty." Everyone in Hollywood knew this was the catch-all phrase when a couple had irreconcilable differences. Jane voiced, for public record, what everyone in Hollywood already knew: that she was bored with Reagan's political diatribes.

The *Los Angeles Times* reported, "Miss Wyman told the court that she and Reagan engaged in continued arguments on his

political views. Despite her lack of interest in his political activities, Miss Wyman continued, Reagan insisted that she attend
meetings with him and that she be present during discussions
among his friends. But her own ideas, she complained, 'were
never considered important.' . . .

" 'Finally, there was nothing in common between us,' said
Jane, 'nothing to sustain our marriage.' "

Years later an account by Jane's friend and advisor, Catholic
priest Robert Perrella, stated that Miss Wyman, recalling the
years with Reagan, "admits it was exasperating to awake in the
middle of the night, prepare for work, and have someone at the
breakfast table, newspaper in hand, expounding on the far right,
far left, the conservative right, the conservative left, the middle-
of-the-roader." He added: "She harbors no ill feeling toward
him."

The Reagans had made an undisclosed property settlement.
Jane would receive no alimony but would receive $500 per
month child support.

After the separation, Jane and Ron saw each other frequently
because of the children. He had complete access to them and
spent a great deal of time with them. And although his ego was
battered, the separation could not be termed anything but ami-
cable. It was assumed Ron was still carrying the torch for Jane
and harbored thoughts that they might yet reconcile before the
decree became final.

The usually cooperative and happy Mr. Reagan now became
very uncooperative, almost hostile, with the press. He even
snapped at a gossip columnist who, on the lot one day, wanted
information on a possible Reagan-Wyman reconciliation.

Jane's name was being linked with others, notably Manny
Sachs, record executive, and actor Peter Lawford. Jane was upset
with the constant gossip that these were romances. "Why
shouldn't I see Manny?" she protested. "He used to be my agent,

and Ronnie and I have known him for years. How can anybody call that a romance?"

But Jane had been in the game too long to really ask that question. She knew the rules. And as the gossips would say, "If you can't stand the heat, get out of the kitchen."

Now that she and Reagan were officially split, her name was linked with Lew Ayres's. There were even stories indicating that they were now having a deep, serious relationship. Everyone naturally assumed the affair had begun while Jane and Lew were on location filming *Johnny Belinda*. Others knew, however, that while he was in Mendocino, Ayres was still romantically involved with actress Audrey Totter. But it was going to be hard to convince anyone that Wyman and Ayres had begun thinking of each other romantically only *after* her separation from Reagan.

Many stories linking Wyman with Ayres were quick to point out that Ayres had had nothing to do with her breakup with Ron. "And this is no whitewash—they never had a date of any sort together until well after Jane and Ronnie had separated," noted Ruth Waterbury, who went out on a limb and further speculated: "They probably will be married this summer when Jane's divorce becomes final. Lew has had Jane down to meet his family. They now are going openly everywhere together, and exclusively with one another. Yet most of the time, no one sees them because they are alone together, talking, reading, studying, painting."

Hedda Hopper did not mince words when she contacted Jane to get "the real story."

"Was there a romance during the shooting of *Johnny Belinda*?"

"No, dear," Jane said patiently.

"Well, everyone says there was," retorted Hedda.

Wyman retained her cool. "They can say what they like. It's not true."

Hedda changed her course. "What about you and Ronnie? I know you two used to have terrible arguments. He'd get on one subject and stick to it. And never get off it. I've seen you at parties. You'd walk away from him and he'd follow you, talking."

Wyman didn't flinch. "That's Hopper's statement, not mine." And Jane said, "Hedda, it's your interview and you can ask any questions you want. But I don't have to answer them."

It was obvious that the columnist was not going to give up. So Wyman sighed, and tried to sum it up: "Ronnie and I have never had career troubles between us. I don't believe the subject ever came up. We see each other quite frequently and talk about the children, and we're getting along fine. Can we let it go at that?" All Jane would say regarding marriage was, "I'm not getting married again for a long, long time."

Certainly all the coverage on the love affair between Wyman and Ayres drummed up interest in their unreleased picture. And long before the film's release, Jane was being touted as a sure Oscar winner for *Johnny Belinda*.

Stories continued that Reagan was still "carrying the torch" for Jane. In addition, with the success of *The Voice of the Turtle* and the hopes for *John Loves Mary*, it seemed Ronald Reagan's career was on course again. He was now working in *The Girl from Jones Beach*, a story about a Vargas-like magazine illustrator. Sex symbol Virginia Mayo, who was at the peak of her stardom, had the title role. The film was filled with beautiful girls, and columnists and publicists alike were trying to get Reagan to date them. Even Reagan has admitted that working on *The Girl from Jones Beach* "went a long way towards solving my social problems."

Virginia Mayo has recalled that during the filming, Reagan "had lots of girl friends visiting the set. He was very handsome."

But Eddie Bracken, who co-starred in the film, recalled: "Reagan was a lonely guy because of his divorce, but a very level-headed guy. He was never for the sexpots. He was never a guy looking for the bed. He was a guy looking for companionship more than anything else. But I wouldn't say he was straitlaced."

Although many have said that in 1948 Ronald Reagan had little to do but carry the torch for Jane Wyman, he continued his political activities, delivering speeches on radio and ardently campaigning for the Democratic ticket, especially President Harry S Truman and the mayor of Minneapolis, Hubert Humphrey, who was running for the Senate.

While Reagan was campaigning for the Democrats, Jane was finishing *A Kiss in the Dark,* after which she prepared for a nine-city tour in conjunction with scheduled openings of *Johnny Belinda.*

Although Miss Wyman contends that the only reason *Belinda* finally got released was that "One day somebody was rummaging around in a lot of dusty cans of film in the New York office and found some reels of the picture," this seems highly dubious.

True, release was held up for almost a year. But certainly, despite Jack Warner's personal feelings toward the film, there had been constant publicity on it. The property was kept alive in people's minds, leading one to believe the "shelve the picture" stories might have been a calculated maneuver by shrewd producer Wald to focus special attention on *Belinda* as an underdog. There is also the possibility that the publicity was masterminded to convince Warner to release the picture *properly.*

In any case, the desired effect had been achieved. By the summer of 1948, Warners was ready to launch *Belinda* in spectacular fashion. Advance screenings and sneak previews had been so successful that the film company's sales department knew they had a potential blockbuster in the offing.

The machinery for launching a "big" film was put into motion. Jane traveled east and was in New York and Boston when the picture opened in those cities. The reception it received from the critics was phenomenal.

According to many people, ever since Jane had lost the Oscar for *The Yearling,* everyone who knew her in Hollywood had consoled her: "You should have won the award, you deserved it." Throughout shooting on *Belinda,* friends kept enthusing over her beautiful portrayal and raising her hopes for an Oscar: "You'll win it for this."

There had been almost a year's wait. But now the critics obviously agreed with Jane's friends. Her performance was praised in every important review.

Bosley Crowther, in *The New York Times*, observed: "Miss Wyman brings superior insight and tenderness to the role. Not once does she speak throughout the picture. Her face is the mirror of her thoughts. Yet she makes this pathetic young woman glow with emotional warmth. . . . Miss Wyman, all the way through, plays her role in a manner which commands compassion and respect."

Variety was a rave: "Her performance is a personal success, a socko demonstration that an artist can shape a mood and sway an audience through projected emotions without a spoken word."

Veteran critic Archer Winsten wrote in the *New York Post:* "Jane Wyman gives a performance surpassingly beautiful in its slow, luminous awakening of joy and understanding. It is all the more beautiful in its accomplishment without words, perhaps *because* it is so wordlessly expressive."

For the studio, this kind of excitement over a performance and a film was equivalent to having a potential winner in the Kentucky Derby. One might hope for a winner, and deserve a winner, but until the horse is over the line there's always that possibility of an upset. . . .

Back in Los Angeles, Jane eagerly awaited the film's Hollywood premiere. On Thursday evening, October 13, 1948, Warners' Hollywood Theater was aglow with stars. It was the same theater where Jane and Ron had attended numerous similar openings for others on Warners' roster of stars—but never for Jane. But now it was her turn; this was Jane Wyman's picture and everyone knew it. Reagan was also at the event.

Special souvenir programs, featuring only a beautiful charcoal drawing of Jane's face as Belinda, had been printed. *Johnny*

Belinda was a class act all the way down the line. There would be no disappointments—the West Coast reception of the film was as enthusiastic as the East Coast's. With all the reviews in, Jane was virtually assured a best-actress Oscar nomination.

In ensuing weeks, fan mail poured in from all parts of the country. The picture was even praised by other stars and producers. Jack Warner accepted all the kudos graciously, as if he alone were responsible for bringing *Belinda* to the screen.

According to Jane's own recollection, she had to force Warner to take out an ad "apologizing" to everyone who had been involved in making *Belinda* for the way they and the film had been treated earlier. But in fact the ad merely "congratulated" everyone concerned with the production, and listed them alphabetically.

While the studio was now mentioning Wyman for every major dramatic role on its agenda, surprisingly the property Jane finally agreed to do was a most undistinguished script, *The Octopus and Miss Smith*.

Meanwhile, Reagan had been cast in a film version of another hit play, *The Hasty Heart*. Though Reagan was to be top-billed, the real star of the screen story was to be newcomer Richard Todd. Patricia Neal was the female star, and both Neal and Reagan were sent to London, where the entire film would be shot.

Many studios were sending their stars to England to make films because income earned on American films released there was frozen in Britain. To utilize the money, film companies had to produce films in England.

Ronald Reagan was unhappy not only with his supporting role in *The Hasty Heart*, but because he didn't like the idea of making a Hollywood film out of Hollywood, taking work away from U.S. technicians. Reagan, however, per his contract, had no choice in the matter, and was cajoled with the promise that on return he would finally get to do a western.

The director of *Hasty Heart*, Vincent Sherman, has recalled, "We were in London for almost six months making *Heart*, during one of the coldest and most bitter winters ever in England." When they first arrived in London, Sherman recalled that he and Reagan "spent an evening or two together, and he told me about his recent divorce from Jane Wyman, and from what I could gather, it hurt him considerably."

Patricia Neal has recalled this London trip as well. She and Reagan "both stayed at the Savoy in London in adjoining suites. And although I was a young, pretty girl, he never made a pass at me. Of course there were splendid reasons. I was wildly in love with Gary Cooper and he was still in love with Jane Wyman, who had just divorced him."

Hollywood was somewhat confused by the amiability of the Reagans' separation. While he was in England, Reagan frequently phoned Jane, both to get news of the children and to talk with them.

While Reagan was in London, he accepted an award for Jane. The London *Daily Express*'s film tribunal had declared Jane best actress of the year for *Johnny Belinda*.

In January 1949, to no one's surprise, Jane received her second Oscar nomination. Her friends clamored, "You'll win this time, you've got to win this time!"

All of this reassurance was mere speculation, and close friends knew the disappointment would be shattering if she lost again. Jane had been around a long time and she knew the realities of the business. How many *Yearling*'s and *Belinda*'s did an actress get a chance at in a career?

This time her competition was even more formidable than the last, and her chances of winning seemed even more problematic. All the other nominees were among Hollywood's favorite actresses. Olivia de Havilland had given an incredible performance this year in *The Snake Pit*, which, like *Johnny Belinda*, was a film with social significance. Ingrid Bergman, who had already won an Oscar for *Gaslight*, and who was acknowledged as possibly the best actress in films, was up for *Joan of Arc*. And there were two strong veterans in the running as well: Barbara Stanwyck for *Sorry Wrong Number* ("Stanny" had been nominated many times and had yet to win), and Irene Dunne for *I Remember Mama*. Miss Dunne had been nominated five times and had yet to win.

The previous year, Loretta Young, who was, like Stanwyck and Dunne, considered one of "Hollywood's own," had finally copped the prize for *The Farmer's Daughter*. There was strong feeling that this year one of the sentimental favorites, Stanwyck or Dunne, would finally join Miss Young as a winner. It was certainly a year in which *all* the actresses were truly deserving. But while Jane's nomination was not a surprise, what was almost unheard of for a seemingly "small" picture like *Johnny Belinda* was that the film received nominations in virtually every major category.

The director, Jean Negulesco, was nominated, and the film was nominated as one of the five best pictures of the year.

Lew Ayres was up for best actor. His competition was keen: Montgomery Clift *(The Search)*; Clifton Webb (as "Mr. Belvedere" in *Sitting Pretty)*; Dan Dailey *(When My Baby Smiles at Me)*; and Laurence Olivier *(Hamlet)*.

Charles Bickford and Agnes Moorehead were nominated in the best supporting actor and actress categories. The odds-on favorite in Bickford's division, however, was Walter Huston for *The Treasure of the Sierra Madre*.

Belinda also received nominations for best screenplay, best cinematography, best set decoration, best sound recording, best film editing, and best musical score.

Despite the stiff competition, however, of all the *Belinda* nominees, Jane was considered the most likely to win.

That winter, Wyman won the Hollywood Foreign Press Association's coveted Golden Globe Award as best actress for her performance in *Johnny Belinda*. Wald and others suggested this recognition was further proof that she was sure to win the Oscar. But, then again, it was Olivia de Havilland, in *The Snake Pit*, who had been picked by the New York Film Critics for their prized annual award.

As the date for the Oscars approached, Jane was before the cameras finishing the silly comedy *The Octopus and Miss Smith*, co-starring Dennis Morgan. People wondered why, after attaining her success, Jane still agreed to do such programmers for Warner Bros. Jane defended her position, arguing that at the time Warners was cutting production and laying off employees, and she had been told that if she took the *Octopus* role three hundred people would go to work. "So I took the picture. You might say it was a mistake but it did help all those unemployed people and that made me happy. I'll admit I blew up when they changed the title from *Octopus and Miss Smith* to *The Sailor and The Lady*. I told them that Dennis Morgan was no sailor and I was no lady."

But Jane was cooperative, maintaining her thoroughly professional approach to her career.

Although the film would not turn out well, it had top-drawer ingredients. The director was Michael Curtiz. The flawless supporting cast included Eve Arden, William Frawley, Allyn Joslyn, Fred Clark, Tom Tully, and a handsome contract player, Craig Stevens, who was married to Alexis Smith.

To defend her return to the comedy genre (with *A Kiss in the Dark* and this film), Wyman observed, "I found my timing had slipped somewhat. I had been away from it too long. Comedy is very tricky and I take my hat off to anyone who can play it well."

Stars like Jane, however, were in a no-win position when it came to all the kibitzing they were constantly subjected to, with challenges such as: "Why didn't you do so-and-so's script?" or "How did you let the studio talk you into doing a turkey like that? You're a star!"

Maintaining a "star" career, however, was no easy task. An interesting explanation concerning the ups and downs, whys and wherefores of careers in the movie business was offered by Dore Schary, the writer-producer who would, in the 1950s, become head of production at MGM: "You have to remember that in the movie business, *no one* has any *real* answers—you simply have some people who are more talented at guessing what the public wants than others."

In Schary's opinion, "There were really only two men that had a terrific and very reliable sense of what it took to be consistently successful with *quality* product—Irving Thalberg and David O. Selznick. Their instincts about what stories would work, *and with which actors,* was extraordinary."

It was these last qualities Schary referred to—what story would work with which actor—which didn't seem to be operating too consistently in Jane Wyman's case at Warner Bros.

Those making *The Lady Takes a Sailor* realized that Jane was doing them a favor. Producer Harry Kurnitz gave Wyman a little gold medal at the end of shooting. It was inscribed "To Jane Wyman—for valor above and beyond the call of duty." For a time Wyman wore the medal and exhibited it proudly on the lot.

After this film Warners supposedly had prestigious dramatic properties under consideration for Wyman, including *A Streetcar Named Desire.*

A behind-the-scenes mini-drama unfolded in the course of the Oscar presentations that year. It concerned the fact that the ceremonies were unexpectedly to be held in the Academy's own small auditorium, located inside the Academy building, a former neighborhood movie house used during the year to screen films for Academy members.

The reason behind the move of the awards to this small space, after two years at the Shrine Auditorium, was that all of the major studios had suddenly stopped their financial support of the awards ceremony. For years accusations had been flying that the studios were exerting undue influence over the voting selections of Academy members. So the studios retaliated by now abruptly deciding not to finance the ceremonies. The move was timed so that the Academy would not have time to raise money to rent the Shrine or a similar space.

It had been a major headache for the Academy to decide, from among the thousands who demanded seats, which "names" would receive the 985 precious tickets. Ultimately, it would be an event with only the top of the "A" list in attendance.

Despite these last-minute problems, the Academy, with a true show-must-go-on attitude, came up with a glittering program produced by William Dozier and emceed by Robert Montgomery. All four of the top acting award winners from the previous year—Loretta Young, Ronald Colman, Celeste Holm, and Edmund Gwenn—were on hand to make presentations. Nothing could dampen the excitement of the evening. Tension was high.

The previous year *Daily Variety* had conducted a poll and successfully predicted every winner in every major category except for the upset in the best-actress award (Loretta Young had beaten the predicted winner, Roz Russell). This year there was no such poll—in many categories, most notably best actress, it was truly a toss-up.

Warner Bros. had received a total of sixteen nominations for three of its films. *Johnny Belinda* had garnered eleven of these; *The Treasure of the Sierra Madre* had received four nominations, including best picture; and *Key Largo* (another Huston picture) had received one nomination, for Claire Trevor as best supporting actress.

As always, the evening progressed slowly for the nominees. As had been expected, Walter Huston was chosen best supporting actor. Then Jane and all the Warners contingent applauded loudly when Jerry Wald was called up to the stage and presented with the prestigious Irving G. Thalberg Memorial Award, given each year to a producer in acknowledgment of the high quality of his work throughout his career and of his contributions to the industry. *Johnny Belinda* had enabled Wald to achieve the recognition he so craved.

As the evening progressed, nearing the final awards, *Belinda,* despite all its nominations, had not yet won anything. Claire Trevor beat out Agnes Moorehead for best supporting actress. Best screenplay went to John Huston for *The Treasure of the Sierra Madre.* Huston got up again a few minutes later when he won the award as best director for the same film.

Finally, Loretta Young took center stage to present the best-actor award—it did not go to Lew Ayres. Laurence Olivier won for *Hamlet.* Douglas Fairbanks, Jr., accepted for Olivier, who was in England.

Then Ronald Colman, the previous year's winner for *A Double Life,* walked to the podium.

Jane was sitting with Jerry Wald and his wife. In Miss Wyman's words: "We were just two rows behind Irene Dunne. There was something about the line of her neck that convinced me she was going to get the prize. I was slumped low in my seat (I've often been told I don't know how to sit like a lady), sort of trying to hide so that I could sneak out."

As Colman read off the nominees, Wyman began "wiping my nose with a handkerchief. It wasn't running, just a nervous habit, I guess."

Colman announced the winner: "Jane Wyman!"

"I was so sure I wouldn't win that when I heard my name called out I didn't recognize it. I didn't get up. But Jerry Wald poked me, and my handbag dropped to my lap. My lipstick and everything went rolling onto the floor."

She has recalled, "I must have been quite a sight trying to pick up things and get to the stage at the same time." She later told James Bacon, "I was the most surprised girl in the world. . . .

"First thing I knew, someone was poking me and saying 'that's you, Janie. Get up there.'

"I started that long walk. And then I began thinking of the craziest thing. I couldn't remember whether I had put my girdle on."

"Did you?" asked Bacon.

"Honey, to tell you the truth, I was so excited I still don't remember."

Jane was in such a state when she reached the stage, it was obvious to others that she was at a loss for words. Her old pal Robert Montgomery smiled at her. "You're on your own, honey, I can't help you now."

Jane had not prepared anything to say, "Just in case I didn't win." But, "You always think of something to say—" When the applause died down, Jane said: "I accept this award very gratefully—for keeping my mouth shut. I think I'll do it again!"

Jane, brunette hair cropped short, was radiant. She was wearing a high-necked, long-sleeved white crepe sheath gown and very little jewelry. To those who had known her from the early days, the dramatic transformation this woman had made in herself in the twelve years since she'd signed her first contract was astonishing. She had won the Hollywood game, persevering long enough to rise from a too blond "chorus cutie" and third-choice Torchy Blane to superstar. Along the way she had played basically ingenues, smart alecks, and glamour girls. Her characters had been brittle, sophisticated, poignant, and flip. And on- and offscreen she had literally gone through every persona the Hollywood Dream Factory could offer. Every struggling player in the business could learn a lesson from Jane Wyman—it *could* be done. One could beat the system and rise even to win the Academy Award.

Backstage at the awards show she was photographed with all the other winners and with Lew Ayres. Ayres and Jack and Ann Warner then accompanied Jane to the gala Warner Bros. party in the Champagne Room of the Mocambo.

It was quite a celebration. Jane's old friend, Warners' musical director Ray Heindorf, who had known her since the *Gold Diggers* movie days, sent Jane a wire: "Dear Bessie Fuffnik—I swim, ride, dive, imitate wild birds, play the trombone, and win Academy Awards."

In ensuing weeks and months, Jane's image took on its final shading. She was now "Jane Wyman"—an *actress* who epitomized *quality* and *class*, a woman who represented taste and style, and a person who had reached her most productive point and was beginning a whole "new" career, not at twenty or twenty-five but at thirty-five.

Unhappily, however, since Jane Wyman's great professional success happened to coincide with the problems in her life with Ronald Reagan, the press was more eager to learn intimate details of her private life than to discuss her career. Jane was not then, nor has she ever been, cooperative in this effort. As a result, along with the Oscar came the implication, and through the years the lasting perception, that Jane Wyman had sacrificed her marriage to get the award.

BOOK TWO

BOOK TWO

7

"OH DEAR, DO YOU, OF ALL PEOPLE, HAVE TO ASK ME that?" Wyman said to Louella Parsons. "I know you love Ronnie and I know you love me, but can't we just once have an interview and not talk about my broken marriage and what caused it? Let's just say I still think Ronnie is a fine man and a wonderful father."

Ron was back from England and Jane was about to leave for England. *A Kiss in the Dark* had been released that March—"Belinda Talks!" screamed the ad line—and the critical reaction toward the light comedy had been harsh. Some called it "a shabby and ridiculous film," and one New York critic said, "The actress gives no hint of the artistry that distinguished *Johnny Belinda.*" Jane's performance was called "woefully inept," and one critic even said, "She should turn the face of her Oscar to the wall."

At least her next film promised her a chance to score a prestigious success and redeem herself in the eyes of the critics. Jane would be working with famed British director Alfred Hitchcock, who had an important production deal at Warners. After the great success scored in the mid-1940s by *"Spellbound"* and *Notorious,* the box office appeal of Mr. Hitchcock's recent pictures had slipped radically. He needed a hit. His two films released through Warner Bros., *Rope* and *Under Capricorn,* had not shown profits. Nor had *The Paradine Case,* his final picture for David Selznick.

Hitchcock personally requested Jane for the lead of his new project, "Stage Fright," shortly after she won the Oscar, reasoning that she was Warner Bros.' biggest star of the moment. The other lead would also be a female: the legendary Marlene Dietrich, currently hot again owing to a big success in Billy Wilder's *A Foreign Affair.*

Jane was set to leave for filming in London in June 1949. Meanwhile, her stature at the studio was reinforced when Bette Davis, finally leaving Warners, "bequeathed" her huge dressing room–trailer to Wyman.

Before leaving for Europe, Jane did a bit in the all-star Warner Bros. pastiche *It's a Great Feeling.* Reagan, too, did a cameo in this Technicolor extravaganza, which starred Jack Carson and newcomer Doris Day. Even little Maureen Reagan (now eight) got into the act by making her film debut. (Jane and Ron, needless to say, were not in the same scenes together.)

Jane's bit in the picture was funny: it called for her to faint when she is told she has to make another film with Jack Carson. Most of Warners' top stars, including Joan Crawford, Errol Flynn, Gary Cooper, Edward G. Robinson, Eleanor Parker, and Patricia Neal, also appeared in cameo roles.

By this time Jane was important enough so that she no longer had to do interviews she didn't want to do. She made it clear that she would not talk to anyone on the press who was going to invade her privacy. On the topic of her ex-husband, she said, "Many 'inside' stories have been written about our breakup, all of them unauthentic and unauthorized. Writers and reporters play an important part in helping all of us get established. I've made many friends who've respected my wishes in refusing to discuss my problems. Unfortunately, there are those who have probed and prodded, so naturally I have avoided them."

Avoiding them did not diminish the flow of stories on Wyman and Reagan. It seemed nothing could be written about one without mention of the other. Wyman and Reagan were "a unit" in people's minds—and, of course, there was a link that would forever tie Jane Wyman and Ronald Reagan together, their children. Furthermore, until either Wyman or Reagan became *seriously* involved with other partners, there was always the chance of a reconciliation. All of this made for good and continuing copy.

Reagan, meanwhile, had had no pictures in release in 1948, but in 1949 there were three: *John Loves Mary,* in January; the dismal *Night Unto Night,* which had been on the shelf for years; and then *The Girl from Jones Beach,* a hit. His ongoing feud with Jack Warner, however, led to Lew Wasserman, his agent, renegotiating Reagan's contract with Warner Bros. The actor would do only one picture a year for the studio for the next three years, in return for only half salary, or approximately $75,000 a year.

Wasserman quickly came up with a five-picture, five-year deal for Reagan at Universal-International, for approximately $75,000 per picture. Universal immediately threw the actor into a crime drama, *Fugitive from Terror,* co-starring Ida Lupino, with shooting to begin in mid-June.

Since Jane was leaving for Europe, Ron could spend as much time as possible with the children while she was away. Michael was four, Maureen eight and a half. Jane told friends, "I haven't sent Michael to school yet, because he is so delicate. I want him to get strong and healthy first. But I think in another year I'll send him to the private school Maureen goes to. It's not far from home."

As far as the children were concerned, Wyman and Reagan made every effort to present a solid front. Long after the children were grown and on their own, Wyman revealed her feelings about this period of her family life. "Raising children . . . having the responsibilities of a house and a career, without a husband, was awesome. What can I tell you? I just coped."

In their social life, Jane and Ron succeeded in remaining close with all their old friends. It was simple—you just did not invite Janie and Ronnie to the *same* party or dinner.

Before Jane left for England, she was pressed for information regarding her romantic life.

"I have no plans to marry."

"Then you won't marry Lew Ayres?" Louella demanded.

"I have no plans to marry *anyone.*" Jane closed the subject. The Wyman-Ayres romance was quickly fading as a topic of conversation, proof for some that it had only been a publicity ploy from the beginning. Others contended it was a serious relationship but had faltered after it had been made public. (It's interesting to note that the twice-divorced Ayres did not marry again until 1964, when he was fifty-six years old. And after great success in his postwar films, he semiretired from the screen and pursued other interests.)

Jane sailed for England. She had been saying that she was willing to experiment and wanted to continue to play character roles after *Belinda*—she saw herself as a young character actress. Her role in *Stage Fright* would give her just that chance. Based on a novel, *Man Running, Stage Fright* is the story of a student (Wyman) at the Royal Academy of Dramatic Art. She encounters a young man, played by British actor Richard Todd, who is suspected of murder and is hiding from the police.

The project featured a superlative supporting cast. Veteran actors Alastair Sim and Sybil Thorndike were playing Jane's parents. Michael Wilding was cast as the police inspector who ultimately wins Wyman's love.

Hitchcock later said one of the reasons he made the film was that it would give him a chance to work in London, where his own daughter, Patricia, was actually a student at the Royal Academy. Pat Hitchcock was anxious to enter the business, so her father gave her a small role in this film, as one of Wyman's friends.

There was enormous preproduction speculation on how Jane would get along with the "real" star of the film, Marlene Dietrich. "I've no illusions," Jane told a friend. "If I worked for forty years I couldn't be a glamour girl like Marlene Dietrich."

Fifty years old, Dietrich—already being publicized as "the world's most glamorous grandmother"—was playing a character very much like herself—a dazzling star. (For this picture, Christian Dior designed Dietrich's "contemporary" wardrobe—*very* dated, in retrospect—and Dietrich's friend Cole Porter wrote the song she sang, "The Laziest Gal in Town.")

In the story, Jane's character must pose as a dowdy maid to try to trap Dietrich into revealing that she is the real killer; it was in this role-within-a-role that, as Hitchcock later said, trouble arose. "I ran into great difficulty with Jane," the director stated. "In her disguise as a ladies' maid she should have been rather unglamorous. After all, she was supposed to be impersonating an unattractive maid. But every time she saw the rushes, and how she looked alongside Marlene, she would burst into tears. She couldn't accept the idea of her face being in character while Dietrich looked so great. She kept improving her appearance every day and that's how she failed to maintain the character."

A few days after shooting began on *Stage Fright,* back in Hollywood Ronald Reagan broke his leg while participating in a Sunday night charity softball game and Universal had to recast his part in *Fugitive from Terror.* To top things off, while he was still in the hospital, the divorce from Jane became final, on July 18, 1949.

In London, Jane enjoyed herself much more than Ronnie had in his recent stay. She posed with Laurence Olivier, both displaying their Oscars. Danny Kaye was in town and palled around with the group. It was generally a festive time for Wyman, since many of her Hollywood friends were in town, including George Burns and Gracie Allen, who were headlining at the Palladium.

Even Jane's old pal Jack Benny had flown over for the Burns and Allen engagement. Louella Parsons was in London as well, and she and many of Jane's other friends thought that Lew Ayres had flown over to be with Wyman. But the man they had seen who looked so much like Ayres turned out to be Clark Hardwicke, whom the press described as a "millionaire sportsman."

"I think she still has it bad for Lew," stated Louella, "but she got over Ronnie and I'm sure she'll get over Lew."

Back on the set of *Stage Fright* there were stories of fireworks between Wyman and Dietrich. Jane denied them and later described Marlene as "The most fascinating person I've ever met. On days when she had no studio call she would come on the set just the same. She'd fix my dress, make suggestions about my hair and makeup, and help me in many ways." Wyman had this to say about Hitchcock: "He looks like a little tubby pixie."

People who worked on the picture recall that Dietrich did, in fact, involve herself in *all* aspects of the production—and that Hitchcock permitted it.

During the filming Marlene had an affair with Michael Wilding. Although Wilding gave a credible performance in the picture, Wyman later said: "We had to redub everything because he mumbled all the way through it and you couldn't understand a word he said."

Jane took her role in *Stage Fright* very seriously. As she had with *Belinda*, she did her research—in this case, mastering a credible Cockney accent for her role-within-a-role. She lived for a week with Kay Walsh, one of the British actresses in the film, in an effort to nail down the accent. And on the set one day, one of the crew told Jane she had "gotten it just right."

One of the keys to Wyman's longevity in the industry was that she was aware that stars who had no concern for running up budgets did not last long. "I have seen many of them come and go," she once said. Jane was a team player, and when she was on location, as now, she knew that budgets could really soar.

Jane said that while in England "It was a temptation to fly to Paris on the weekends and get some good food. After all, it was only fifteen minutes by air." But Wyman and Dietrich agreed that they wouldn't take a chance on leaving London: "If weather should keep us from returning, the already swollen budget would really take a beating." Studio executives were not unaware of the statistics—that Wyman and the few stars like her were helpful in keeping budgets and schedules tight because of their professional attitudes.

The picture was completed by mid-September, and on September 22 Jane sailed from Southampton to return to the States. *The Lady Takes a Sailor* was about to be released. Like *A Kiss in the Dark,* it was not very good; it would have to be Jane's star power that provided respectable box office. But Jane and the studio had high hopes for *Stage Fright.*

Upon her return to America, the actress said: "I realize the press was very good to me in England. We had one big meeting, but I watched myself to see that I wouldn't make any mistakes because I felt I was not only acting for myself, but for all of Hollywood, and I didn't want to disillusion any of the reporters." With emphasis she stated: "Art and politics, you know, should never be mixed—so I feel that actresses who go to a foreign country should try to talk about the things they know."

Statements such as this reflect the fact that Jane had a new attitude toward her responsibility as "a star." And obviously she was determined to avoid controversy and explosive subjects like politics.

In her private life Jane sometimes still used stationery with the letterhead "Mrs. Ronald Reagan, Hollywood, California." On this stationery she wrote a note to lawyer Lloyd Wright, asking him to accept an enclosed check for $5,000 as payment in full for his $7,500 bill in handling her divorce from Reagan.

In later years, when this letter and check became collector's items, there was conjecture about Wyman's being "financially strapped" at the time. But a more realistic explanation is simply that it is more or less standard procedure to make a counteroffer on a bill that has been submitted. Seventy-five hundred dollars was not an inconsiderable sum. Wright accepted Wyman's proposition and settled for $5,000.

Reagan had been living in Jane's house while recovering from his accident, so that he could be near the children. Now he moved back into his own apartment, and soon afterward he met a twenty-eight-year-old MGM contract player, Nancy Davis. The socially connected Miss Davis had arranged the meeting via Mervyn LeRoy, contending that she needed Reagan's help (he was still president of SAG). The facts indicate that Ron thought the matter could easily be taken care of via the telephone, but Miss Davis insisted she had to meet him personally.

Reagan subsequently began dating the demure young woman while continuing to date others. At the premiere of his film *The Hasty Heart*, he escorted beautiful brunette Ruth Roman, Warners' "answer" to Ava Gardner. (Jane attended the premiere with her pal, costume designer Milo Anderson.) But Hollywood was still abuzz that Ron's heart belonged to Jane and to no other, despite whom each might be seen with.

While Reagan was completing a small but pleasant comedy, *Louisa,* at Universal, Jane had started a new picture with Jerry Wald, the much heralded, eagerly awaited film version of Tennessee Williams's famous play *The Glass Menagerie.* Again, as with *Belinda*, Wyman was, at thirty-six, technically too old for the role of the fragile, introverted daughter, Laura. But as with her previous roles in dramas, Jane threw herself into the part.

Producer Wald noted, "Jane isn't fresh anymore. She's mellowed. . . . In the old days, she'd read a script and ten minutes later be in the picture; a script was a script and to hell with it. Now she reads a script, studies the character for weeks and months, discusses it thoroughly, and has a deep and perfect understanding of the part before she goes before the cameras."

For *Glass Menagerie*, at first there were plans for Jane to wear a leg brace to simulate the crippled character's affliction. The device proved unwieldy, however, and instead of a brace a special shoe was designed to create the limp.

To give Jane an added look of youth and vulnerability, it was decided that she should have long blond hair. There was no bleach bottle this time—it was a wig. And according to Frank Westmore, his brother Perc, head of the makeup department at Warner Bros., told him that "Jane complained every morning that the hairpiece made her head look too big. Perc talked her into letting him cut her own hair and designed the short, fluffy bob she has worn ever since. The wig fit smoothly over her shorn locks, and both she and Perc were happy."

Although Tallulah Bankhead had first been mentioned for the role of the domineering mother in *Menagerie* (created so memorably on Broadway by Laurette Taylor), British star Gertrude Lawrence eventually was signed for the part.

The character of Tom (autobiographically Williams) would be played by Arthur Kennedy, and the gentleman caller was being played by Kirk Douglas, then in the first flush of his stardom. The director of the production was Irving Rapper. Williams and Peter Berneis had written the screenplay.

Although Wyman and Douglas were given top billing, Gertrude Lawrence's part was by far the largest. Unfortunately, the role had been rewritten to such an extent that the poignancy of the original play was lost. In production, however, the package had the earmarks of a blockbuster.

In January, Ron was at Jane's house to help celebrate her thirty-sixth birthday (he gave her a poodle). The children, of course, were always happy when their parents were together for such occasions. Jane and Ron kept close counsel on how the children should be educated. They had conferred on sending

Maureen to a boarding school and had finally decided that she should go to one not too far from home so that she could stay overnight during the week but be home on weekends. The prestigious Chadwick School, in nearby Palos Verdes, was decided on (Joan Crawford's daughter, Christina, was a student there). Jane felt that Michael, only five, was too young for boarding school.

While Jane was completing *Menagerie, Stage Fright* was released. To everyone's chagrin, it received mediocre reviews and did only moderate box office business. Most people blamed the muddled script and the misleading of the audience in the film's initial flashback sequence. Certainly the performances were good.

Hitchcock still needed a hit—and now, it appeared, so did Jane. One is reminded of prima ballerina Dame Margot Fonteyn's assessment of being Number One: "Staying at the top is like running up a down escalator—the moment you stop running, down you go!"

Jane and Warners could not agree on her next film, although Jane maintained her good relationship with Jack Warner. When the studio did not have a film they could agree on, Jane, as her contract stipulated, simply perused offers from other studios. She and her agents would discuss what was available, and they now chose a vehicle at MGM that would co-star Wyman with heart-throb Van Johnson and up-and-coming Howard Keel. It was a comedy called *Three Guys Named Mike*. (The third "Mike" was Barry Sullivan.)

Jerry Wald had said, "Jane should never do comedies again. Comediennes in this town are a dime a dozen. She is a great dramatic actress. . . . The remarkable thing about Jane is that she has grown up. Most actresses never do."

"Mike" was a comedy.

Jane's name was not linked with anyone's romantically during this period, but Reagan's name was in the columns frequently— he was finally leading the life of the roving bachelor. His dates included Doris Lilly (then an actress, soon an author-columnist), actress Penny Edwards, and model Betty Underwood. His name was also linked with actress Adele Jergens and singer Monica Lewis. But according to Doris Lilly, "I don't think he went with anyone for very long."

That year the Friars Club honored Ron at the Crystal Room of the Beverly Hills Hotel. Jane was in the audience. Reagan's status in town was a unique one—as a star he had never achieved the highest ranks, but as SAG president he associated with the top people in Hollywood, both stars and executives.

A few nights later, again in the Crystal Room, *Photoplay* magazine held its Gold Medal Awards ceremonies, during which Jane received the award for *Johnny Belinda.* This time Ron was in the audience, prompting even more talk that the Reagans were reconciling.

And in May 1950, Wyman even attended the premiere of Ron's first movie for Universal, *Louisa.* (Reagan's date that night was his mother.) Once again there was more talk of a reconciliation, but insiders knew that this was not probable. Reagan continued to date others and had become, according to some sources, quite a lothario. Producer-writer Dore Schary has recalled being in Boca Raton, Florida, around this time, where he was surprised "to find Ronald Reagan, a fellow liberal, was in residence with an attractive blond lady as an escort."

Obviously, through 1950, Reagan's dating of Nancy Davis could not be termed serious. Although reports were that she had ended her romance with MGM executive Benjamin Thau shortly after meeting Reagan, she, too, dated others, including Robert Stack and Peter Lawford.

Meanwhile, Jerry Wald approached Reagan about playing the lead in *Storm Warning.* It was a powerful script dealing with the Ku Klux Klan that could be made into a socially important as well as a commercially successful film. It was to star Ginger Rogers, along with fast-rising Doris Day and Steve Cochran. This would be Reagan's first picture at Warners under his new contract, and it certainly seemed a step in the right direction.

Ginger Rogers has recalled that during production of this film, "We'd sit around at lunch and Ronnie would talk—guess what? Politics. He talked politics the whole hour at every lunch time."

During this time Reagan dated Doris Day. Her comments illuminate what life with Reagan must have been like for Jane Wyman. In Day's words: "There were two things about Ronnie that impressed me: how much he liked to dance and how much he liked to talk. Ronnie is really the only man I've ever known who loved dancing. . . . When he wasn't dancing, he was talking. It really wasn't conversation, it was rather talking at you, sort of long discourses on subjects that interested him."

The Glass Menagerie was released in September. In retrospect this film has been perceived as an outright bomb for Wyman personally, but this is not at all the case. Although the film itself got bad reviews and Gertrude Lawrence was booed by most critics, personally Jane Wyman received excellent notices and was, in fact, believable and moving in her portrayal of Laura. When the picture is viewed today, her performance holds up.

The New York Times wrote at the time, "Modest Jane Wyman is beautifully sensitive in the role of the crippled and timid daughter who finds escape in her menagerie of glass." Other critics agreed. The *Herald Tribune* noted, "She duplicated much of the same fragile sweetness which she displayed in *Johnny Belinda.*"

However, despite these fine reviews, the picture was another disappointment at the box office. The general atmosphere in the entire movie industry at the time was very bleak. Television had drawn the vast audiences from the theaters, and although this wouldn't directly affect big stars like Jane Wyman immediately, it certainly did change the atmosphere at the studios where they worked. Top executives were taking salary cuts and the "good old days" were entering a final phase.

Jane had flatly turned down a role in Warners' *Along the Great*

Divide, and after completing *Three Guys Named Mike,* instead of returning to her home studio she headed for Paramount and an exciting new project, one that offered an opportunity to "stretch" and to work with her singing idol, Bing Crosby, and with legendary director Frank Capra.

Capra had been feuding with Paramount's head of production, Y. Frank Freeman. The director didn't like the kind of films the studio wanted him to make and he wanted out of his contract. Freeman came up with a deal: there was a new Crosby picture, and if Capra would direct it, they would call it the last of Capra's two-film commitment. It was a light musical-comedy, *Here Comes the Groom,* in which Crosby would play a man who had to get married quickly in order to adopt children. There was a strong comedy part for an actress who could sing, and the plum role went to Jane.

Capra sought a special song for a Crosby-Wyman duet. One of the director's pals, Joe Sistrom, came up with an old Johnny Mercer–Hoagy Carmichael ditty that had been in the studio's files for years. It had been written originally for a proposed Betty Hutton picture about the life of Mabel Normand. Capra had a demo record of the song dug out of the files and on it Johnny Mercer sang "In the Cool Cool Cool of the Evening." He liked the song, Crosby and Jane liked the song, and the director hired choreographer Charlie O'Curran to work it into a big production number.

Veteran character actors Connie Gilchrist and James Barton were portraying Jane's parents in the film. Miss Gilchrist has recalled that during a break, "Jane was going through an odd tune which I considered quaint when she should have been having lunch.

" 'Why are you knocking yourself out with that? Wait till they hand you the music they're gonna use,' I said."

" 'This *is* the music they're gonna use,' " retorted Wyman, her sense of humor never at a loss.

When Jane moved onto the Paramount lot, she had tried to take her huge dressing room–trailer with her, but it would not fit through the studio gate (eventually the unwieldy vehicle had to be sold). Nevertheless, working on the Paramount lot was invigorating.

Jane's friend Harold Lloyd visited the set and saw that this was an exciting time creatively for Wyman. *Groom* was a top-notch production with many stimulating elements. The second leads were stars also: Franchot Tone as Jane's fiancé, and Alexis Smith as Crosby's love interest. Fourteen-year-old operatic singer Anna Maria Alberghetti would be making her motion picture debut. And for additional insurance the film had stars (and Crosby pals) Dorothy Lamour, Louis Armstrong, Phil Harris, and Cass Daley playing themselves.

In an innovative move, it was decided by Capra to record the big production number with Crosby and Wyman singing *live*, in one continuous take. The technical people had devised tiny radios to fit into Jane's and Bing's ears so they would hear the orchestra as they performed the number, which consisted of them singing while walking through a number of elaborate sets— from an office, through a corridor, in an elevator, through the lobby of a building, and out into the street.

There are few stars who could have brought off this feat. Frank Capra has said that the big news about "Cool Cool Cool of the Evening" was not the various innovations. "No, the news about the song was Jane Wyman—the way she traded in her crying towel for a glamour girl's raiment and became a dish to behold." In addition Capra has noted that the screen chemistry between Bing and Jane was electric, and he compared it to that between Spencer Tracy and Katharine Hepburn, Clark Gable and Claudette Colbert, and Jimmy Stewart and Jean Arthur—all of whom Capra had directed. Jane later said, "It was a holiday doing this picture with Frank and Bing."

In the movie industry, insiders always seemed to know which

pictures would really "click" and which wouldn't. From the beginning, all instinctively knew *Groom* was a hit, and Paramount was already preparing a Crosby-Wyman reteaming.

Since Warners still had nothing suitable for Jane, she next accepted a role from her old pal Jerry Wald, who had left Warners and set up independent production at RKO. It was a sudser of a script, to be sure—*The Blue Veil*—a reworking of a very popular 1942 French film. Wald had initially sought Garbo for this picture, as a comeback vehicle for her. Even Ingrid Bergman had been mentioned.

The Blue Veil certainly offered Wyman a challenge: from being a glamorous singer-comedienne in *Groom,* she would go to another extreme in *Veil,* playing a character who ages forty years in the tale of a children's nurse who has no life of her own but lives through the children she raises.

As usual, Wald had assembled a fabulous supporting cast: Charles Laughton, Joan Blondell, Agnes Moorehead, Cyril Cusack, Everett Sloane, Dan O'Herlihy, Richard Carlson, Don Taylor, Vivian Vance, and child star Natalie Wood. Curtis Bernhardt was signed to direct.

As they began production, Wald was enthusiastic. "Let's shoot for another Oscar," he told Jane. Wyman retorted, "Let's just make a good movie."

Ironically, although Jane was supposedly too old for *Johnny Belinda* and *The Glass Menagerie,* for this part her youthful face was not an asset. She had to wear complicated makeup appliances to age convincingly. Jane had insisted that Perc Westmore be hired to do her makeup. He designed the latex "pieces" that would be applied to Jane's face to produce the proper "aging" effect. As production progressed, Wyman noticed that Westmore was not his usual chipper, fun-loving self. Back at Warners, in the old days, Jane and Westmore used to kid each other a great deal, but he no longer did this. Jane sensed something was terribly wrong. A few weeks into shooting *Veil,* Jane arrived at the studio one morning to learn that Perc had suffered a heart attack and was in the hospital. She was shocked and very sad, but not altogether surprised.

Jane would not let any other makeup man near her and attempted to handle the chore herself. She was having difficulty, however, so Westmore arranged for his brother Bud, who was under contract to Universal, to be lent to RKO. Thereafter, each morning before reporting to work at Universal, Bud would help Wyman with her involved makeup.

Jane had approached the *Blue Veil* role with her usual intensity. "I put a lot of research into it. First of all, I started studying old people—at the club, on the lot or in restaurants. I know a lot of them must have thought me crazy. I would just sit and stare. Then, I went to the library and read up on the subject. It was an education. I found out that as people age, their bone structure changes. That's why they stoop and walk the way they do." She noted that she and Perc Westmore had spent many late nights in her den sketching the various postures of old people.

Wyman even met with co-star Laughton to discuss the script and her approach to it. Laughton and his wife, Elsa Lanchester, had a little theater and acting group in Hollywood. Laughton was a recognized teacher of acting, and top stars such as Tyrone Power turned to him for advice.

For Jane, Laughton "was an experience." She felt he had a phenomenal brain and was the most learned man she had ever met. "To sit and talk with him was an intellectual bath. I learned more about acting from him in ten days than I had learned before in ten years." They pored over the script. "Then, he gave the most amazing performance I have ever witnessed. He enacted the entire screenplay without once looking at the script. He had memorized every line of each role. He gave each line a distinctive reading."

Before the cameras Jane began "using little tricks and devices Laughton had used in his one-man performance of the script. He

had indoctrinated me subconsciously." This was the most difficult
and demanding role Jane Wyman had ever attempted. But with
the help of Laughton and veteran director Bernhardt, her performance was exceptional.

In February 1951 *Three Guys Named Mike* was released. Jane
had ceased to be major copy for the fan magazines—her personal
life was quiet and her publicity was "puff" pieces. She was concentrating totally on her career and her children.

When Ronald Reagan emceed the *Photoplay* Gold Medal
Awards ceremonies early in the year, Wyman was on hand as a
presenter. Her date that night was the famous and very attractive attorney Greg Bautzer, who had for years been squiring
around Hollywood's most beautiful women, all of whom he was
at one time or another reportedly engaged to. In fact, Bautzer
was divorced. In the early 1940s he had married seventeen-year-
old Buff Cobb, granddaughter of humorist Irvin S. Cobb. Buff
later married and divorced Mike Wallace.

The Bautzer-Wyman relationship was a serious one and some
of Jane's close friends warned her that she might be leaving
herself open for disappointment.

Meanwhile, Jane returned to Warners for another cameo, playing herself and singing a song in another all-star conglomeration
called *Starlift*.

In late June, she went into a recording studio with Bing Crosby
and the duo cut their first record. Accompanied by Matty
Matlock's All Stars and the singing group Six Hits and a Miss, Jane
and Bing recreated "In the Cool Cool Cool of the Evening." For
the flip side, Bing recorded "Misto Christofo Columbo," also
from the film.

Here Comes the Groom was soon released, and with this picture
Jane Wyman had finally found another blockbuster. It was an
even bigger hit than had been anticipated at a time when few
movies were registering really big grosses. And there was a further dividend—after fifteen years Jane Wyman was suddenly

discovered to be "a singer"! "Cool Cool Cool of the Evening" became a hit record throughout the country.

Jane's reviews for the picture were excellent. The fact that she could hold her own with Crosby as a singer astonished everyone. Suddenly, singing offers poured in. The London Palladium wanted to sign Wyman for a personal appearance. Jane even signed a recording contract with Decca.

Paramount's followup for Crosby-Wyman was not, unfortunately, in a league with *Here Comes the Groom*. The swiftly fashioned *Just for You* wouldn't have Frank Capra as director (Elliott Nugent got the job), and it was a weak story of a Broadway producer (Crosby) who has lost touch with his children (Natalie Wood and Robert Arthur played the kids). Jane played a Broadway star (Crosby's fiancée) and as such got the opportunity to wear leotards and sexy, strapless outfits—one costume displayed Jane's shapely legs in mesh stockings and the photo was distributed by Paramount's publicity department as a "cheesecake" shot.

The new song created for Wyman and Crosby, "Zing a Little Zong," was no "Cool Cool Cool of the Evening." Jane continued to record for Decca, doing solos and even duets with artists like Danny Kaye. For one session she teamed up with Kaye, Jimmy Durante, and Groucho Marx for two comedy songs: "Black Strap Molasses" and, on the flip side, "How Di Ye Do and Shake Hands."

The Reagan children were often taken to see their parents' films. Dad's latest release was *Bedtime for Bonzo*. While it is assumed today that *Bonzo* was the nadir in the film career of Ronald Reagan, and also his swan song, this is not true. *Bonzo* was in fact a successful enterprise, followed by *The Last Outpost*, Reagan's first western (Rhonda Fleming was his leading lady).

In September 1951, *The Blue Veil* premiered. Jane attended the glittering event with ten-year-old daughter Maureen and Greg Bautzer. Ronald Reagan was there, escorting Nancy Davis.

It wasn't generally known at the time, but both couples were contemplating marriage. Bautzer and Jane had even gone so far as to have blood tests, and had cleverly done so at the office of the Reagan children's doctor in order to keep their plans secret.

Jane and Greg and Ron and Nancy were even photographed together, seated at the same table at Ciro's after the premiere. Reagan appeared uncomfortable; undoubtedly the role of modern divorcé who could be seen on a double date with his ex-wife and her new lover was unappealing to him.

Reagan, as SAG president, was talking about launching a campaign to prevent fan magazines from printing stories about the private lives of established stars! Obviously this was a direct reaction to the treatment he and Jane had received for the past few years. Reagan was implying that reportage on private lives was all right if the subjects were youngsters on their way up. But after achieving stardom, an actor or actress should have control over stories published about them.

The editors of *Motion Picture* magazine ran a scathing editorial in response to Reagan's suggestion. Speaking directly to him, they said: "You cited fan magazine stories about your divorce from Jane Wyman as 'false and irresponsible' invasions of your privacy. We disagree. We disagree because you apparently didn't feel the marriage itself was a private affair." The editors noted that during the marriage Reagan had opened his home to photographers and reporters and had allowed pictures of his home, his wife, and his family. "But if a happy marriage was news, then it seems to follow that the *breakup* of that marriage also was news," noted *Motion Picture*. "Yours is a business, Mr. Reagan, which is built on publicity. In this sense, actors are like politicians."

The magazine further stated that by allowing publicity only on upcoming young actors, the assumption was that fans weren't important to an actor once he no longer needed them. "We suggest that you take another look at your bank account, Mr. Reagan," the editorial concluded.

Needless to say, Reagan's campaign to try to control publicity was abandoned.

Although Jane was seeing Bautzer, publicly she admitted to no involvement and still parried the inevitable questions about reteaming with Reagan. "I don't have time for romance. Ronnie and I have a wonderful understanding. We discuss the children and I make no move where they are concerned without him. But that romance died a long time ago."

Friends noted that if they began to discuss Ronnie, Jane soon realized she had a pressing previous engagement elsewhere.

The Blue Veil was labeled a tearjerker by most critics, but *Variety* had cleverly noted that it was "a personal triumph that ranks with, if not surpassing, any for which Jane Wyman has been previously kudoed."

The tradepaper predicted correctly. Jane's fans flocked to theaters to watch her character, devoted to raising children after being widowed and losing her own child, go through thirty years of joy and heartbreak, self-sacrificing all the way.

Toward the end of the film she is a janitor too old to get a job as a governess. But then, of course, one of the children Jane had helped to raise, now a successful doctor (portrayed by Don Taylor), rescues her—and assembles at a party many of the others she has raised. All pay tribute to her. The film ends with the happy old woman being taken into Don Taylor's home to raise his children.

The Blue Veil would go on to gross nearly $4 million, the highest grosser that year for RKO. With the receipts from this film and *Here Comes the Groom*, Jane Wyman, for the first time ever, ascended to the ranks of top-ten box office draws.

After years of investment in her career, Wyman was reaping gratifying dividends. But there had been yet another major shake-up in her personal life, and within the next twelve months there would be a number of dramatic developments.

○ ○ ○ ○ ○ ○ ○ ○ ○ ○ ○ ○ ○ ○ ○ ○ ○ ○ ○

8

NINETEEN FIFTY-TWO WAS AN IMPORTANT YEAR IN the lives of Jane Wyman, Ronald Reagan, and their children. Before the year was out, Michael and Maureen Reagan would have a new stepmother *and* a new stepfather. There was a new man in Jane's life and her social set was abuzz with the news.

Meanwhile, her prestige as an actress was further enhanced when the Oscar nominations were announced. Jane was tapped for one of the five best-actress nominations for her performance in *The Blue Veil*. Joan Blondell received a nomination for best supporting actress in the film. Both actresses, however, faced very stiff competition. It was another boost for Wyman to learn that her hit duet with Crosby, "In the Cool Cool Cool of the Evening," was nominated for best song.

It was another year of magnificent performances by women. Jane was matched against Vivien Leigh for *A Streetcar Named Desire*, Katharine Hepburn for *The African Queen*, Shelley Winters for *A Place in the Sun*, and Eleanor Parker for *Detective Story*. Blondell would have to win out over the odds-on favorite Kim Hunter, who had recreated her Broadway role in the film version of *Streetcar*.

On the heels of the Oscar nominations, Jane won the Golden Globe Award as best actress for her performance in *The Blue Veil*. The Golden Globe choices were often harbingers of who would win the Academy Awards, and, since this was her second Golden Globe, could it mean that Wyman really had a chance for a second Oscar? It could also be seen as a favorable omen that Jane was also awarded the Golden Globe as World Film Favorite Actress of the year. Her former co-star, Gregory Peck, won as World Film Favorite Actor.

That January, Wyman was back on the Warners lot, filming *The Story of Will Rogers*. Like many projects at the studio, it had been kicking around for years. In 1942, Michael Curtiz had directed Will Rogers, Jr., in a screen test for the part. Then, for the next decade, a half-dozen other tests were made, with people like Charles Drake and Herb Shriner tested for the role of Will Rogers, and Eleanor Parker and Phyllis Thaxter for the part of Mrs. Rogers. Eventually, when Rogers, Jr., was tested again in Technicolor, Curtiz gave him the part.

Jane agreed to do the co-starring but relatively minor role of Mrs. Will Rogers because they needed her star power at the box office and she did have commitments to the studio. But it was also another case where she could proudly display her medal "for services above and beyond the call of duty."

That spring Ronald Reagan surprised many in Hollywood when he married Nancy Davis at the Little Brown Church in the Valley. The story goes that the actor had made the impulsive decision to wed while attending a meeting of the Motion Picture Industry Council with his pal William Holden. It was hardly impulsive: Reagan and Nancy had been dating for more than two years. All reports claim that Miss Davis had worked long and hard to win over Maureen and Michael, spending much time with the children and Ron at his new 350-acre ranch in the Malibu hills.

In later years Maureen denied any resentment that her father was getting remarried. As an adult, Maureen recalled, "I was delighted when he married her. I named my horse after her—I don't know what more an eleven-year-old can do to show undying devotion, though maybe she didn't take it that way."

There is a general theory that no matter how many times one marries, one tends to wed someone with the same characteristics and personality of one's original mate. Although some say that Nancy Davis is totally different from Jane Wyman, others point out that while their interests definitely differ, both of Ronald Reagan's wives are considered strong-willed women who on occasion display fiery tempers.

On March 13, nine days after Reagan had married Nancy Davis, Louella Parsons announced Jane's engagement to Travis Kleefeld, a twenty-six-year-old building contractor and the son of socially prominent Mrs. Sylvia Kleefeld of Beverly Hills. Louella did not fail to mention that Ron and Nancy had wed the previous week—the obvious implication was that Jane was on the rebound from Reagan.

Jane was on the rebound, all right, but it was not from Ronald Reagan. What the fans didn't know—but Jane's close friends did —was that her relationship with Greg Bautzer had ended abruptly. Bautzer, it appears, was attracted to beautiful women whose careers were riding high, and since Jane's career was at its peak, many wondered why the sudden split. The answer, it seems, is that Bautzer preferred the appellation attached to him by the press—"the elusive bachelor." All his relationships with stars up to this point had stopped just short of the altar.

But Jane was a beautiful, desirable woman in the prime of her life. Perhaps Sheilah Graham described the Wyman of this period most succinctly: "Jane *does* like to gadabout and she does like to have fun. She likes to dance. She likes to dress up. She likes men. And they find her dangerously desirable. She has a clean look that seems to arouse them. She's smart, emotional, ambitious. . . . This, added to everything else, makes her someone to be reckoned with."

One evening at a nightclub Jane was introduced by friends to a handsome young man, Travis Kleefeld. There was an instant attraction between them. Today, Kleefeld remembers, "It was all very romantic." The couple loved to dance, and later Jane invited Travis to be her escort to a party that some of her friends were giving. Kleefeld was somewhat apprehensive because it was to be a "top" Hollywood party, filled with big stars. He wouldn't know anyone there.

"Well, invite another couple to join us," Jane suggested.

Kleefeld knew Dick Haymes and his then wife, Nora Eddington, so he asked them to the party; they were to meet Wyman there. It was a huge outdoor tent affair on the lawn of a Beverly Hills estate. Almost as if planned, the orchestra had just stopped playing and the dance floor was clearing as Kleefeld entered and saw Jane across the floor. She turned and they headed toward each other. They met just as the orchestra resumed playing. It was literally, according to Kleefeld, like a scene from a film. Kleefeld knew that all eyes were on them.

Over the next few weeks the romance progressed rapidly, and Kleefeld found himself in the whirl of Hollywood "society." Within ten weeks the couple became engaged and Louella had broken the story.

Unlike Reagan's quick wedding, Jane was planning an elaborate affair. It would be a June wedding, followed by a European honeymoon. Edith Head was designing Jane's trousseau.

At the Academy Awards ceremonies that year, Jane lost the Oscar to Vivien Leigh for her performance in *A Streetcar Named Desire*. But "In the Cool Cool Cool of the Evening" won as best song, beating out "Too Late Now" and "A Kiss to Build a Dream On." Jane was at the awards with Travis. The newlywed Reagans had returned from their honeymoon and were also in attendance.

Although Wyman hadn't won the Oscar, her name was in the papers and on the lips of thousands across the country. She had just turned thirty-eight; her fiancé, Kleefeld, was only twenty-six —in the staid early 1950s this was *news*. The press wasn't kind. The difference in their ages was the talk of Hollywood. Many in the film colony were shocked: how could a down-to-earth, dignified star like Jane Wyman expose herself to this kind of publicity? To complicate matters further, there was, it was reported, a hue and cry from the Kleefeld family.

In fact, although thirty-eight, Jane did not look any older than Kleefeld. She was a very youthful woman both in looks and in spirit. In the 1980s, of course, such a relationship would be met with congratulations and envy. But at the time, it was a situation that generated endless speculation and gossip.

One fact was clear: Kleefeld was an established businessman from a wealthy family. He had an identity and career of his own. He was not interested in getting into the movies. The couple had been swept into the romance of their mutual attraction for each other. But soon both decided that they had better think *seriously* about what they were doing.

Within three weeks Jane announced that the engagement was broken. She said vehemently, "Age had nothing whatever to do with our decision not to marry. I guess we're the only two people who are not conscious of the difference in our ages."

Jane went on to say, "It was just that we decided that the marriage was wrong for us and it was silly to go into as serious a matter as matrimony without being perfectly sure it was what we both wanted. Believe me, Travis and I will always be friends. I think Travis is one of the finest men I have ever met. But we have both been realizing that we went into this thing too quickly and that it's better to break up before marriage than to go into the divorce court later."

Wyman continued to see Kleefeld socially, and said, "It's best this way, no entangling alliances."

In April, Jane finally finished shooting *The Story of Will Rogers.*
It had been a long three-month schedule with location work in
Santa Monica. Atypical of Jane was that on this production she
had been ill for several days during shooting.

As with the Will Rogers project, there was another script that
had been kicking around the studio for over ten years—a revised
version of Edna Ferber's *So Big.* The story had been filmed twice
before—once as a silent with Colleen Moore and as an early
talkie with Barbara Stanwyck.

Jerry Wald had wanted to do a remake of *So Big* as early as 1943
—he had had a new treatment prepared but could not convince
Steve Trilling or Jack Warner to do it. In 1945 he again approached Trilling and Warner: "It would be great for Paul
Henreid and Eleanor Parker. Or Henreid and Ida Lupino. Or
any other combination you wish."

It was a pet project of Wald's, and whenever a new female star
came along, he tried again to sell it. At one point he suggested
Alexis Smith. In early 1948 he wrote to Trilling, "I think Pat Neal
is the girl." In March of that year he again appealed to Warner:
"Dear Jack: Everyone these days is trying to secure good wom-
en's stories. Again I call your attention to the script I have on *So
Big.* As you know, Jane Wyman read the script some time ago and
is most anxious to do it."

However, at that point, *Johnny Belinda* had not yet been released, and Wald knew that Warner did not consider Wyman a
box office star. So in his memo he noted, "I doubt very much
whether you would have trouble getting a top female personality
for this story," leaving the way open for the studio to cast *anyone.*
Wald concluded with "What would you like to do about it?"
Obviously, in 1948 Warner's answer had been "Nothing."

But now the studio needed a vehicle suitable for its biggest
remaining contract star (by this time, Jane had been there longer
than any other actor on the lot). Wald had left Warners for

greener pastures, so producer Henry Blanke was assigned *So Big* and Robert Wise was set to direct.

The film would be in preproduction for many months, so Jane would have time off and her agents could even arrange for an outside picture.

That spring, Maureen and Michael learned that they would soon have a little baby brother or sister. When the press revealed that Ronald and Nancy Reagan were expecting a baby, the announcement said the baby was due in December.

That year Maureen and Michael's grandma, Nelle Reagan, momentarily joined Jane, Ron, and Nancy as a film actor. She had a small part in a low-budget film. This was a lark for Mrs. Reagan, who actually spent most of her time volunteering at hospitals and doing other social work.

Nelle, of course, saw the children whenever she wanted. Reagan, too, tried to spend as much time with them as he could, but in later years he expressed regret that he had missed watching them grow up on a day-to-day basis.

The Reagan children were at a stage in their lives where they required attention. Someone who knew Jane well recalls that when he went to the house, eleven-year-old Maureen was "emotionally needy"—like most girls her age, she wanted to be included in all discussions and activities.

As the children were growing up, the usual roles of the indulgent mother/disciplinarian father were reversed. Michael Reagan has revealed that his father "never spanked me in my life," nor did he even yell at him. "He doesn't yell, he tries to talk it out with you."

Someone close to Jane recalls, "She was a good mother but sometimes a bit too strict with the children. I told her so one day, when she was discussing the punishment she had meted out to Maureen for some small mischief. Jane answered, 'But I do it for their own good. They must learn, as all of us have to, that life can't always be just the way we want it.'"

In regard to disciplining the children, Maureen has recalled that her mother used a tactic different from physical punishment. "Mom is a great actress, and she could make me cry on or off the screen. If I did something wrong she'd put on her wounded act and that would hurt me more than any spanking would."

Both Wyman and Reagan have been described by their daughter as "strong-willed, opinionated individuals." Undoubtedly, Jane was determined to instill a sense of independence and self-reliance in the children. Years later Maureen recalled: "My mother's favorite line was 'If I get hit by a Mack truck tomorrow, you're going to have to take care of yourself.'"

The adult Michael Reagan has remembered that he was disciplined by Jane, and often the discipline included the use of a riding crop. However, young Reagan has stated that he believes in corporal punishment and has said, "Lord knows where I would be if I never had discipline."

Michael, more than Maureen, has expressed regrets about his parents not spending enough time with him. He, more than his sister, seems to have been a victim of their breakup, since he was at a much more impressionable age during the years when his parents turned their attention to their own emotional lives.

Ironically, *Just for You*, released that summer, was about this very situation—a single parent who is a star and, because of professional demands and his own personal life, is distanced from his children. The film was an okay vehicle but certainly not in a league with *Here Comes the Groom*. Jane and Crosby had recorded the song from the film, "Zing a Little Zong," and, although it had respectable sales, it was in no way a hit.

Even at the time, Jane was blasé about her singing career: "Records are a whole new field. I'm just coasting. I think I can make a few more sides before they get wise to me, though." When people suggested that she record albums and perhaps do another picture with Crosby, Jane frowned and shook her head:

"I think we've about had it. We should just let it lie there." She noted, "Records are great fun but I'm not that serious about it."

However, Jane *had* signed for another musical. Over at Columbia they were remaking a classic—*The Awful Truth*—and had added songs. The studio had signed both Jane and Ray Milland, and the film was being called *Love Story*. Screenwriter-producer Oscar Saul was handling the producing chores. He recalls Jane as "a lovely woman. She was a pro, interested in her life, her work, her children."

Saul mentioned to tough Columbia studio chief Harry Cohn, "Hey, we've got both Wyman and Milland in this picture. It's the first time they've been together since *Lost Weekend* and both have won Academy Awards!"

"Big deal," snorted Cohn. "Let's wait and see the box office."

Jane would be working closely with people in the Columbia music department, and there she met Fred Karger, a handsome, affable man who was Morris Stoloff's assistant. Jane had met Karger socially—she knew he was a bandleader and that his band often played the Escoffier Room at the Beverly Hills Hotel. He was charming and fun to be with, and they enjoyed each other's company.

Karger and Wyman seemed to have a lot in common. Like Jane, Fred was divorced and had a daughter by his first marriage. The girl lived with him. Like Jane, he enjoyed music and night-clubs but was basically a serious, one-on-one person.

That fall Jane and Fred quietly and discreetly saw a great deal of each other. Even their close friends were unaware of how serious they had become in such a short time.

Maureen and Michael had a new baby sister when, on October 22, Patti Reagan was born. Far more newsworthy than the birth of Nancy and Ronald Reagan's first child, however, was the surprise elopement, a week later, of Jane Wyman and Fred Karger.

Wyman and Karger had sneaked away to Santa Barbara on Saturday, November 1, 1952, and were married at the El Montecito Presbyterian Church. Fred's best man, actor-director Richard Quine, accompanied them. No one could accuse Jane Wyman of being a publicity seeker. Her elopement with Karger took the Hollywood press corps completely by surprise and hurt the feelings of Jane's old pal Louella Parsons, who *certainly* expected to be informed—ahead of time—of such news.

When Louella ran the story of the elopement, to set herself apart from others who carried the story she noted that upon Jane and Fred's return she would be one of the guests at an exclusive dinner party with "a few others of us who are close friends." The others included Lew and Edie Wasserman, and Quine and Betty Lou Frederick. And, of course, Jane's two children and Fred's family, including his daughter, Terry.

Parsons had a unique way of expressing her pique in print and those astute enough to know how to read her column got the real story. "I hope none of my other friends decides to get married on a Saturday night, when it's difficult to get telephone calls through and there's a political rally going on." (It was only three days before the 1952 presidential election.)

Fred and Jane had returned from Santa Barbara almost immediately and they would be back at work on Monday. Karger was well known and universally liked throughout the industry, but the public wanted to know more about this mystery man that Jane Wyman had married.

Only a handful of people knew that rising young star Marilyn Monroe had been longing to marry Fred Karger.

Frederick Maxwell Karger, the son of Ann and Max Karger, had been born in 1916 (he was two years younger than Jane). Max Karger was one of the founders and a producer at Metro Pictures Corporation before it merged and became Metro-Goldwyn-Mayer. The elder Karger produced many films before he died suddenly in 1921, when Fred was only five. Ann Karger, however, remained an active, very well-liked and respected figure on the Hollywood social scene. She had an incredibly warm and winning personality, and knew and entertained—and was entertained by—all the greats of the silent picture era.

Fred became a musician and eventually went to work for Columbia Pictures, where he remained for twenty-eight years. (He worked on many of Rita Hayworth's films, including *The Loves of Carmen* and *Affair in Trinidad.* Karger had recently co-written "The Re-Enlistment Blues," better known as the theme of Columbia's soon-to-be all-time blockbuster, *From Here to Eternity.)*

Back in August 1940 (the same year Jane had wed Reagan), Karger had married Patti Sachs. Described once as an actress, Sachs later became an attorney. Fred and Patti had one daughter, Terence Meredith, but the couple separated in 1948 and were officially divorced a year later. Fred, who had custody of Terry, moved back with his mother.

Fred had met Marilyn Monroe on the Columbia lot when he was assigned to give the girl vocal coaching. Monroe was making *Ladies of the Chorus,* and had a six-month contract with the studio. Marilyn was attracted to Karger's gentle manner and attached herself to him. Then she fell in love with him. He, in turn, offered the girl friendship, but nothing more. After he introduced her to his mother, the Karger household became a second home for the young waif.

Maurice Zolotow, one of Monroe's biographers, described Karger as the "epitome of courtliness" but noted that at the time of his involvement with Marilyn, Karger was very sour on women. "When he talked of love, it was to express a world-weary hopelessness about the honor of women . . . he said women were not capable of genuine love. He believed no one could give herself honestly and entirely up to one man for whom she cared. Women, he said, were too shrewd—too practical."

It should be remembered that Karger was on the heels of a divorce, and that these sentiments were filtered through Marilyn's point of view.

While Karger's relationship with Marilyn had been very private, his marriage to Jane Wyman now catapulted him into public view. However, like Jane, Karger had the ability to be polite to the press without revealing any of his inner self.

The elopement had been so sudden—and had taken place over a weekend, when most people didn't read the papers—that even Oscar Saul, the producer of the aptly titled *Love Story*, was taken by surprise. He remembers, "We were winding up the movie, and at the end of one day's shooting, there was a surprise party on the set. I called the assistant director and said, 'What's going on?' He told me that Jane and Fred Karger had just returned from their elopement and the crew was throwing them a party."

Another party was held at Chasen's, the posh restaurant in Beverly Hills. The late columnist Sidney Skolsky once told a colorful tale regarding this event. Skolsky was an intimate friend and booster of Marilyn Monroe's during this period of her career. It happened that Skolsky and Marilyn were dining at Chasen's that night. Skolsky has recalled, "The only bitchy thing I ever saw Marilyn do" occurred that night at Chasen's. Marilyn and the columnist noticed that a dinner was taking place in the private party room.

"What's going on?" Skolsky asked the maître d'.

In Skolsky's words: "Marilyn and I were told that the Fred Karger and Jane Wyman wedding party was in the room. . . . Marilyn said she had to go inside and congratulate Fred. She knew this would burn up Jane Wyman. She boldly crashed the reception and congratulated Fred. As Marilyn and Jane were pretending that they didn't know the other was in the same room, the tension in the atmosphere would have been as easy to cut as the wedding cake."

Shortly after their marriage, Karger accompanied Jane to a party at the Jean Negulescos'. Screenwriter-wit Nunnally Johnson was there, and a few days later he wrote a note to his pal Claudette Colbert, who was in Barbados and had missed the party. Along with other chitchat and gossip, Johnson said: "Met Jane Wyman's new husband, and that's all there is to that."

There were high hopes for the Wyman-Milland film, which was retitled *Let's Do It Again*. It had several elaborate numbers, including Jane doing a song that producer Saul felt had great commercial possibilities. Ned Washington and Lester Lee had written "It Was Great While It Lasted." Jane had recorded it commercially as well as sung it in the picture. But according to Saul, it never became a hit because the studio "never pushed it."

After the first of the year, Jane was back at Warners to begin her first prestigious role there since *Belinda*, playing "Selena DeJong" in *So Big*. By now Jane's agents had again renegotiated her contract. Instead of $3,500 per week she would receive six figures per film. While reports were that she would be paid $200,000 per picture, studio documents indicate the figure was less. But then, inflating salaries was, of course, standard procedure. After all, if you read someone was getting $120,000 per picture, you'd know they were really only receiving $60,000.

In all fairness to Wyman, it must be noted that, unlike Gable and certain others where money was the primary consideration, with her the stories and career direction were paramount. Jane was one of those rare individuals who are capable of giving highly emotional, sensitive performances, but at the same time, off-screen, she was a practical businesswoman about her career. She often observed, "Acting is a business. The only way an actress can keep alive is to get variety into her roles. But you don't get variety sitting back on your fanny. Waiting for jobs to come to you. That's the quickest way to die, professionally speaking of course. A girl's got to plan."

And plan she did. Each year, usually in the summer, Wyman would get together with her manager, her agents, her press agents, "and everyone else who has anything to do with my career." The Wyman team would confer on the future. It was an informal gathering, but, at the same time, there were specific goals. The group would review all that Jane had done in the previous year, analyzing what was good, what was bad, what had been benign. Then they'd discuss scripts that had been submitted. They discussed books, plays, foreign films that might make good vehicles for Jane as remakes. They'd weigh what was available at Warners versus what the other studios in town might offer her, and how much time she should devote to the various aspects of her career.

Jane was such a professional that on many occasions she even literally prepared for interviews, choosing to leave as little to chance as possible. She went so far as to "try to speak and behave in interviews, in a way, similar to the character" she had portrayed in her last film. She wasn't the only star to do this. "Barbara Stanwyck does the same thing," Wyman observed.

In *So Big*, Jane was re-creating the role Stanwyck had essayed to perfection twenty years earlier. From a box office point of view, with *So Big* Wyman would have the responsibility of being the sole name draw. Sterling Hayden, Steve Forrest, Nancy Olson, and Martha Hyer were featured, but it was Jane's picture all the way. As she had in *The Blue Veil*, Wyman's character would age from a young woman to an old lady.

After her last three fluffy roles, *So Big* was a challenging drama in which, once again, she would have to immerse herself totally. But she was a seasoned trouper, and although it took an enormous amount of energy to sustain her character, Wyman was up to the challenge. The film's director, Robert Wise, was not noted for his work with actors, but he was a master at capturing the physical elements necessary for a film with vast visual scope. When *So Big* was completed that April, the studio was enthusiastic with the results and many said Jane would surely receive another Oscar nomination.

In June 1953, Columbia released *Let's Do It Again* with the highest of hopes. This time Jane was top-billed over Milland. Although the film received generally good reviews, and especially favorable ones for Jane, mentioning her renditions of the songs and how fabulous she looked in Jean Louis's gowns, almost every critic noted that it was not nearly as good a picture as the original, *The Awful Truth.*

After the grueling months on *So Big,* Jane again had time to spend with her family. She and Fred enjoyed nightclubbing and socializing with friends. That summer they went up to San Francisco with songwriter Jimmy McHugh and Louella Parsons (who, to everyone's disbelief, were in the midst of a love affair).

But Jane's marriage to Karger was proving to be a rocky one. Wyman's all-absorbing career, and Karger's work schedule as a musician, meant major adjustments to be made on all sides. When Jane broke up with Kleefeld, she had said, "I would certainly never subject a new marriage to the pressure of living against an old background. You know how that can ruin things. I began to wonder where we would live."

With Karger, there was no such problem. They had rented a house on Beverly Glen Boulevard. He had brought two pianos with him and Jane had one, making it, in Jane's words, "a three-piano house." Their respective children, Maureen and Michael, and Karger's daughter, Terry, lived there when not away at boarding school.

Their house was tastefully furnished and some of the paintings hanging on the walls were by Jane herself. She had continued to pursue what had started as a hobby on the set of *Johnny Belinda.* In addition, Jane was understandably proud of three portraits she owned of herself, all done by noted artist Paul Clemens. One was of Wyman as the character of Ma Baxter, one as Belinda, and one, of course, as herself.

The Kargers were shopping for a house to buy, which many claim posed difficulties, since the couple was trying to live on Fred's salary, which was relatively modest compared with Jane's.

There was another difficulty as well: Karger was having health problems. Some say he had a mild heart attack that spring; others say he was just suffering from physical exhaustion and overwork. Socially the Kargers had curtailed their activities. "It was embarrassing when they were invited to a party and Freddie's band had been hired to play at the same party," remembers one on the scene.

Implications were now strong that the couple had rushed into marriage, and now had some regrets. This time, however—unlike with her marriage to Ronald Reagan—Wyman was not willing to share the details of her new relationship with the press and her fans. "I feel an obligation to the public that is twofold—to make good pictures and to lead the best possible life," she stated. "Outside of that, what else can there be? You can't take the public into your home; there isn't room. If you open that front door and let the world in, how do you maintain an intimate relationship with your husband, with your children? It's as simple as this—would the public rather live in my house or see me on the screen?"

So Big was released in October and Jane received terrific personal reviews. Bosley Crowther wrote, "Miss Wyman, whose acting of drudges has become a virtual standard on the screen, is remarkably strong and effective in every forthright little bit she does. . . .

"The virtue of Miss Wyman's acting is in the simplicity of her style and in the earnestness with which she makes expressive her wistful face and eyes. These are most potent contributions to this particular tale, which depends entirely upon integrity and forcefulness in the leading role."

So Big did good business.

Although Wyman was supposed to do at least two pictures a year at Warners, through the fifties she worked very seldom for that studio. She was blunt about the situation: "If they don't have the right stories for me, I tell the studio, 'You haven't found the story and neither have I. So let's postpone my commitment. Don't send me my check for the next six months.' "

Jane was represented by Lew Wasserman (she and Mrs. Wasserman are best friends). Wasserman was now the most powerful agent in Hollywood, and his MCA agency had become the most formidable in the business. It was Lew Wasserman who masterminded the concept of a star's getting a percentage of the profits. Some, like Wasserman client James Stewart, could forgo big salaries up front in lieu of a piece of the profits (gambling on the likelihood there would *be* profits). Others weren't important enough stars to warrant this arrangement. Still others preferred the security of a guaranteed six-figure income.

Jane was satisfied with her Warner Bros. deal. At the time Jane said, "It's a good arrangement and I'm happy there. I'll never leave the company. I've been with Warners for seventeen years. For a good many of those years I didn't make any money for them. And after all, I'm not the ungrateful type."

Her strong will and determination, however, were by now well known, and it was around this time that Jane started becoming vocal about her years as a contract player: "I've been pushed around by experts. I don't have to take it anymore."

○○○○○○○○○○○○○○○○○○○○

9

THE 1950S WAS A TIME OF TURMOIL AND ANXIETY IN the motion picture industry. The little David known as television had almost fatally wounded the Goliath that was the motion picture industry. Films now *had* to be good. The studios no longer had their theater chains to guarantee play dates for their mediocre product. And public tastes were changing—stars who were once favorites and still contractually received huge salaries were no longer box office draws.

Reeling from the blow of the loss of its market to the small screen, the movie industry searched frantically for ways to lure an audience. The major studios were floundering. At 20th Century-Fox they came up with CinemaScope and Stereophonic Sound. Warner Bros. hoped that their 3-D process would be the gimmick to bring back the crowds. Cinerama was yet another new big-screen process.

There was one studio that had never had a chain of theaters, nor had it ever had a huge roster of highly paid stars. Universal, now Universal-International, had always succeeded by producing thirty or forty films a year, concentrating on action-adventures, programmers, and series. U-I had produced the Ma and Pa

Kettle, Francis the Talking Mule, and Abbott and Costello films. Budgets were kept low and exploitation values high.

Still, Universal would produce three or four top-quality films each year. In the fifties, while the other studios were flailing about for mechanical innovations, Universal was relying on "good, old-fashioned women's stories" for their two or three big pictures.

There had always been a formula at Universal: Sign stars who had been built into major attractions by other studios, but whose careers were slipping (Claudette Colbert, Linda Darnell, Ida Lupino, Loretta Young, Alexis Smith, and Irene Dunne were recent examples), and then team them with Universal's contract players and rely on a good director and a strong story.

Actor-turned-producer Ross Hunter had taken the studio's formula and was raising it to new heights. With his talent for making films with great production values that screamed Big Budgets but in reality were brought in for low cost, Hunter was becoming well known in the industry. He had produced *All I Desire* with Barbara Stanwyck (Douglas Sirk had directed). Then he had revived the career of Ann Sheridan with *Take Me to Town*, a western-comedy with music (Sirk again directed). It turned out to be one of the surprise hits of the year, as had the Hunter-Sirk film *Has Anybody Seen My Gal?*

When people heard that Jane Wyman had signed for a film at Universal, however, it seemed somewhat incongruous. It was a studio for slipping stars, and Jane was at her peak. What people did not realize was that the move to Universal had been Jane's own idea.

Douglas Sirk was a Danish-born director who had scored great success in pre-Nazi Germany and had come to America during World War II. He made a few films at Columbia before moving over to Universal and becoming one of the studio's stock directors. In fact, along with producer Hunter and other crew members, the group (which also often included actor Rock Hudson) referred to themselves affectionately as "the stock company."

Sirk loved working at U-I. He knew their formula for success and respected it. There was one simple requirement: A film had to make money. If he could get a star, the studio would give him more production money, perhaps even let him film in color.

Sirk recalls that it was after directing the Stanwyck picture *All I Desire* that Ross Hunter then came to him and said, "I have Jane Wyman."

"Oh!" Sirk was impressed. As he later said, "She was still a real star then and I was terribly interested." But then Sirk's enthusiasm was dampened when Hunter told him that Jane wanted to remake an old Universal picture. According to Sirk there was *always* an actress remembering this particular old film and wanting to remake it. The film, of course, was John Stahl's version of Lloyd C. Douglas's famed novel, *Magnificent Obsession.*

"Ross Hunter gave me the book and I tried to read it, but I just couldn't," recalled Sirk. "It is the most confused book you can imagine—it is so abstract in many respects that I didn't see a picture in it."

But then Hunter brought Sirk an outline that he'd had done on the original Irene Dunne–Robert Taylor film, directed by Stahl. (Sirk has noted, "By the way, I did not see the Stahl picture.")

Sirk recalls that the outline was "quite different from the book." But he still had reservations. "I said to Ross, 'Look, we'll be buried under this thing,' and I went home and wandered around the house in a deep depression for a couple of days. But then, thinking it over, I realized that maybe Jane Wyman could be right and this goddamn awful story could be a success."

Magnificent Obsession was the granddaddy tearjerker of them all, a story about a handsome, reckless playboy who accidentally blinds a woman but then falls in love with her. He finds spiritual meaning in his life, returns to medical school to become a doctor, and ultimately saves the woman's life and cures her blindness.

When Irene Dunne played the part opposite Robert Taylor in the 1935 version, the picture had established Taylor as a matinee idol.

Sirk has confirmed that with *Magnificent Obsession*, he and the studio had a great opportunity to boost Rock Hudson's career. "I was still working on turning Hudson into a star," recalls Sirk. "Now this meant the first occasion for him to ride into stardom on the name of Jane Wyman."

Up to this point Hudson had starred mostly in western and adventure yarns. He was, like the studio's other rising contract players Tony Curtis and Jeff Chandler, receiving a lot of fan mail. But Universal knew that to launch Hudson as a romantic leading man, they needed a very special star and property.

In the novel *Magnificent Obsession*, the woman is *much* older than the playboy. She has a grown daughter. In the movie versions, of course, the daughter character became a stepdaughter, so the mother needed only be ten rather than twenty years older than the girl. Although the matter of age never comes up in the script, it is well established at the beginning of the story that the woman is mature while the man is a callow, irresponsible youth. Wyman was around ten years older than Hudson, but they looked close to the same age. It would not be a ludicrous romantic pairing.

The project moved forward with great expectations. Jane's old friend Agnes Moorehead was signed for the supporting cast, which also included Barbara Rush, Otto Kruger, Paul Cavanagh, and Mae Clarke.

Jane was once again playing a character with a major handicap, and as with *Belinda*, she did her homework. She talked to blind people, who made her realize that the blind do not careen around rooms knocking over things or groping wildly in the air. "My greatest problem would be the tendency to overact . . . I learned the importance of knowing how blind persons feel inside. In transmitting that sense of blindness and emotion, the

Left to right: Jack Carson, Jane, John Garfield, and Bette Davis in the all-star 1944 extravaganza *Hollywood Canteen.* (Davis and Garfield had actually founded the Canteen.)

Charles Brackett and Billy Wilder's 1945 film *The Lost Weekend,* co-starring Wyman and Ray Milland, was the turning point in Wyman's career.

Modern Screen

OCTOBER
15¢

DELL

CAPT. RONALD REAGAN

Ronald Reagan was still a far bigger name than his wife as far as the public was concerned—he remained "cover boy" material, even though not making movies.

Above: The Yearling (1946), with Jane as Ma Baxter, Gregory Peck as Pa Baxter, and Claude Jarman, Jr., as their son, Jody, established Wyman as a star.

Right: An inadvertently symbolic photograph: While Wyman and Gregory Peck are front-and-center at the gala Los Angeles premiere of *The Yearling,* Ronald Reagan (behind Peck's shoulder) is blocked from view.

Left: Wyman and James Stewart teamed for William Wellman's *Magic Town* (1947).

Below: Producer Jerry Wald, an important man in Jane's career, on the set with Wyman, Agnes Moorehead, and Charles Bickford. They were filming *Johnny Belinda* (1948).

Right: Seven-year-old Maureen visits Mommy and co-star Lew Ayres on the *Johnny Belinda* set.

Below: Belinda learns sign language from the compassionate doctor. Wyman and Ayres were superb in the now classic motion picture.

The ultimate accolade—an Academy Award as best actress for *Johnny Belinda.* Loretta Young, pictured with Jane, had won the previous year for *The Farmer's Daughter.*

Not a trace of makeup on Jane's sad face as she testifies in court at her divorce from Ronald Reagan.

On the town with Lew
Ayres. The press had
them altar-bound.

Below: With recording
executive Manny Sachs.
Another romance,
according to columnists.
In fact, they were
longtime friends and
business associates.

With famed attorney Greg Bautzer. This was a serious relationship that many thought would result in marriage for Hollywood's "most elusive bachelor." It didn't.

Below: With Marlene Dietrich in *Stage Fright* (1950).

Betty Delmont, Jane's longtime hairdresser, adjusts Wyman's blond wig on the set of *The Glass Menagerie* (1950).

Below: Charles Laughton worked closely with Jane on her interpretation of her difficult role in *The Blue Veil* (1951), which garnered her another best actress Oscar nomination.

With Bing Crosby in Frank Capra's *Here Comes the Groom* (1951), a big hit in which the duo sang the standard-to-be "In the Cool, Cool, Cool of the Evening."

Jane, thirty-eight, and Travis Kleefeld, twenty-six, were engaged to be married. Public opinion was against them.

A radiant thirty-eight-year-old Jane after her wedding to thirty-five-year-old musician-bandleader Fred Karger. They eloped on a Saturday to avoid publicity.

Wyman and Sterling Hayden in *So Big* (1953), a successful screen version of Edna Ferber's classic novel.

A teary-eyed Wyman at the divorce hearing that ended her marriage to Karger. Their relationship, however, was far from over.

Above and right: The quintessential woman's movie—*Magnificent Obsession.* The 1954 Wyman–Ross Hunter blockbuster established Rock Hudson as a star.

With Charlton Heston in *Lucy Gallant* (1955). *No Magnificent Obsession* at the box office.

In *Miracle in the Rain* (1956), Wyman's final Warner Bros. picture. Paul Picerni portrayed the young priest.

Jane Wyman today: as Angela Channing, the empress of *Falcon Crest,* which debuted almost one year after Ronald Reagan was inaugurated President. Wyman is currently the highest-paid actress on television.

problem, as with all acting, is to make the audience emote for you."

Under Sirk's expert direction, Jane delivered a subtle yet powerful and poignant performance.

The title, *Magnificent Obsession*, refers to the fact that the playboy is told that if he adopts the philosophy of helping others, without credit or remuneration of any kind, it will become an obsession—"but it will be a magnificent obsession." The appeal of the story rests upon this spiritual message commingled with the love the man feels for the woman—with the implication that this, too, is a "magnificent obsession."

By the time *Magnificent Obsession* had completed shooting, in late 1953, Hedda Hopper had a scoop: "The marriage of Jane Wyman has hit the rocks." The feisty Hedda got through to Karger: "Freddie, who has moved into his mother's home, verified the situation but said: 'Please, no comment.' Jane does not answer her phone."

A few weeks later Louella reported the Kargers had reconciled. "I told them they were equally to blame. There were a few problems, but not important ones. It looks like everything will be all right." Louella was wrong.

That Christmas was a very tense time in the Wyman-Karger household. Jane was supposedly on edge for weeks and then overreacted when there was a minor accident. The story goes that eight-year-old Michael, in attempting to light the Christmas candles on the centerpiece of the dining room table, had accidentally set the table on fire. The expensive table was ruined, the ceiling was blackened, but no one was hurt. Jane was not home at the time, and when she arrived and learned what happened, she was furious.

All had expected a reaction of some sort, of course, but reports were "that she blew sky-high," and that she was on edge all through the holidays. There were rumors of another blowup with

Karger, and they were confirmed when shortly after the new year Jane filed for divorce.

In a move that seemed odd, Karger took action as well, filing for a legal separation in preparation for his own filing for divorce. Men generally didn't countersue unless they were publicity seekers, and Karger was certainly not interested in publicity.

As the elopement had been a surprise, these actions shocked Jane's fans. The couple had been married only fourteen months. Jane was a vulnerable target for the press. There was embarrassing publicity, and she was very sensitive to the criticism leveled at her. She especially didn't want to look foolish.

The divorce hearing was scheduled for January 25. Wyman, ill with a virus, didn't attend. It was soon learned that Wyman and Fred were dropping the divorce and getting back together again.

In all fairness, it should be noted that both were serious people when it concerned marriage, and both honestly felt they should give every effort to making the union work.

Nineteen fifty-four was a very big year professionally for Jane Wyman. *Magnificent Obsession* opened in May and was a resounding success. Today Rock Hudson says that it was with this film, his twenty-fourth, that he realized he had made it. When the film was sneak-previewed at the Encino Theater, the audience reaction was precisely what the studio had anticipated and *Variety* had predicted. Hudson recalls: "I fled the theater before the film was over." Referring to his new status as a star attraction, Hudson has recalled that at this preview, "I knew, I knew, and I knew I had to get out of there before the lights went on." Mr. Hudson reveals that this was a very emotional moment for him.

While today the picture is viewed as trite and saccharine, at the time, it received good reviews, and Jane, especially, was lauded by the critics. "In appealing contrast to Miss Dunne's pristine languor, Miss Wyman is, as usual, refreshingly believable throughout," the *New York Times* critic noted. Rock Hudson, too, received good reviews.

The public, especially women, loved *Magnificent Obsession.* Although in the film there is no mention of age, the fans knew that Jane was forty and Rock was almost ten years younger. It was a pairing that apparently offered wide appeal.

That summer Jane did a publicity tour for the picture, accompanied by her husband. It was "first cabin, all the way," as her former husband might have said. In New York the couple were domiciled at the Waldorf Towers.

As was frequently the case, the children were away from home that summer, Maureen visiting friends in Cape Cod, and Michael in a boys' camp in Montana. During the school year they were in boarding schools. As an adult, Michael Reagan said: "I didn't get to know my mother and father personally until I was twenty-five. Mom was working double time. I was more or less raised by Carrie, who was Mom's cook. I would go to her with my problems and inner feelings."

Wyman was certainly working nonstop. Ever practical and with an eye to the future, Jane cautiously entered a new medium: television. She filmed an episode of the *General Electric Theater,* co-starring with Bill Goodwin and Louise Beavers in a story called "Amelia," scheduled to be aired the following year. It was a newsworthy event because Jane's film career was still in high gear and she was not considered an actress who needed to do television. Stars who were making appearances on TV were people like Margaret Sullavan, Mary Astor, Ann Sheridan, and others whose film careers were virtually over.

Ronald Reagan had already done TV, first showing up on the small screen back in 1950. That appearance had been followed by over a half-dozen more in TV dramas. In truth, Reagan's film career was slipping badly, and early in 1954 he had even appeared as a nightclub entertainer in Las Vegas. So, when approached with a lucrative offer to act as host for the *G. E. Theater* television program, Reagan—despite his earlier statements of disdain for the new medium—readily accepted.

His old friend Ann Sheridan later observed: "I remember Ronnie telling me—all of us—not to join TV because it was the enemy of the movies. Next thing, he was on *G. E. Theater* with his contact lenses reading the commercials."

Ironically, therefore, Jane Wyman made her television debut on a show hosted by her ex-husband. Wyman said she had wanted to get into television before this time but hadn't because she would not perform live. *G. E. Theater* alternated between live broadcasting and filmed shows in its anthology series, unlike *Studio One, Playhouse 90,* and others that were only "live."

"In those days everything was live, and I knew that wasn't for me," recalled Jane. "I'm strictly a movie actress—this is a profession all by itself, completely distinct from the theater, and I knew that I wouldn't and couldn't go in and compete with the Broadway actresses who easily adapted themselves to this new medium. I had to wait until film became acceptable to the networks and the sponsors."

"What's the matter?" Louella Parsons wanted to know. She had of course heard the latest rumors.

"The same old thing. You know. We just weren't able to work out a reconciliation," confessed Jane. She had made a final decision about her seesaw marriage and had once again officially filed for a separation from Karger. "However, believe me, we parted very amicably. We both realized our problems couldn't be solved so we decided to go through with the divorce."

"Any chances of making up?"

"Absolutely not," said Wyman.

"The way she said it left no doubt," Miss Parsons concluded.

Said Mr. Karger: "I don't want to say anything. I'd rather Jane made all the statements. Anything she says is all right with me."

By December, Wyman was awarded her interlocutory decree

and the Karger marriage was over, although, as events would prove, their relationship wasn't.

Fortunately, there wasn't much time on Jane's schedule for brooding. When the receipts from *Magnificent Obsession* began pouring in, Universal immediately planned another feature with the Wyman-Hudson duo. Douglas Sirk admitted that Jane had been right and he wrong in assessing the possible success of a remake of *Magnificent Obsession.* "It topped the receipts of the old Stahl picture by more than ten times," recalled Sirk. "The picture was an enormous success, for both Hudson and Jane Wyman, and that's why the studio wanted to make *All That Heaven Allows* right afterwards."

All That Heaven Allows, produced, of course, by Ross Hunter, went into production in January 1955. It was another book—believe it or not, *Walden,* by Henry David Thoreau—that inspired the film. The book was a favorite of Sirk's (his father had given him a copy of it when he was fourteen), and he made the philosophy of *Walden* the key element of the story of the new film. He even used a shot of the book in close-up in one scene.

All That Heaven Allows would not pussyfoot around the issue of older woman–younger man. That, in fact, would be the central theme of this story. *Magnificent Obsession* had proven that "mature" women across the country could and did identify with the fortyish Jane Wyman. She radiated dignity and warmth, and her youthful appearance made it perfectly sensible that a younger—but not *too* much younger—man could fall in love with her. To her fans, Wyman embodied the perfect wife-mother-friend. She, and the characters she played, were good-looking, nice, and, above all, *likable.*

With *All That Heaven Allows* the script pulled out all the stops. Although the screenplay tried to inject a *Magnificent Obsession*–like spiritual aspect (the character played by Rock has learned the "secret of happiness"—being true to oneself, finding answers within oneself), this part of the story is not clearly presented and certainly not believable.

Essentially it is a film about an older woman, a widow, who has a sexual attraction for a younger man, her gardener. When he wants to marry her, she is faced with a dilemma: What will her friends in the community say? She is willing to continue the romance without marriage—it is the man who insists upon sealing the union both spiritually and legally.

To underscore the age difference, in this script Jane's character has two grown children—not stepchildren. Her son is a senior at Princeton and her daughter is a social worker. When the children make it clear that by marrying a younger man—and a gardener at that—their mother is ruining their lives, she gives him up. Later, however, when she learns that he has pneumonia and is near death, she returns to nurse him back to health, and it becomes clear as the picture ends that eventually they will defy convention and marry. The obvious parallels between *All That Heaven Allows* and Jane's private life did not go unrecognized. She *had,* of course, been close to marriage with a younger man.

In addition, the spiritual themes of her recent films coincided with a major development in her personal life. It was apparent that Wyman was searching for answers in her life beyond what script to do next or what medium to appear in. She had converted to Catholicism; Maureen and Michael, too, were baptized as Catholics. Their father and stepmother were invited to the services.

In Hollywood the group of stars and industry people who are Catholic is large and, for the most part, they are friendly with each other. They often have a sense of humor about themselves —Jane once told a friend that they referred to Loretta Young as the "Mother Superior."

During these years Jane was close to Catholic priest Robert Perrella, known to his friends as "Father Bob." They met on the set during a rehearsal of a Perry Como TV show (Father Bob was

an old pal of Rosemary Clooney, who was on the show that week).
There was obviously an immediate rapport between Jane and
Father Bob. They shared a similar sense of humor and joy of
living. Reverend Perrella has noted, "Her outlook on life—her
savoir-vivre—startles me. It always culminates in five short words
—'Play it by ear, honey.'"

Jane's nickname for herself with Father Perrella is "Jeanie
Weenie." He has characterized Wyman as someone who has a
great sense of humor and no pretensions about any "star status."

Her star status was once again reinforced, however, when, in
February, Wyman was nominated for the fourth time for an
Academy Award as best actress. With this nomination for *Magnificent Obsession,* Jane entered the league of other grandes
dames of the screen in that she was being nominated for a star
performance in a star vehicle, but in a movie that was not recognized in any other category.

For the first—and, as it would turn out, the last—time, the
Academy had decided to televise the announcement of the
nominations. Actors, producers, directors, and other industry
people were gathered at various restaurants around Hollywood.
The plan was to intercut between the main telecast at NBC's
Burbank Studios and the various restaurants and nightclubs
(Romanoff's, Ciro's, the Cocoanut Grove) where stars were gath-
ered.

The noble experiment was, however, a disaster as television
entertainment. Nonetheless it was exciting for the participants.
Jane was seated at a table with Judy Garland when both women
received their nominations (Judy for her bravura performance in
A Star Is Born). Again it was a banner year for women. Others
nominated were Audrey Hepburn for *Sabrina,* Grace Kelly for
The Country Girl, and—the first black woman ever nominated in
this category—the beautiful Dorothy Dandridge for her performance in *Carmen Jones.*

Garland was the overwhelming favorite to win the award. The

former child star had made a stupendous comeback in the brilliant remake of *A Star Is Born*, and the public's sympathy and emotions were with her. Still, Wyman couldn't be counted out—one never knew how the awards would turn out.

When the envelope was opened, however, Jane lost the Oscar—but not to Garland as expected. Newcomer Grace Kelly was named best actress.

Paramount wanted to try for a "woman's picture" bull's-eye, and producers William Pine and William Thomas had signed Wyman for *Lucy Gallant*. Her co-star this time would be the young Charlton Heston. Robert Parrish was signed to direct, and the supporting cast included Claire Trevor, Thelma Ritter, and William Demarest. *Gallant* was the story of a dress designer (Wyman) in a boomtown in Oklahoma, and gave Jane the opportunity to wear a lavish Edith Head wardrobe.

Wyman went straight from *Lucy Gallant* into a new film (her workload in 1955 was heavier than in the old five-films-a-year days at Warners). Warners had finally come up with a script that both Jane and the studio found acceptable, *Miracle in the Rain*, fashioned by veteran writer Ben Hecht from his own short story.

It was a property that offered Jane a wonderful part in a very effective story. It was another "plain" character, the tale of a girl who falls in love with a soldier on leave during World War II. (Ironically, television, the arch rival, was now providing motion pictures with story ideas. *Miracle in the Rain* had already been a TV drama, two years earlier, starring Phyllis Thaxter and William Prince.) Van Johnson was signed to co-star with Jane. Although his days as a bobby-sox idol were long over, Johnson was still commanding top dollar. In fact, his salary for this film was $150,000, and, although publicity said Jane was receiving more, in reality she received only $120,000.

Rudolph Maté was chosen to direct, and the line producer was Frank Rosenberg. A superb supporting cast was assembled: Eileen Heckart, who had just made a hit on Broadway in *The Bad*

Seed, would play Jane's best friend. Josephine Hutchinson would portray Wyman's mother; William Gargan, her alcoholic father. Fred Clark, Marcel Dalio, Barbara Nichols, Alan King, and Arte Johnson rounded out the cast. Paul Picerni had a pivotal role as a priest in St. Patrick's Cathedral.

It was a nicely budgeted feature, over $1.1 million, respectable for a black-and-white picture, and the location work in New York's Central Park and at St. Patrick's Cathedral would give the picture an authentic feel.

In the story, the soldier (Johnson) has gone off to war and is killed. Jane goes to St. Patrick's every day to pray for him. (Shooting inside St. Patrick's Cathedral had to be done between ten at night and five in the morning.) The key scene of the film is the ending, where the girl staggers in from the rain and tells the priest and her friend that her lover is not dead—she has seen him. She then dies in the priest's arms. They think she had been hallucinating until they look down and see that in her hand she is clasping the coin the soldier had taken with him overseas.

Jane's formidable acting skill was never more evident than in this picture, especially in the scenes where she, as an old maid under the domination of her mother, allows herself to fall in love with the soldier. Wyman displayed enormous depth and vulnerability in the part and there were many who felt this performance would garner her yet another Oscar nomination.

When the company returned to Hollywood to shoot interiors at the studio, Jane and Van recorded a song for the film, "I'll Always Believe in You," which was released on disc as "Miracle in the Rain."

With the completion of this film in early July, Wyman had three pictures, all major productions at major studios, ready for release. Any one of these might prove to match the success of *Magnificent Obsession*. It was indisputable that Jane Wyman, unlike most of her peers, was still, after twenty years in the business, a movie star.

But she now surprised the industry by abruptly and dramatically changing career direction.

○ ○ ○ ○ ○ ○ ○ ○ ○ ○ ○ ○ ○ ○ ○ ○ ○ ○

10

"IT WAS A WEIRD PERIOD OF HER LIFE," RECALLS PRO-
ducer Eva Wolas, the woman who had been picked to produce
Jane's new television series. Mrs. Wolas's expertise at selecting
stories for television shows—such as the highly successful *Climax*
—had made her one of the most sought-after talents in the industry.

Jane would be taking over the already established *Fireside
Theatre*. The anthology series had been on the air for seven years,
and for the last two, Gene Raymond, a leading man of films in the
1930s and husband of Jeanette MacDonald, had been the host.

Jane, however, entered TV as more than a mere "actress": she
was president of the company that produced the series, and as
such she would set all the policies. "We'll do everything from
comedy to drama. It's part of our policy to get the best available
talent and stories."

For her premiere season, the title of the series was changed to
Jane Wyman Presents the Fireside Theatre. And instead of forty-
two half-hour episodes, the season was cut to thirty-four, with
Jane slated to star in fourteen.

Although in later years Wyman said that she had made the

move to television because she saw the handwriting on the wall
—that her kind of pictures were going out of fashion—this re-
mark is obviously hindsight. Unlike Loretta Young, who had gone
into television (two years earlier) when her film career was dramatically on the wane, and she was reduced to doing programmers, Wyman was still on top.

Jane's entree into the TV world was not all smooth sailing,
however. According to Eva Wolas, the chemistry between her
and the star was not exactly perfect. Today Mrs. Wolas recalls,
"One of the 'tests' to see if we could get along—after I had
already been hired—was, in the presence of Lew Wasserman and
others in her inner circle, a showing of *Love Is a Many
Splendored Thing.*"

This immensely popular 1955 film featured Jennifer Jones and
William Holden as star-crossed lovers. Mrs. Wolas recalls that this
was a movie with which Jane was very taken. "It had the kind of
story that greatly appealed to her. I didn't like the picture at all."

Mrs. Wolas reiterates that this "test" of how they would get
along happened *after* she had already been hired. Obviously she
had been hired because, at the time, she was the top story-editor
in television. Sixteen of the programs she had bought for *Climax*
had subsequently been bought by motion picture companies for
development into full-length features.

Today, Wolas notes that prior to her being hired, she and Wyman "never sat down and discussed a philosophy of what each of
us wanted to do." According to Mrs. Wolas's recollections, during
the time they worked together Wyman was involved "with a
nice-looking young man from the advertising agency. They were
having a thing." There was also a priest on the scene—"Always a
priest being talked about and referred to," recalls Mrs. Wolas.

She relates that subsequently the agency man became executive producer of the show, and she left shortly afterward and
returned to CBS.

Even before Jane's show was on the air, she was badgered on

all sides as to why she was abandoning films and going into TV, and, like Loretta Young, she said, "I don't intend to forsake pictures." Her agenda called for two features a year, and when queried if she was still "secure" in the film business, she answered, "I'm not certain that such a state of affairs exists. But if it does, yes, I suppose I'm fairly secure in pictures." Wyman noted, however, that security "can be a frightening word. It gets confused in my mind with complacency.

"Idleness makes me jumpy and lack of purpose drives me to distraction. I love to work at the work I love." She compared television to nothing more than making movies. And noted that from the very beginning she viewed television as an inevitable adjunct to her acting career, pointing out that her contracts in the late forties had stipulated she had the right, unlike other stars, to appear on TV if she chose.

At this juncture the challenge truly did appeal to her. "Naturally," she admitted, "I can fall on my face. But does one stay in bed all day for fear of being hit by a car? Don't we take chances, respond to challenges?"

Many people told her she had everything to lose and nothing to gain by going into the new medium. But forty-one-year-old Jane said that she had "personal pleasure to gain. A sense of achievement . . . I turned to television simply because I like it. The more audience an actress has to work to, the more stimulating it is. I want to spread things around a little. I think TV will help my picture career, and vice versa."

Jane was sensitive about people reading psychological messages into her need for work. "They all want to know whether I'm working myself into a tizzy in order to escape from something in my personal life. The answer is 'no.' "

At this point, Jane's personal life took a definite backseat to work, but almost immediately an obstacle was thrown in her path. They had been filming the show only a few weeks when a SAG strike was called against all filmed television shows. As a member of SAG, Jane of course honored the strike, although she wouldn't say whether or not she was in favor of it. As producer and as an actress, she was on both sides of the fence. All Jane would say was that the strike was hurting their show more than others because "we don't have a backlog from last year to throw into the breach in case the strike lasts a long time."

Jane contended that each of the episodes was being made "as if it were a major movie." At the time the strike was called, the company had completed six half-hour films with Jane playing the lead in two of them. Four that Jane only hosted starred friends like Jack Carson, Peter Lawford, and Dane Clark and Rod Cameron.

Eventually, of course, the SAG strike was settled and Jane resumed work. Her statements that she would continue making movies raised the question of where she would find the time— even Jane Wyman couldn't add additional hours to the twenty-four-hour day.

She later admitted, "When I first got into TV it really was in its embryonic stages. . . . And the pace! I had no idea you began work at six in the morning and quit at ten at night, and that after shooting you went to your office to get the next script started— and it goes on and on and on. I'd limp home over that lousy Coldwater Canyon and I'd say, 'Well, Lord, if you want me there tomorrow, you goin' to have to git me there!' Of course it becomes second nature."

Jane's series was shot at the Republic Studios in North Hollywood, just over the hill from Beverly Hills, where she lived.

The new *Jane Wyman Presents the Fireside Theatre* debuted on August 30, 1955, on the NBC television network. The first show in which Jane was both hostess and star was broadcast September 29. "Holiday in Autumn" co-starred Jane with Fay Wray and was the fourth episode of the season.

Then *Lucy Gallant* was released in October, and *All That Heaven Allows* followed a few weeks later. Both films were lambasted by the critics. Warners, which had rushed *Miracle in the Rain* through postproduction so it could be released in time to qualify for the Oscars, now held up release—there were already too many Jane Wyman pictures in the marketplace.

All That Heaven Allows, though not the success *Magnificent Obsession* was at the box office, was a money-maker. Today the film is a curiosity piece because it did mirror a coming social change in American attitudes about older women–younger men (in real life the romance between Jane and Travis Kleefeld was perhaps a decade and a half too early).

In her private life, Jane was at a loss as to whom she could date without causing a flurry of unfavorable publicity. "What am I supposed to do?" she asked a publicist at Universal. "I'm trapped! I like to go out and have fun but anyone I go out with I'm said to be engaged to. And if I go out with several different fellas over the course of several months, it's 'playgirl Janie is at it again' publicity and I don't want it or like it."

She received her final divorce decree from Karger in December 1955. Meanwhile, she continued with *Fireside Theatre*. The series was done with "class" and a high budget. Jane was an immediate success with the television audience. During the season, Wyman played in both drama and comedy, starring with such people as Carolyn Jones, Patric Knowles, Charles Coburn, and newcomers like Chuck Connors, Don Murray, and Jack Kelly.

Miracle in the Rain was released in April 1956 to generally mixed reviews and generally small audiences. Critics said it had moments of insight, sensitivity, and compassion. Abe Weiler, in the *New York Times*, said, "it hits high, lovely notes on occasion but too often lapses into soap opera."

Jane attributed the box office failure of the film to Jack Warner. "I hate to bring up my own work, honey," she told Rex Reed years later, "but what a wonderful movie! But by the time we got that one out, Van Johnson and I weren't so big, and Warners was already spending all its money promoting *Giant*, so it never got any attention."

From now on, Jane would devote all her energies to television. In later years she said, "I realized the time for my kind of film was passing, that the blockbuster was now in. So I got out while the going was good." She signed for another TV season. Once again the title of the show was changed—now it would be known as *The Jane Wyman Theatre*. William Asher, who produced the show its first season, has described Jane Wyman: "She is a very astute businesswoman and a devoted and hard worker. She can—and does—jump into any kind of business negotiation in competition with men. She has a tremendous understanding of the value of a dollar."

A familiar question arose: Could men work for a female boss? A Wyman business associate said her male employees didn't resent her: "After all, it's her show. And if you agreed to accept that proposition in the first place, then it's certainly not your place to be resentful. . . . Janie has come to rely more and more on the judgment of her key staff people. She makes the decisions, but most of them are based on our recommendations."

Jane was too busy to concern herself with publicity or interviews, and she was especially not interested in talking about her private life. One of the people who worked on *The Jane Wyman Theatre* was quoted: "Janie believes she has a right to her privacy and just plain resents it when some stranger starts asking questions about her personal affairs. Janie isn't that extroverted. A lot of stars will talk freely, even airily, about their former marriages, but Janie just isn't built that way. She's never felt that she owes it to the public to get up on a box and bare her soul."

Her attitude, of course, didn't prevent noted show business reporters from sleuthing out the facts. In March, Dorothy Kilgallen reported that Jane's friends believed she was "wildly serious" about Gail Smith, identified as "a big executive with the company sponsoring Jane's show." Kilgallen predicted a wedding.

Walter Winchell reported a month later that there would be no marriage.

Louella Parsons confirmed the couple were indeed having a big romance, and Ed Sullivan wrote: "Jane Wyman and Gail Smith blazing." Sheilah Graham predicted the new year would find Jane Wyman and Gail Smith as Mr. and Mrs.

To Wyman's chagrin, some columnists even now rehashed the whole Reagan matter, ridiculously stating that Reagan was still the one true love of her life until Gail Smith had come along!

In this era of Debbie, Natalie, and Doris Day receiving the lion's share of the public's attention, Wyman quietly let these stories die and pressed on with her show.

Since Jane wouldn't talk about her personal life, publicists tried to pitch Jane-the-executive as the "hook" for keeping publicity going on *The Jane Wyman Theatre*. But Jane didn't like that approach, either: "I'm in the glamour business. Glamour is what's kept me going for never mind how many years. I don't honestly think the public is interested in the fact that I'm a business girl or that I get up at five in the morning. A lot of people get up at five or six in the morning. What's so great about that?"

But there was no doubt that behind the scenes Jane was, like Loretta Young on her television program, totally involved in every aspect of production. She later revealed, "My eyes went to pot reading three thousand scripts a month, just to get thirty-eight shows. Loretta Young and I used to trade scripts. I'd say, 'This part's too pretty for me, you do it' or 'That one's too ugly for you, let me do it.' We used to trade leading men, too. One of my best shows came from a garage mechanic who handed us two pages of paper while he was filling the car with gas. I gave him $100 for it and the damned thing won an Emmy nomination."

Jane was well suited to her role as a lady mogul. Someone who worked on the show noted, "Janie is essentially lonely. She doesn't have anyone to lean on; there's no one there to protect her. So she feels she has to fight it out for herself. It's her show, her reputation as an artist, that's on the line, and there's nobody else to carry the burden for her or even help her with it. Instead of crying on a strong man's shoulder, she lets off steam by being an executive whirlwind. Fortunately, she has the ability and the temperament and the energy to carry it off. I think any lesser girl would have cracked up under the strain long ago."

Wyman was a no-nonsense individual and expected total professionalism from other actors. On one episode of her show, she was playing a love scene with an actor. When they kissed, he began attempting to French-kiss her. She didn't stop the scene, didn't speak, and seemingly did not react. But when the scene was over, she fired the man. Years later she told a friend: "The son of a bitch hasn't gotten a job since."

For three years Jane was incredibly busy. In her second season, she starred in eighteen out of thirty-four episodes, and, of course, she hosted all of them. As a result, she had virtually no time for a social life. Certain gatherings, however, were "musts." When the Jules Steins hosted their famous parties at their Bel-Air estate, Jane was frequently a guest. Louella Parsons was present on one of these occasions, and expressed her delight at how well Jane again looked—because, "For a time, when she was so very busy on her TV show last year, it didn't seem to be that Jane was too interested in her appearance."

During the years of filming her series, Jane helped launch the careers of many budding young talents. One such was an actor-turned-writer, Aaron Spelling, who previously had enjoyed some success selling story ideas to such top dramatic shows as *Studio One* and *Alcoa Presents*. Spelling's agent sent him to see Jane Wyman. Her company bought his story idea, but his agent told him that unfortunately they didn't want him to write the screenplay.

Spelling said: "It was the saddest day of my life. I had gotten three hundred and eighty dollars for writing the story, which was a godsend to me—I could now pay the rent. But I couldn't write the screenplay. Four weeks later Stan tells me to go out and see Jane Wyman again. I was all pumped up to say, 'Thank you, Miss Wyman, but I'm not going to write another story unless I write the screenplay.' I walk in and she says, 'What the hell happened to your story?' I said, 'I don't know. I didn't write the screenplay.' She said, 'But I loved your story. Go home and write the screenplay.'"

He delivered his screenplay to Wyman the following Monday and she began shooting it a week later.

Spelling went on to write for *Dick Powell's Zane Grey Theater* and would eventually turn producer and become the most successful mogul working on the small screen.

In the third and final season of *The Jane Wyman Theatre*, only twenty-four episodes were produced, with Jane headlining nine, her most notable performance being in "My Sister Susan," in which she played twins.

More than in previous seasons, this final year utilized guest stars—Joseph Cotten, Fernando Lamas, Paul Henreid, Linda Darnell, Ruth Roman, among others. It is a matter of opinion as to whether this ploy was an attempt to save the series or to go out in a blaze of glory. Perhaps it is just that more film actors, not getting work on the big screen, were willing to appear on television, and Wyman took advantage of the opportunity and hired them.

Of these years Jane later said, "It was very grueling work. I had to cast, produce, do the office work. I used to go down to the airport and hand the film to the pilot myself to get it to New York by Tuesday night so it could go on the air. Things are more sophisticated now—bigger budgets, shorter working hours. But the reason I got out of it was because of a cycle again. The anthology show went out of style overnight and the series with regular characters came in. But I learned one thing—you can always get quality if you *are* quality."

Jane was duly recognized for her work on television. She had twice been nominated for an Emmy, but both times she lost to Loretta Young.

Close friends of Wyman's were pleased she was leaving the hard grind—her physical appearance had again begun to reflect the constant pressure she was under.

It is interesting that during the mid-1950s, both Jane Wyman and Ronald Reagan were big stars on the new medium of television. *G. E. Theater* was one of the staples of Sunday night viewing; it would remain on the air for eight years, gaining Reagan a following he had never enjoyed in films. One can speculate that if Reagan and Wyman had stayed together, they might have become star moguls of TV, like Lucy and Desi, and Reagan's pal Dick Powell.

Maureen was now seventeen, Michael thirteen. Their dad had already provided them with a baby sister, and now a baby brother entered the scene. Ronald Prescott Reagan was born on May 20, 1958.

Maribe Nowell, a neighbor of the Reagans', has been quoted as saying that Nancy always felt "that she was in competition with Jane Wyman and her children. And wanted them [her kids] to be just as good, or better, so Ronnie couldn't compare them."

Despite whatever efforts were made over the years at getting the two sets of Reagan children close together, it was never accomplished. Maureen Reagan has admitted that where Patti is concerned: "We're not really like sisters. We don't have much of a relationship." And Michael has said that Nancy, Patti, and "Skip" are the "real" First Family. He has noted that before "Skip" and Patti were around, Maureen and he were closer to Nancy.

Although she had bowed out of the weekly TV grind, Jane Wyman was not out of the public eye for very long. Her series was sold instantly into syndication, and would be seen continuously on the air through the early 1960s.

She returned briefly to the television soundstages to co-star with Philip Carey in an episode for the *Lux Playhouse* entitled "The Deadly Game." Immediately thereafter she resumed her movie career. Twentieth Century-Fox had asked Jane to replace Gene Tierney when illness forced the actress to drop out of *Holiday for Lovers,* a CinemaScope production co-starring Clifton Webb. They played parents taking their brood on a foreign vacation.

Jane's friend Jerry Wald, who had produced the Oscar telecast in 1958, was repeating the chore in 1959 and invited her to appear on the program. Wald had assembled a dazzling array of presenters, and Wyman joined Ingrid Bergman, Maurice Chevalier, Gary Cooper, Bette Davis, Susan Hayward, Rosalind Russell, Elizabeth Taylor, John Wayne, and many others on the most-watched television program of the year.

Over the next several years Jane would bounce back and forth between occasional film and television roles. She went to the Disney studio to star in Walt Disney's live-action feature *Pollyanna.* As he did with all the films produced by his studio during his lifetime, Disney personally supervised the production. He was fond of the ad line that *Pollyanna* had assembled "the most important star cast in the history of the Disney studios." Along with Jane, the film starred Richard Egan, Adolphe Menjou, Agnes Moorehead, Donald Crisp, Nancy Olson, and introduced the British child actress Hayley Mills, daughter of John Mills.

An interesting observation on the Disney studios: Although working there meant first-class treatment, salaries were notoriously low. For example, Fred MacMurray's film career was revitalized at Disney around this time, via such pictures as *The Absent-Minded Professor.* However, MacMurray reportedly never received more than $50,000 per picture from Disney. It is probable that Jane received no more than this amount for her role in *Pollyanna,* but she was top-billed and presented beautifully on screen. In addition, the working conditions at Disney were the most favorable any star could imagine.

For her role as Aunt Polly, Jane undoubtedly called on both her own real-life experience with her mother and her role as Ma Baxter, for Aunt Polly was a loving woman, but stern and unable to express her feelings.

After the film opened at Radio City Music Hall and went into general release, it was a box office disappointment. In those years the Disney organization expected every film to gross at least $5 million—*Pollyanna* grossed only $3.75 million. Walt Disney attributed this to the title: "Because of the title, we had the women and the children, but the men stayed away." Although the film received generally good reviews when it was released, viewing *Pollyanna* today one realizes that, despite superb performances and top-notch production values, the pace of the film is almost unendurably slow.

Since her entry into television, Jane had been able to keep her private life very much out of the press. But in 1961 there were unexpected headlines when on a Saturday in March she remarried her ex-husband, Fred Karger. As with their elopement years earlier, the couple had picked a Saturday to avoid publicity. This time, Jane and Fred were married in a Catholic ceremony.

Wyman's close friends knew that she and Karger had been seeing each other, and this second try at marriage was obviously a decision arrived at after serious consideration—after all, they had already been married and knew the differences in each other's personalities and what problems those differences would pose when they lived together. They also realized that if a second marriage did not work out, they would open themselves to ridicule. And most importantly, Jane was now a Catholic and a religious ceremony meant that the marriage, in the eyes of the Church, was until death do them part.

One advantage they would have this time around was that Jane's career was winding down. They would be out of the constant glare of the spotlight, and perhaps this time the marriage would be left alone by the press and the gossip mongers. In addition, they would mainly have each other to be concerned about. Their children were older, and for the most part out of their day-to-day lives. Maureen had gone east to attend Marymount Junior College in Arlington, Virginia, but she dropped out of school and continued living and working in the Washington, D.C., area. For a while she was employed as a secretary in a real estate office.

During the first year of Jane's remarriage to Karger, twenty-year-old Maureen married John Filippone, a thirty-two-year-old police officer. The marriage lasted only a year.

The Wyman-Karger remarriage would last somewhat longer. Jane seemed to have found a new peace. The burden of her harrowing work schedule no longer existed, and there was space in her life to accommodate a relationship. Now she worked just enough to maintain her status in the industry.

She starred in several television dramas in 1961. The first was none other than the *G. E. Theater*, hosted by Ronald Reagan. Jane and David Brian co-starred in a story called "Labor of Love." Later in the year she did an episode of *The Investigators* and an episode of *Rawhide*, the popular MCA-produced series starring Clint Eastwood. Jane's co-stars on that particular episode were Ed Wynn and Anne Seymour.

She returned to the big screen in 1962. Walt Disney signed her to co-star in *Bon Voyage*, in which she played Fred MacMurray's wife. It was another story of a couple taking their teenage children abroad, but it was typical pleasant Disney family entertainment and was a success at the box office, grossing in excess of $5 million.

With this film, as with *Pollyanna*, the Disney organization was utilizing Jane Wyman effectively—her audience was their audience. Older women could identify with still-youthful-but-mature Jane as a mother of teenagers, and Jane's status in the industry was maintained.

Although her career had wound down dramatically, it was not

petering out as were the careers of Claudette Colbert, Irene Dunne, Barbara Stanwyck, and other former first ladies of the screen who could be seen in low-budget programmers and westerns. Jane was still top-billed in "class" product that was successful at the box office.

And throughout this period, the old *Jane Wyman Presents* episodes were shown on daytime TV on ABC (and they even resurfaced as a nighttime entry on NBC in the summer of 1963).

For all its glamour, Hollywood with its community of people is, in some aspects, a very small town. As in any small town, ex-husbands and ex-wives often run into each other, and often this occurs at very solemn occasions.

Ronald Reagan's beloved mother, Nelle, passed away in 1962, one day after her seventy-seventh birthday. A few days into the next year, Jane and Ron both attended the funeral of their old friend Dick Powell, who had died of cancer. Reagan had been offering his services to Powell's Four Star company, introducing several of the Powell shows while Powell was ailing. Around this time the *General Electric Theater* went off the air and Reagan was hired to host the series *Death Valley Days*.

Over the next couple of years, television provided Jane Wyman with at least one or two shows a season to spotlight her talent. By the mid-1960s, however, there were no offers from either the big screen or the small screen that Jane felt were appropriate for her.

The release of *What Ever Happened to Baby Jane?*, teaming Bette Davis and Joan Crawford in a Grand Guignol–gothic melodrama directed by Robert Aldrich, had begun a trend: bringing back Hollywood's former top stars in what were in effect "monster movies"—with the actresses portraying the monsters.

"I wouldn't believe myself in those roles, so I'd be doing the producers an injustice. Furthermore, I don't like all the sick pictures being made," said Jane. "I won't lower myself to act in the type of films that are selling these days. I simply refuse to play a prostitute, a dope addict . . ." Or worse.

It was a dismal time for many in the industry. "Something happened in the sixties," noted Wyman accurately. "It seemed that the time didn't permit women to be a part of it, except in a sort of secondary way, which I resented. I kept telling myself, 'I don't want to play a *What Ever Happened to Baby Jane?* I just don't want to do it.'" She didn't.

She later recalled that most of the offers she received were to play "Murderers, old ladies that were senile—they were awful. The weirdest kind of writing. And every time I'd read one of those scripts, I'd look in the mirror and say, 'How could they think of me for this?'"

But with characteristic candor she noted: "I wasn't unreceptive to working. . . . I don't think they were exactly looking for me with a fine-tooth comb."

Nor were the studios exactly combing the country searching for Ronald Reagan. MCA came to his rescue (the company had recently bought Universal Pictures, and was on its way to becoming one of the largest entertainment conglomerates in the country).

For the first time on screen—albeit the small screen—Reagan would play the role of a villain. The project was a two-hour movie for television starring John Cassavetes, Lee Marvin, and Angie Dickinson. The story was loosely based on Ernest Hemingway's *The Killers.*

When the completed film was deemed too violent for television, the studio released it theatrically. The 1964 action-adventure proved to be Ronald Reagan's last film, and to this day he reportedly regrets doing the picture. Meanwhile, Wyman continued to search for suitable acting assignments. A further sign of how radically times had changed was driven home one day by an incident that occurred on the Universal lot. Perc Westmore was there giving lectures and makeup demonstrations for the recently inaugurated Universal City Studios Tour.

Jane was horrified at what she considered the spectacle of her old friend Perc, the dean of the legendary Hollywood makeup wizards, delivering a spiel as if he were an open-air pitchman. She attempted to sneak away unnoticed, but Westmore spotted her. He raced over to her, grabbed her hand, dragged her in front of the audience, and told the crowd, "Always remember, ladies, if you look like Jane Wyman, don't wear any makeup at all."

The Hollywood that Jane—and Reagan—"grew up with" was obviously gone forever. While she has said in recent years she never wanted to appear in, nor ever liked, live theater, in 1964 she was for all practical purposes semiretired and there was talk that she would finally make her Broadway debut in a comedy, *Not in Her Stars*, with Anita Louise as her co-star and Nancy Walker as their director. The project never materialized.

Trouble on the home front had materialized, however. The Kargers were not getting along. In addition, her children were going through major changes. Michael had entered Arizona State University. His father paid for his tuition, but young Michael left ASU after only one semester and returned to Los Angeles to attend Los Angeles Valley College in Van Nuys. By now he was not receiving any financial help from either Jane or Ron, and he soon dropped out of Valley College as well.

Maureen, after her divorce, had returned to Los Angeles to try her hand in show business. Although no longer living in the nation's capital, Maureen found herself more and more interested in politics, but not to the exclusion of her personal life. On February 8, 1964, in Beverly Hills, she married David Sills.

For her second marriage Maureen decided to have a fancy lawn reception. Many people were surprised at the civility of the Wyman-Reagan divorce when they noted that Jane stood in the reception line and so did Ron *and* Nancy.

Maureen shared her interest in politics with her father. Few people today realize that it was not only Nancy Reagan and Neil Reagan but Maureen as well who was instrumental in her father's decision to become a serious candidate for public office. ("One thing I know about Maureen is that she will always be able to take care of herself," noted her father. "She has what in the old days we would call spunk; today they call it assertiveness.")

Reagan had switched over from the Democratic to the Republican party in the early 1960s. Although Ronald Reagan had spoken at national Republican conventions, most notably giving a speech later that year for Senator Barry Goldwater in his bid for the presidency, up until now no one had considered the actor (he was still an actor by profession) to be a serious candidate.

After the beating the Republicans took at the polls in the 1964 presidential election, California millionaire Republican Holmes P. Tuttle, along with A. C. ("Cy") Rubel and Henry Salvatori, decided to approach Reagan to be a Republican candidate in the next California gubernatorial election. After all, Reagan's old pal George Murphy had just been elected a U.S. Senator from California, proving that former actors could indeed successfully transfer to the arena of politics, so why shouldn't Ron be willing to try.

The Republicans hired a top political management firm, Spencer-Roberts, to mastermind Reagan's campaign. The Republican primary wasn't until the spring of 1966—but throughout 1965, Spencer-Roberts and the corps of Republican millionaires who had backed Reagan were working to make sure that he would win.

One can imagine their dismay when they picked up the newspapers in March 1965 to discover that Reagan's ex-wife was in the news. Her husband, Fred Karger, was suing for divorce, claiming that Jane had deserted him. Of course, Wyman soon countercharged "grievous mental cruelty," and claimed that Karger had "an uncontrollable temper."

From a political point of view, this publicity served negatively to remind voters that Ronald Reagan was a divorced man. However, the primary was still a year away and this was, after all, California, not the Bible Belt. One divorce did not ruin a politician's career in this part of the country.

From the Hollywood gossip point of view, the interesting aspect to the Wyman-Karger split was that he was divorcing her. This turnabout may have developed because it is very difficult for practicing Catholics—such as Wyman—to obtain permission to seek a civil divorce. And if Mr. Karger need not worry about the Catholic Church's attitude, it would be easier for him to seek and obtain the divorce.

Of course, the Catholic Church does not recognize any divorce —in its eyes a marriage is valid unless annulled by the Church. But under certain conditions "the Church permits an innocent and aggrieved party, whether wife or husband, to seek and obtain a civil divorce." Once divorced, a practicing Catholic may continue to receive the sacraments as long as he or she does not seek to remarry.

To this date, Miss Wyman has never again married. Karger remarried in later years, and remained married until his death of leukemia in 1979, at the age of sixty-three.

As with Wyman's divorce from Reagan, this breakup with Karger was not publicly discussed by either party involved, then or ever.

Jane returned to work—she had found a script she liked, one scheduled to be filmed for Bob Hope's *Chrysler Theatre*. In it she would play a farm woman, *circa* 1919. "I accepted the role because I liked the sort of woman I'm playing. I have no desire to play a part I can't be proud of." She defended her waiting around for the right script by saying, "Sometimes nonexposure is better than appearing in the wrong thing."

Returning to work after semiretirement was not easy, even for Jane Wyman. "You ask yourself if you've become rusty after three years away from the cameras. And that five A.M. call comes awfully early. But once I was down on the set and the first scene was shot, everything went beautifully."

The episode, entitled "When Hell Froze Over," had Jane playing a housewife who gives aid to a wandering war veteran. The cast also included Leslie Nielsen, Martin Milner, and Jeff Corey. Her return to TV was widely publicized, but now her name only appeared on the entertainment pages. Meanwhile, her ex-husband, Ronald Reagan, was making the front pages across the country. In January 1966, he announced what everyone was speculating: that he was going to compete in the upcoming primary to become the Republican candidate for governor of California.

Jane's episode on *Bob Hope Presents the Chrysler Theatre* was aired in February and she received excellent reviews. There was more talk of Broadway when a proposed play, *Wonderful Us* by Reginald Denham and Mary Orr, was mentioned for Jane. Orr had written the story, on which the legendary film *All About Eve* was based. This new play was heavy drama. In it Wyman would portray a reporter who tracks down a murderer. However, she did not appear in the play.

Instead she turned her attention to a nightclub act she was planning to do with Donald O'Connor. Jane had given up singing, and her recording contract, back in the mid-1950s when TV usurped most of her time. But now she would return to singing with this engagement. Describing the proposed act, Jane said, "I had the white furs and the Spanish guitars and I was going to make a very glamorous movie star entrance on a white staircase."

In June, Reagan won the primary and became the Republican candidate for governor. (One of the most oft-repeated stories in Hollywood is that when Jack Warner heard that Ronald Reagan was running for governor, he said, "Oh no, no. Jimmy Stewart for governor, Reagan for best friend.")

There was discussion on the Reagan staff as to how to present

Maureen and Michael, whose appearances would serve to point up the fact that the candidate was divorced and had children by both marriages. Jane's children might be further public relations problems in that Michael was considered "boisterous" and not of the image that the PR people wanted Reagan and his current family to project. Furthermore, twenty-five-year-old Maureen had already divorced her second husband.

It finally evolved that in their father's 1966 campaign for governor, Maureen and Michael were shunned by Reagan's people. "His managers were gun-shy about the divorce issue," Maureen has stated. "They sort of pretended that Michael and I didn't exist. I guess I understand."

Maureen, however, was proving herself a good politician. She was young and pretty (she looked very much like her mother), plus—like her father—she was a conservative in her political views. Maureen was also a good speaker and would ultimately prove to be a great asset to her father's political career.

While the candidate, along with his wife and children, was stumping the state for the November election, his famous ex-wife was preparing her Tahoe nightclub debut. But a week before the opening, Jane was rushed to Cedars of Lebanon Hospital in Los Angeles. "I got peritonitis of the pancreas and nearly died, so that was off," she later said.

So in the fall of that year, while Jane Wyman's career was temporarily in limbo, the new career of Ronald Reagan was launched spectacularly when he was elected governor of California by a huge margin.

As everyone now recognizes, Reagan's greatest asset as a candidate—at least in the earliest years—was his affinity for the camera. All his show business training in radio, movies, and television hadn't been wasted. Not since John Kennedy had there been an office seeker so photogenic and so capable of projecting likability and sincerity in a relaxed manner.

"Politics," said Reagan during this period, "is just like show business. You have a hell of an opening, you coast for a while, you have a hell of a closing."

Republican leaders across the country were eagerly thinking of Ronald Reagan in terms of national office.

THROUGH THE YEARS, MAUREEN REAGAN HAS bounced in and out of a career in show business, but she has always had Jane Wyman's support when working as an actress.

Several years ago Maureen had the lead in a San Diego dinner theater production of *Guys and Dolls*. Wyman naturally went to see her.

"Jane Wyman was in our group and sat at our table," recalls Jane Dulo, a leading character actress who has worked with some of the screen's great comedians, including Buster Keaton. Recalling the San Diego junket, Miss Dulo relates that "Jane was friendly and seemed very politically astute even though she says she isn't politically involved." After the performance, when Miss Dulo met Maureen, Miss Reagan made comments about Charles Chaplin being a Communist. "I laced into her," Miss Dulo recalls, and the two were arguing heatedly when Wyman turned to Dulo, patted her on the arm, and said kindly, "Don't waste your breath, honey." Miss Dulo's opinion is that Wyman had heard it all before and knew there was no point arguing politics with Maureen.

As an actress, "Maureen was damn good," according to Miss

Dulo. And like many in Hollywood, Dulo wonders why Maureen Reagan didn't pursue a career in show business.

For the past two decades Maureen has alternated between jobs in the entertainment world—actress, radio commentator, show business reporter for syndicated television shows—and positions in the business and political communities.

In the sixties, while her father was governor and a shining light of the Republican party, Maureen worked for PSA, the California airline, in a public relations position. Michael, then in his early twenties, was "racing boats for a living."

Jane Wyman's children were now making news far more than their mother because of their father's new prominence. Michael Reagan said he raced boats "to try to get an identity of my own." And Maureen Reagan was quoted as saying: "I have a career of my own and I'm getting awfully sick of being known as somebody's kid." Both of Jane's children were obviously searching for identities outside those of being the offspring of their famous parents.

It was inevitable, with her ex-husband in the governor's mansion, that there would be talk about Jane Wyman. In the first year Reagan was in office, there were whispers that he was giving Jane financial aid. Michael Reagan subsequently said that his father never gave his mother any money. Wyman never deigned to comment on these ridiculous rumors.

If there was any fear on the part of Reagan's key advisors that Wyman might exploit her position as the governor's ex-wife, Reagan certainly knew better. He and Jane were simply not the kind of people who would use each other in this way.

In fact, Jane kept a very low profile during the first year of Reagan's governorship. She obviously wanted to work, however, and was mentioned as Angela Lansbury's replacement in the Broadway hit *Mame.* "I sang a few songs for them—it was the first time in my life I ever auditioned for anything."

Show business executive Frank Little was at the audition and recalls, "She was fantastic. She looked wonderful and delivered a great performance. But it seemed to me the producers had already decided on someone else." What surprised Little was that in his opinion Wyman was treated like any other actress trying out for a part and not given the special treatment one assumes a former Academy Award winner should be accorded.

Jane later gave her explanation as to why she didn't get the part: "They were willing to give me only a week's rehearsal. I need a lot longer than that."

Then the actress turned her attention to a new and all-consuming activity: She began to work for the Arthritis Foundation. Many people thought (and still think) that Jane was working for this group because she herself suffered from arthritis. Such is not the case. What is true is that a close friend of hers had been stricken so severely that Wyman felt compelled to help. "I didn't even know how to spell arthritis before I became involved with the foundation," said Jane. "But it turned out to be rewarding and exhilarating because I was doing something that was contributive."

In 1968 she hosted the Southern California telethon to raise money to combat the disease, and she continued to do so yearly. Her free time was spent mostly painting and playing golf.

Her old pal Bob Hope sought Wyman for a part in a film he was making with Jackie Gleason, *How to Commit Marriage*. Originally Lana Turner, then Ava Gardner, had been mentioned for the role that now went to Jane. Wyman's waiting had paid off in one sense—this was a "class" production. Norman Panama was directing from a screenplay by Ben Starr and Michael Kanin. Wyman didn't try to make it appear she had been mulling over countless offers and finally settled on this one. At the time, she candidly noted, "This is the first movie I've been offered that I figured I could have a good time with, and working with Bob and Gleason is a ball. I'm not complaining."

Why had she waited so *long* to return to the big screen? "I dropped out for a while because all they offered me were ax-murderers and lesbians. I won't play lesbians, honey, not this kid," she told Rex Reed.

She certainly had no illusions about her status as a box office commodity: "The studios are afraid to hire the old stars because they're afraid we might bomb. Then they bring in people who bomb anyway because they have no experience."

Jane hated the implications that this film with Hope and Gleason was "a comeback." But she *had* been off the big screen for seven years, and admitted, "I haven't worked in so many years that I just wanted to get back in front of the cameras and see if I could do it. It's not a return. What do you call it? A reentrance? Anyway, it's a lot of fun, and comedy is harder to play than drama."

The film, like most of Hope's products in the late sixties, was overblown, half-baked, and a dud at the box office. Jane later astutely noted, "It was a Mickey Mouse job. It was dated stuff about gurus." She did a Bob Hope special that year, however, to publicize the film.

Although she tried, Jane couldn't totally avoid questions about the governor of California. She wouldn't discuss issues, but Earl Wilson got her to talk about one subject. There was a burning question about Ronald Reagan that was sweeping the country: Did he dye his hair?

"Ron dye his hair!" exclaimed Jane. "Oh, no. The Reagans have marvelous hair. Ron's the image of his father, who didn't have more than about three gray hairs when he died. I don't think Ron has a gray hair in his head and never will have more than two or three. I wish," Miss Wyman added, "I could say the same."

In 1970, Jane Wyman appeared with old friends Fred MacMur-ray and William Demarest on an episode of MacMurray's hit television series, *My Three Sons*. She played a flamboyant old girl friend of MacMurray's—sort of a brunette reincarnation of the dumb-bunny blondes she had created so memorably in Warner Bros. films more than thirty years earlier.

Maureen, during this period, was becoming more and more involved in political issues of the day, even traveling with the USO on a thirty-five-day tour of Vietnam. Like many who visited Vietnam at that time, Maureen returned with very definite and outspoken views on America's involvement there. Her trip deepened her commitment to politics and, in her words, "getting people involved in their government." She campaigned valiantly for her father, and in November, Ronald Reagan was elected to his second term as governor of California.

The following year Jane Wyman did a motion picture–for–television, *The Failing of Raymond*. It had a top-notch cast: Wyman, Dean Stockwell, Dana Andrews, Paul Henreid. It was a thriller about a teacher (Jane) who is at the mercy of a former dropout student—now a mental patient—whom she had flunked ten years earlier. The production was ably directed by Boris Sagal.

Despite later statements and denials, it seems clear that Jane was interested, in the early seventies, in getting back to television on a full-time basis. In late 1971 she filmed an episode of *The Bold Ones* in which she played a pediatrician, Dr. Amanda Fallon. Mike Farrell and David Hartman portrayed fellow doctors. Jane's character was treating a fourteen-year-old (Ron Howard) who was suffering from bleeding ulcers. The boy's father was played by Jim Davis. Unfortunately for Jane, the attempt to spin off "Dr. Amanda Fallon" into its own series did not succeed.

Jane continued her work for the Arthritis Foundation and later confessed that when she had begun working for the foundation, "I didn't really know too much about arthritis, but I decided to do my best, and the next thing I knew I was the national chairman. . . . I certainly didn't plan it that way, but I've enjoyed it because we have accomplished wonderful things."

Another attempt at creating a television series for Wyman was made the following year in another episode of *The Bold Ones*, with Jane again playing Dr. Amanda Fallon. Again, a superb cast had been assembled: Pat O'Brien, Leslie Nielsen, Kathleen Nolan, Steve Dunne. Once again, however, the proposed spin-off did not materialize.

Jane worked on other television programs. She appeared in an episode of *The Sixth Sense* on ABC, followed by an episode of *Owen Marshall.* Then she starred in a drama on the syndicated religious series *Insight.*

In 1975, Ronald Reagan completed his second and last term as governor and returned to private life. Although Miss Wyman would certainly take issue with the supposition that her career as an actress and his career as a politician in the 1960s and 1970s had any link, after Reagan left office Wyman seemed to fall back into semiretirement.

Reagan, however, was rising fast in national political ranks. He soon announced he would challenge incumbent President Gerald Ford for the 1976 Republican presidential nomination.

Meanwhile, Michael Reagan (who back in 1971 had married for the first time—his wife was a dental assistant) had divorced and remarried. This time all the Reagans campaigned for Ron's nomination, with the entire family often presented as a single unit. Even at the Republican convention that year, when interviewed by reporters, Maureen Reagan would say in referring to the family, "My father and mother," rather than "My father and stepmother."

In a bitterly fought battle, Ronald Reagan, who was viewed as an ultraconservative, narrowly lost the nomination to Ford. But when Ford lost the national election to Jimmy Carter, the road ahead was clear. The Reagan family was now politically seasoned enough to know their time was imminent.

Jane Wyman seemed totally out of the picture. She had moved from Los Angeles to Carmel, a beautiful, serene seaside community near Monterey, California. She appeared finally to be joining the ranks of others of her era by being seen only on telethons or attending awards ceremonies, premieres, or tributes to other former stars. Wyman was at the American Film Institute's tribute to Bette Davis in March 1977, and at the Directors Guild salute to Clarence Brown (director of *The Yearling*) in early 1978.

She had let her hair go totally gray and was spending most of her time in Carmel, painting. She was now sixty-four years old and it certainly seemed that the career of Jane Wyman, actress, was over. The age-old cycle seemed to be complete: in the life of a celebrity there are four phases: Who's Jane Wyman? Get me Jane Wyman! Get me a young Jane Wyman! Who's Jane Wyman?

In the mid-1970s, painting had become her passion. All the energy and concentration that had been focused on her career now seemed to center around creating her canvases. The rewards, however, obviously weren't sufficient to sustain the intensity of her commitment: "I really enjoyed it at first. Then it became a trap. I was painting eight hours a day, sometimes into the night. Finally, I just packed up my paints and put them away."

Since Ronald Reagan was obviously going to continue to seek the presidency, Jane was still sought for comments on her ex-husband's political career—she wouldn't ever discuss it. She had once said, "It's not because I'm bitter or because I disagree with him politically. I've always been a registered Republican. But it's bad taste to talk about ex-husbands and ex-wives, that's all."

She stood by this statement. And if she and Reagan had been childless, undoubtedly the connection between them in the public's mind would have faded with the years. But this was not the case, and invariably their names would always be linked.

Maureen Reagan was more and more in the spotlight. She became friends with Judy Carter, wife of President Carter's oldest son, Jack. They met in Indiana in 1977 when both were stumping for the Equal Rights Amendment. Mrs. Carter said that Maureen is "fiercely loyal" to Ronald Reagan in spite of their political disagreements. And she also noted that "Maureen claims to be a doting aunt for her brother Michael's son." Jane and Ron had become grandparents on May 30, 1978, when their daughter-in-law, Colleen, gave birth to a boy.

Ironically, it was Ronald Reagan's children by Jane who were now providing the "traditional" image. Michael was happily married and a father; Maureen was a successful single business-woman. Reagan's children with Nancy, however, were now perceived as "rebels" and were leading life-styles very different from those of their conservative Republican parents.

In the final analysis, however, this situation only seemed to add color and humanity, not controversy, to the aura of Ronald Reagan.

Some political analysts have suggested that at the beginning of his political career, Ronald Reagan just "let it happen," that he did not take the initiative in seeking public office. However, if that was true before his election as governor, after eight years in Sacramento the political bug had certainly bitten Mr. Reagan and he had set his sights on the presidency. The sixty-seven-year-old former actor was now exhibiting fierce career ambitions.

Jane Wyman's fierce career aspirations, years before, had been labeled the reason for her breakup with Reagan. But by the late 1970s, Jane's career seemed to mean little to her. She said, concerning a possible return to films, "I'm just not that ambitious anymore. I'm through clawing after parts. I've got other things going."

When a part did come along, however, Jane certainly was available. Television producer Ron Samuels approached her in mid-1978 about a script he was prepping for a three-hour television movie-of-the-week. It was a property that could spin off into a potential series for Jane, *The Incredible Journey of Dr. Meg Laurel.* Lindsay Wagner would play the lead, and get top billing. Jane would be billed second, as "Miss Jane Wyman." It was a character part, to be sure, but one that promised to get all the attention and reviews. And indeed it did.

The story concerned Meg Laurel (Wagner), an idealistic young female doctor who in 1931 leaves her Boston practice and returns to her roots in Appalachia. Before she can get through to the townspeople, Meg must first make a separate peace with feisty old Granny Arrowroot (Wyman), a practitioner of folk medicine. The film was shot near Nevada City in northern California in an effort to re-create the proper woodsy effect, and Dorothy McGuire, Brock Peters, Andrew Duggan, Gary Lockwood, and James Woods rounded out the top-notch cast.

When the picture was aired, Jane's reviews were spectacular. Judith Crist wrote: "Jane Wyman as the local medicine woman is simply firstrate." The *Hollywood Reporter* said that Jane, as "a backwoods granny doctor, manifests a credible sturdiness and wisdom." *Variety* noted that the story was "upgraded by a very professional reading of the healer's part by Wyman," and that Wyman's "underplaying" was responsible for "saving" what could have been "cornpone dialogue."

Her old pal Aaron Spelling, now a top TV producer, contacted Jane. He wanted her for a *Love Boat* segment that would reteam her with Dennis Morgan; they would play childhood sweethearts who meet in old age. Jane's first reaction: What in the world would she do on *The Love Boat*? But then Spelling told her the twist: She'd be playing the part of a nun.

In Jane's words: "A nun? But then I thought, why not?"

The *Love Boat* episode was aired in early 1980, and Spelling then inked Jane for an episode of *Charlie's Angels,* which was then in its fifth season. Jane played a small role, that of a psychic. It appeared that if she chose to continue her career, all that lay ahead would be cameo roles in television fare, with her around to give the programs a touch of glamour and name value.

The presidential primaries of 1980 had fallen into place. Michael and Maureen were widely covered by the press as they campaigned for their father. They joined their half brother and half sister, Patti and Ron and their stepmother, Nancy, in Detroit that July for the Republican National Convention and Ronald Reagan's nomination to run for President. Reagan proudly displayed his children and his only grandchild, Cameron.

Jane avoided giving any interviews during the year. When, in November 1980, Ronald Reagan was elected to the most prestigious and powerful office in the world, Wyman was once again a star—but, for the moment, by reflection.

Although she had made every effort to avoid the tidal wave of attention poised to roll her way, she was inevitably caught up in it.

And Wyman was not the kind of person who was unprepared for what might be ahead.

12

JANE WAS TRACKED DOWN BY THE PRESS SHORTLY AFter the election. She was quick to tell reporters that she had "no regrets" about not being the First Lady: "Oh no, the White House is not for me. . . . Mark you, I have perfectly wonderful memories of him. We are good friends and we will always remain good friends."

President-elect Reagan, even before his inauguration, revealed his true feelings about being a divorced man: "I was divorced in the sense that the decision was made by somebody else."

Michael and Maureen (and Michael's family) naturally attended their father's inauguration in January 1981. The appearance that the Reagans were a devoted, united family was not exactly accurate—the Reagan children are "unforgiving with each other in some respects," according to many reports.

Michael has said that in campaigning, "Sometimes I felt like I was fighting to volunteer." He guessed that it made his father "look old, having older children," and reasoned that "Headquarters may feel it's embarrassing if Maureen and I are in the forefront and the real kids are not."

However, the "real" kids (Reagan's two offspring by Nancy) were not as interested in campaigning for their father in his presidential bid as were Maureen and Michael. Maureen was critical of Patti's attitude in the 1980 campaign—"I don't know what she means when she says that she's not political. She's out getting signatures when it's something she believes in."

A few weeks after the inauguration, Ronald Reagan celebrated his seventieth birthday. Historians would soon note several "firsts" regarding Reagan and the presidency. He was: the oldest president ever inaugurated; the first president to be born in Illinois; the first president to have headed a union; and the first president to have been divorced.

Meanwhile, Jane, sixty-seven, was going back to work. Her professional situation was shrewdly summed up by one industry insider's observation: "There's no disputing that Jane Wyman is a top-notch actress, but her current status, as President Reagan's first wife, isn't hurting her show-biz marketability."

Lorimar, one of the most successful producers of TV programs in the industry *(The Waltons, Dallas, Knot's Landing)* had signed Wyman for a proposed series, *The Vintage Years,* to be produced by Earl Hamner. It would be set in California's wine country.

The leading character, Angela Channing, in the words of CBS and Lorimar, was: "A strong-willed matriarch of a legendary vineyard—brooding in the mansion on the hill, empress of a vineyard kingdom but determined to enlarge her power further still (even if it means driving her own nephew off his land)." Angela was tough and ruthless, qualities hardly typified by Jane Wyman's most memorable characterizations in films. She seemed a character more suited to the style of actresses like Bette Davis, Anne Baxter, or Eleanor Parker.

However, Wyman had represented a special image to moviegoers of the 1940s, and her women's audience had followed her into the 1950s and 1960s, on television as well as in films. Lorimar was obviously hoping that Jane Wyman of the

1980s had retained that older female following—women, who along with their daughters and granddaughters, were the backbone of nighttime soap opera audiences.

In casting Wyman, Hamner had chosen someone with name value. In his words: "We wanted a star of Jane's stature, and certainly she comes from a legendary time in filmmaking." But Hamner also wanted, and needed, another quality Jane possessed, a quality that had served her well through four decades— her likability. "For all of her power and seeming ruthlessness," Hamner says of dowager Angela Channing, "The audience must *like* Angie—and who could not like Jane Wyman?"

The role of Angela certainly offered Wyman a challenge. "I read the pilot script . . . and all of a sudden, it just struck a bell," she later stated. "I thought, 'Well, I've always done the four-handkerchief hits—you know, everybody walking outside and saying, "Wasn't it marvelous?" . . . In contrast, Angie Channing is a very heads-up lady, so why don't we just go ahead and play her? I really like her. A lot. She's very much a 1981 kind of lady. You just can't miss on a thing like this. You really can't. If you do, you're dumb."

And no one has ever accused Jane Wyman of being dumb.

To co-star with Wyman in *The Vintage Years* pilot, Lorimar signed Clu Gulager and Samantha Eggar. The group was up in the California wine country filming the show when they, and the rest of the world, received the shocking news that President Reagan had been shot in the chest by a would-be assassin. At this point he had only been president for two months and nine days.

Reagan had again made the record books. He was the eighth president to be the victim of an assassination attempt while in office, but he was the only president to survive a wound.

After the assassination attempt, Jane momentarily abandoned her "no comment" attitude: "Thank God he was alive. That was a very dramatic thing." It was impossible not to answer the inevitable next question: How did she think her former husband was handling the job of president? "I think he's doing a marvelous job, I really do. We're very good friends and I just adore him."

As soon as the President's health was no longer an issue—he was in extraordinary physical condition for a man his age and made a remarkably fast recovery—the burning question among some became, Would he attend his daughter Maureen's upcoming wedding in California? Maureen Reagan, now forty, was engaged to a young law clerk, Dennis Revell, twelve years younger than she. They had known each other for years, having met via the Young Republican Club when her father was still governor.

The wedding was going to be a ticklish social situation for President and Mrs. Reagan. This would be Maureen's third marriage, and one of the guests, naturally, would be Jane. In addition, the wedding was not going to be a quiet affair. There were more than 365 people invited to the reception at the Trianon Room of the Beverly Wilshire Hotel, and Jane was throwing a small dinner for twenty at the Beverly Hills Rangoon Racquet Club the night before the wedding.

Naturally, after the attempted assassination all the Reagan children had immediately been surrounded by Secret Service agents, and reports were that Jane, too, was surrounded by the Secret Service "after the assassination attempt on her ex-husband," while she was "trying to finish the arrangements for the wedding, and to complete fittings."

The White House announced officially that the President would not make the trip. But other reports said that friends of the family expected him to be in attendance. "Moon" and his wife, Bess, would of course be there.

On April 24, Maureen became Mrs. Dennis Revell. Uncle "Moon" escorted Maureen down the aisle. Michael and his family were present. But everyone noted that Patti and "Skip" were not in attendance, and the President and First Lady had stayed in Washington. The President phoned his congratulations.

After the reception the couple left for their honeymoon to Europe. Six Secret Service agents traveled with them.

In addition to a new husband, Maureen had a new job. She was now president of an organization called Sell Overseas America, whose object was to boost U.S. exports. But her interest in politics and her father's stunning victory had intrigued Maureen with the idea of running for U.S. Senator from California on the Republican ticket. Her father was not happy about the possibility that she would pursue this matter.

Nor was Ronald Reagan happy when it was revealed that Michael had written a letter while vice-president of sales for Dana Ingalls Profile, Inc., which began with the statement "I know that with my father's leadership in the White House, the Armed Services are going to be rebuilt and strengthened. We at Dana Ingalls Profile want to be involved in that process."

The President was understandably embarrassed and Michael subsequently retracted the letter with a statement to the effect that he had not thought the matter out and was misusing his family relationship.

Michael continued receiving adverse publicity about certain business dealings. One case involved a gasohol project. Another involved stock fraud, in which young Reagan was a victim. All the press coverage was disturbing to Michael and his family. "I was vindicated," Michael noted, "but it was maddening. I got more publicity than the average man. It upset me, it affected my wife and child."

Meanwhile, CBS Television bought *The Vintage Years*. Robert Raison, Jane's agent, announced that there had been "some conceptual changes in the series." In the new version, Wyman's character would be stressed and several characters who were predominant in the pilot would be eliminated or downplayed.

The story, however, would still focus on Angela Channing trying to "drive her nephew off his land." One television reporter noted, "Wyman apparently *drives* very well where land and series are concerned," implying that to keep Wyman, major changes in the program had been made. Clu Gulager and Samantha Eggar were out. Even the title was being discarded. There was talk that the producers would expand the locale from the Napa Valley to nearby San Francisco and set Wyman up in a swank Frisco apartment. It was obvious they wanted the character to be a female J. R. Ewing, the highly popular villain on the series *Dallas.* Wyman's Angela had to be treacherous, conniving, and yet still vulnerable.

The show went into production. Abby Dalton would play Wyman's alcoholic daughter; Margaret Ladd won the role of Jane's mentally ill daughter. Robert Foxworth and soap opera star Susan Sullivan would play Wyman's nephew and his wife. Lorenzo Lamas, the handsome young son of Arlene Dahl and Fernando Lamas, would play Angela's grandson. Jamie Rose and Billy R. Moses played Sullivan and Foxworth's grown children.

The series went into production under its new title, *Falcon Crest.* CBS was scheduling it as a possible midseason entry.

From the absolute beginning Wyman was involved in the creative process. Wyman, who has a dry sense of humor and is a master of understatement, will say things like: "I'm not a stranger to this business." Comments such as these give everyone concerned with the series pause to reflect that Wyman *must* know more than they.

"It's the old voice of experience," quips someone on the production staff, "and we'd be fools not to listen."

The late Fernando Lamas directed several episodes of *Falcon Crest.* There have been other guest directors as well. Generally the work goes smoothly and according to schedule. Although the script is trite and senseless, the producers have always had the good sense to hire top-notch actors to read the inane lines.

Jane approaches her role as a job—she takes pride in her performances but has little use for the usual Hollywood flattery. Someone frequently present on the set recalls that on more than one occasion, when complimented on her work, Jane has snapped, "Of course it was good."

"She's a no-nonsense tough cookie on that set," notes a crew member.

Meanwhile, daughter Maureen continued to make news on her own by announcing that she was seeking the bid for the Republican nomination to the U.S. Senate from the state of California. It was a wide-open race. Incumbent Senator S. I. Hayakawa was being challenged in the Republican primary by a field of other candidates.

Jane Wyman wouldn't publicly endorse Maureen. She later noted, "I never get involved in politics. I hate politics, and Maureen knows it. She said, 'Well, Mother, couldn't you just say that I belong to you?' I told her, 'I've done that, I've said, *That's my daughter!* But I've never been political, and I don't intend to start now—or ever."

Maureen's father was taciturn but vocal about Maureen's ambition. When asked if his daughter was going to run for the Senate, President Reagan commented, "I hope not."

Uncle "Moon" was more vocal: "Just because your father is president is no reason to get very busy and very ambitious." In fact, he co-chaired the campaign of one of the other candidates, San Diego Mayor Pete Wilson. Subsequently, Maureen was soundly defeated in the primary and to this date has not again sought public office.

In early December, CBS debuted *Falcon Crest,* cleverly programming it to follow *Dallas* on Friday nights. Both shows combined would provide viewers with two solid hours of serial entertainment.

John J. O'Connor, the *New York Times* television critic, observed that *Falcon Crest* was "the standard stuff of soaps with a crisis bubble bursting at least three times between commercial breaks." Of its star, he noted: "Adding a fillip of interest to the project, Angie is played by Jane Wyman, the former Mrs. Ronald

Reagan." O'Connor related the plot of the first episode and concluded: "Everybody keeps telling steely-eyed Angie what a gracious hostess she is. At the fadeout, she is meaningfully stroking a live falcon on the grounds of her estate. The stage is set for anything. Miss Wyman seems to be in remarkable control."

As always, once Wyman commits herself to a new project she throws herself into it wholeheartedly. Sources say she is constantly working on bits of business for the character she portrays. She concerns herself with all aspects of the character's psychological makeup and physical appearance. She personally chooses Angela Channing's wardrobe—"I found a little wholesale house that makes the most charming and aristocratic suits, very 'new' looking, very tailored, but very lovely and feminine."

All her years of experience in crafting a character were brought into play. Almost instantly, *Falcon Crest* was a success with TV audiences. Wyman later related how her daughter had phoned her: "Maureen's so funny. She called after *Falcon Crest* first came on and said, 'Well, mother, the world knows you're still here.' "

Wyman was more than just *here*—she fast became one of TV's leading stars. Her face was soon back on national magazine covers and in newspapers across the country.

With *Falcon Crest*, Jane was top-billed, just as in the old days. This was no second-billing situation, as with *Meg Laurel*, and no last-billed "And Miss Jane Wyman as Angela Channing" to set her apart.

From the beginning, the other cast members of the show were very respectful toward Wyman. However, the cast and crew genuinely like her.

Co-star Abby Dalton admitted that Wyman was demanding and wanted perfection, but said: "She's a realist, but she wants everyone around her to do everything they can to make it good." According to Miss Dalton, although Jane was receptive "and open and very social," the star was someone "you really don't get close to." In Miss Dalton's opinion, "She's just private and observes all of the protocol until she gets to know and trust you. Then she's willing to show you just a little more of herself. She's very careful. I think she has to be. I think she resents being referred to as someone's ex-wife, and why shouldn't she?"

Billy R. Moses has noted that Jane sometimes directed the other actors: "If she doesn't like what you're doing, she'll tell you right away." Moses has said that it's "a little disconcerting at first —you don't often have the other actor directing you—but you relax and you roll with the punches and you learn."

Lorenzo Lamas has observed: "She never actually pressures changes, but people on the set feel compelled to listen."

Because of Jane's connection to Reagan, there were inevitable pitfalls for *Falcon Crest*'s co-stars when they were interviewed.

Susan Sullivan appeared on the *Tonight* show hosted by Joan Rivers, and the irrepressible—and more than occasionally irreverent—Rivers lost no time in asking about Jane Wyman: "Do you ever call her 'Second Lady'?"

"She would have been a superb First Lady," replied Miss Sullivan, unflustered. "She's very smart."

"Ever talked politics with her?" pressed the blond comedienne.

"Never. I like my job," answered Miss Sullivan, tongue-in-cheek. She added: "She has a way of letting you know she doesn't want to talk about something. Her face expression changes."

Joan Rivers was undaunted. "Ever say, 'Who you gonna vote for?—whoops!' . . . I guess the IRS is never gonna audit her! Bet she wishes she never had that last argument!" quipped Rivers.

While the Reagan connection might have caused some viewers to tune in to *Falcon Crest* out of curiosity, there was no doubt that the show, and Wyman, had clicked on their own. Wyman, in fact, seems to be the catalyst that holds the show's synthetic story together. All the actors are first-rate, but many reviewers and fans alike agree that *Falcon Crest* scripts are not in the same league with those of *Dallas* and not even as good as those of other nighttime soaps such as Knot's Landing or *Dynasty.*

And from the beginning there was no doubt who the star off-camera was. Assistant cameraman Steve Wollenberg noted: "When you work with Jane, you dance to her tune. But it's a pleasant tune. She's a very sweet, no-nonsense woman, but that does not detract from the softness of the person. Jane's a star, there's no question about it. She stems from the old star system, but in no way is she a prima donna."

Then another star from the old system joined the group. As with most soap operas, *Falcon Crest* constantly adds new and dramatic characters to keep up viewer interest. Toward the end of the first season, the "dazzling, glamorous" character of "Jacqueline Perrault"—Angela's sister-in-law—made her debut. If one big star from an earlier era meant big ratings, then perhaps two big stars would lure even more viewers. In a move *Falcon Crest*'s producers hoped would result in lots of publicity, Lana Turner, the screen's former golden girl, was signed to portray Jacqueline.

In fact, signing Lana produced far more attention and publicity than Lorimar could possibly have anticipated. The time was obviously right for renewed interest in Turner. The seven-times-married-and-divorced, plagued-by-scandal star was writing her memoirs, an eagerly awaited event. And apparently the public was fascinated and intrigued by Lana's pending reemergence on the small screen via *Falcon Crest.*

Turner was seven years younger than Wyman. She had not been on television in years, and, to the surprise of many, was successfully performing in the medium Jane Wyman had never entered—live theater. By now people had forgotten that Lana had had her own series, *The Survivors,* back in 1969, and that it had fared disastrously. Somehow, Turner had never permitted the aura of glamour that surrounded her to dim.

It may have been a long time since Lana had had a screen hit, but in true movie star fashion her demands to appear on *Falcon Crest* were almost the same as in her heyday, including a limousine to be available to her at all times.

Like Jane Wyman, Lana Turner was a big favorite with women. To many fans the pairing was exciting; they seemed perfectly matched adversaries. It was to be the blonde who had been Hollywood's premiere sex symbol versus the brunette who epitomized cinema class and dignity.

Offscreen, however, there were major differences between the two ladies.

Wyman was gracious with Lana and both posed together for widely circulated publicity pictures. When reporters on the *Falcon Crest* set later queried Miss Turner about "dates" she had been reported to have had years ago with Ronald Reagan, Lana replied she hadn't dated him, it had all been publicity—but Lana's mother was quoted as saying Lana *had* dated Reagan.

That Lana Turner and members of her family were publicly discussing Ronald Reagan was not, one must assume, appreciated by Jane Wyman. (Susan Sullivan has stated: "Jane never mentions Reagan and nobody ever brings it up.") It is also likely that Wyman did not appreciate the fact that all of Miss Turner's "star" demands were so readily met by *Falcon Crest*'s producers.

Contrary to gossip, however, Wyman was hardly wary of Lana Turner taking over her territory. She was too secure—and too professional. It was only good business sense that anything that made *Falcon Crest* a continuing big attraction was good for everyone connected with the show.

Susan Sullivan has provided a fascinating "inside" perspective on how the two stars differed. Discussing Lana, she observed, "She's really of another era, another style of acting, another style of working. It's fascinating to watch."

Were there any problems between Wyman and Lana? According to Sullivan, "They appeared to get along. But I couldn't tell if they liked each other or not. Their personalities are so very different. Jane, who chalked up considerable television experience fifteen years ago, likes to play poker with the crew on lunch breaks, and Lana stays very much to herself. They're from the same Hollywood period but it's interesting to watch them because their styles are so different. Lana likes to retain the glamorous star image."

Jane was not averse to projecting a glamorous star image herself when the occasion warranted it. Miss Sullivan has recalled a CBS affiliates meeting: "Jane appeared on stage in a long gown and a white ermine wrap and the affiliate members went wild. They loved it. She got a loud ovation. She's still very much the star."

It turned out that Lana Turner's appearance on *Falcon Crest* *did* raise the show's ratings. The first episode Turner appeared on was one of the highest-rated since the series' debut. She was immediately set for five more appearances for the next season; but by then there was definitely no love lost between Jane Wyman and Lana Turner.

When questioned as to whether Jane and Lana's "feud" was real or merely publicity, one crew member, who requests anonymity, says: "Let's put it this way—between shots one afternoon the boy was setting up chairs for the cast and Wyman saw her chair next to Lana's and said, 'Move me into the other room.' She was never bitchy, but she let it be known that she thought Lana's star demands were pretty foolish. And then . . . of course . . . she simply wanted everything that Lana got. If Turner had a limo to pick her up in the mornings, then Jane wanted one too. Before then—and by the way, since then—Wyman's always driven herself to work."

"You know exactly where you stand with her," series producer Earl Hamner has noted. "She tells you what she knows and how she feels about things. It's been an honest relationship from the very beginning. I suspect her input will always be affirmative and useful, and I certainly plan to listen to it."

While it had appeared to the industry that Lana Turner was to become a semi-regular on *Falcon Crest*, her character was killed off at the end of the second season and literally buried at the start of the third. (This, of course, does not preclude—in true soap opera fashion—Miss Turner's twin sister from visiting the show at some future point.)

Of the incident, respected TV columnist Kay Gardella wrote that Turner "lasted just one season before her 'big star' act got under the skin of the show's star, Jane Wyman, referred to as 'The Iron Lady.'" From this point on Wyman's reputation became that of one who had both the desire and *the power* to control who would be signed for the show.

When talking with people who are involved with *Falcon Crest*, a clear picture emerges that Jane Wyman is, as the popular press is so eager to report, a benevolent dowager empress. If she rules over her minions, she does so with grace and humor, and from the point of view that she has the experience to know what is right and the ability to correct what is wrong.

As with all actresses whose private lives have been lived more or less in public over a long period of years, Wyman sometimes speaks lines as her character that fans are sure reflect her *real* feelings. For example, Angela Channing has dialogue such as: "Every time I've ever cared for anybody, I've lived to regret it"; and, "I, and I alone, am responsible for the survival of Falcon Crest. I don't need any of them."

In her private life, Jane continues to quietly work for various charities, including speaking at Catholic fund-raisers. A woman who is involved in Catholic Charities states that "Jane is a lovely woman, always gracious and giving of her time. An excellent speaker. On one occasion she had to rush through a speech and leave early, because she had to get to the hospital to see her new grandchild."

Michael's wife, Colleen, had given birth to their second child. Subsequently, Michael Reagan revealed that his father had not displayed enough interest in this new granddaughter, Ashley, even to make an effort to see the baby. However, Ronald Reagan writes to Michael's children. He sends the notes on White House stationery, and after signing them "Love—Grandpa," he puts a dash and adds—"Ronald Reagan." Michael has said, "This is his way of giving his grandchildren a piece of Americana. Dad jokes that it's also a way of paying for their college education—if they want to sell the letters."

Michael Reagan feels he has "inherited" his father's sense of humor but also his mother's "steadiness," and he classifies himself and Wyman by saying: "We're both thinkers."

In a sense, Jane Wyman represents a typical, astute mother of grown children. She is there when they need or want her for moral and emotional support, but she does not interfere in their day-to-day lives—nor do they in hers. She keeps in touch with her children and undoubtedly has a sense of humor about them and is not judgmental—at least not publicly so.

Away from the set, Wyman lives quietly in an apartment in Beverly Hills. "I prefer it to a house because I can just pack my bags, lock the door, and go out. I don't have to worry about gardeners, dogs, and whatnot." She loves to read and has said she barely watches TV. Although she is the focal point on her television show, she has noted, "Working on the series isn't strenuous and I wouldn't have taken it if the emphasis had been on me alone."

Wyman, of course, has no control over the continual linking of her name with Reagan's. She often gets peeved when questioned about her relationship with her former husband, and has been known to turn on her heel and silently walk away from an interviewer who breaks the unspoken rule and asks her questions about her old marriage. Someone close to Wyman says: "She feels that all ended thirty-seven years ago and has nothing to do with her life today."

Sometimes the linking of the Wyman-Reagan names is humorous. In November 1983, *The Wall Street Journal* carried a front-page story with the headline: THIS PRESIDENTIAL CANDIDATE WANTS JANE WYMAN AS HIS RUNNING MATE. It seems that Richard Grayson, a thirty-two-year-old former English teacher, had decided to run for president. He apparently had quit his teaching job to pursue a career as humorist and author, but in the meantime was collecting unemployment benefits. Hounded by the unemployment office to prove he was looking for work, he had decided that his new job would be seeking the presidency, and he announced that as his running mate he would draft Jane Wyman, "because she has experience dumping Ronald Reagan."

Over the next few months, this story was rehashed in other publications. It was no wonder that people in the media found Jane a "tough interview." She became even more wary because she knew the inevitable questions about Reagan would arise. Consequently, she does *very* few interviews.

As to her personal life and the possibility of her remarrying, she has recently said: "I still think marriage is a marvelous thing. But for me—at my age, my stage in life—I don't want to get involved again. I just have too much fun being single. I enjoy coming and going as I please."

While marriage was not on Jane's personal agenda, on the show it would be a major plot point when Wyman, as Angela Channing, wed *Falcon Crest* lawyer Phillip Ericson, portrayed by Mel Ferrer. (Of course, the plot called for Angela to marry not only for love but for power.)

All along, the characters' relationship had been depicted in a frank and rather "modern" manner. It was perfectly clear on more than one occasion that Phillip Ericson was an overnight guest at Falcon Crest, and that he had not occupied one of the many guest bedrooms. When, at the end of an evening, he accompanied Angela Channing upstairs, it was her young grandson (portrayed by Lorenzo Lamas) who strongly—and usually silently—disapproved!

The "wedding" between Angela and Phillip provided Jane's fans the opportunity to see a lavish, let's-pull-out-all-the-stops grand wedding with Jane in a long, elaborate beige gown and veil. It was a scene worthy of any movie star of *any* era. Jane's friend, handsome Catholic priest Robert Curtis, portrayed the priest and performed the "marriage" on this particular episode. (Father Bob Curtis had also presided over Lana Turner's "funeral" when Jacqueline Perrault was laid to rest.)

With the marriage episode, it seemed as if Ferrer's role was assured on the continuing soap. However, at the end of the third season, in true serial fashion, there was a cliffhanger finish. The characters played by Ferrer and actor Cliff Robertson were, along with other major members of the cast including Wyman, involved in a plane crash. Would all—or none—return to the show the following season?

The question was soon answered when news leaked out that Ferrer had been written out of *Falcon Crest*. Supposedly the actor was surprised—he and Jane had become friends, and he apparently assumed that he was guaranteed a spot on the show. Once again Jane was painted by the popular press as being instrumental in the demise of a co-star's character, and her "Iron Lady" tag was reactivated. There is little doubt that this publicity helps the audience identify the actress with the character of Angela Channing and may even contribute to the series' high ratings. Each time a new star has joined *Falcon Crest*, there has been speculation as to whether Jane would "approve."

In the spring of 1984, Sophia Loren was announced as a potential co-star on the series. There followed a good deal of publicity alleging that Wyman was unhappy about this choice, and Loren subsequently did not join the show. Sources report, however, that the decision had nothing to do with Wyman but rather was due to Loren's extraordinary salary demands.

Soon thereafter Gina Lollobrigida was signed for the part that Loren was to have done, that of Angela's half sister. Instantly the former sex symbol from Italy was deluged with questions about "The Iron Lady."

"Why should I be intimidated?" said the gorgeous fifty-six-year-old Lollobrigida, looking not too different than she had in her heyday. "I think she's a lovely lady and a beautiful actress. It will be a pleasure to work with her and the entire cast." Lollobrigida was subsequently most definite and vocal on one point: *She* would *not* be permanently written out of the show at the end of the season.

Around this time it was reported that Ginger Rogers was tested for the proposed role of Susan Sullivan's mother. The legendary Miss Rogers, of course, belongs to the crème de la crème of Hollywood's "old society." She is occasionally even a visitor at the White House. However, after she made the test, it was announced that the blond septuagenarian would not be joining *Falcon Crest*—she was "not quite the right type" for the role. Instead, Jane Greer, a popular RKO leading lady in the late 1940s, got the part.

Wyman agreed to publicize the launching of the fourth season of *Falcon Crest* and appeared on Merv Griffin's TV talk show. There was to be no talk of politics or of her private life, of course. Jane and Merv (whom she had known since they worked together thirty years ago at Warner Bros.) chatted amiably about wine, restaurants, and such. They carefully skirted most aspects of her private life.

However, unwanted publicity linking Wyman's name with Reagan's soon made its way into newspapers and newsmagazines. The public was alerted that there was a major rift between Jane's son, Michael Reagan, and the First Family. While Jane had retained close ties with Michael and his wife and children, Reagan apparently hadn't. Ultimately, it was a situation that was to result in embarrassment to the president.

During Ronald Reagan's reelection campaign of 1984, political analyst Lou Cannon of *The Washington Post* noted: "There are those even in the Reagan camp who are offended by the contradictions between Reagan's espousal of 'family values' on the stump and the remote relationships he has with some members of his family. He has rarely seen his only grandson, and confused his name when they met."

In early 1984, when President Reagan's staff knew he would be seeking a second term, there was again concern about Maureen's outspokenness. Terry Dolan, whom *Time* magazine describes as an archconservative activist, requested that Maureen be "muzzled" because of her support of the Equal Rights Amendment. The President, however, announced that he was "completely satisfied" with Maureen's work as a consultant on women's issues to the Republican National Committee.

Michael Reagan announced that he would not campaign for his father as vigorously this time as he had in 1980. That campaign, he said, had left him financially devastated and he now had to concentrate on his own family's future. Michael was described as "passionate to the point of obsession about family togetherness." It is easy to speculate that he was reacting to the torment of his own broken-home childhood.

True to his word, Michael did not actively campaign for his father in the 1984 election. In fact, of all the Reagan children, only Maureen was active in the reelection bid.

Despite Wyman's distaste for being linked with Reagan's current life, it was inevitable that her name would come up during the election year. Reagan's opponents used slogans such as: "Do what Wyman did—dump Reagan." There were even campaign buttons stating: "Jane Wyman was right."

The public didn't agree, however, and President Reagan won a second term in a landslide victory that gave him 59 percent of the popular vote.

Just as Jane Wyman had not escaped publicity prior to the election, post-election coverage prominently featured mention of the actress. Only two days after the election, the *New York Times*, in a full-page pictorial feature on Reagan's past, prominently displayed a shot of "Mr. Reagan with his first wife, Jane Wyman, and their daughter, Maureen, in 1941."

Memories of the "dream house" Ron and Jane had built in the Hollywood Hills back in the early days of the couple's marriage suddenly exploded into potentially ugly headlines. Back in the forties Ron and Jane had bought and sold several pieces of property in the Hills area. And now, in October 1984, it was revealed in a UPI story that county documents stated that "four of those lots were covered by deeds or 'protective covenants' that barred non-Caucasians unless they were servants."

Through spokesmen, Reagan and Wyman each made forceful statements of denial. Not only had President Reagan never known of such a restriction, but Wyman was " 'appalled' that anyone would think she would endorse a racial policy."

Even Lorimar got into the act. UPI noted, "Robert Crutchfield of Lorimar Productions also pointed out that movie stars like Mr. Reagan and Miss Wyman often left details such as deeds and contracts to their business managers."

That was the end of the incident. But soon there was another that placed the Reagans' private lives back on the front pages. "At Thanksgiving time, the president was at his California ranch celebrating the holiday. The entire family was present—all except Michael. Nancy Reagan told an interviewer that the president and his thirty-eight-year-old son were "estranged." "We are sorry about it," said Mrs. Reagan. "We hope someday it will be solved."

Michael Reagan lost no time in replying publicly to Nancy's remarks. He stated that he was "shocked and hurt" by the First

Lady's statement. The result was that once again a barrage of public attention was focused on the private lives of the Reagan family. This was the kind of "family feud" that was guaranteed to make worldwide headlines, and it did.

"The estrangement seems to date back to 1981," observed one account, "when Michael—then a sales executive for an aerospace supplier—wrote a letter to military bases that appeared to try to capitalize on his White House connections."

Even the staid *New York Times* couldn't ignore the gossipy story: "Maureen Reagan . . . said today that her brother Michael Reagan was conducting a 'vendetta' against Nancy Reagan that had left the President and his wife 'just agonized.' "

Time magazine observed that Nancy Reagan's "relationships with her husband's two children from his earlier marriage to actress Jane Wyman have seemed more fundamentally troubled [than those of her relationships with her own children]."

Was Michael, in fact, a "victim" in this episode? Maureen was emphatic that he was not. "He's been estranged from all of us," she was quoted as saying. She defended her father, and observed: "He certainly does not want someone to declare war on his wife."

Did Maureen have any opinions on why Michael was motivated to pursue the "feud" via interviews on TV and in the press? She replied that it might be because "he is constantly singled out as the adopted son. I never did that, nor has anyone else in the family."

By Christmas, however, the storm had passed. "Reagan Meets Son and His Family in 3-Hour Reunion in Los Angeles," reported the *New York Times.* The "fence-mending" was successful and the White House issued a statement: "Everybody loves each other."

All the while, Jane Wyman had somehow managed to completely avoid being publicly queried on the contretemps, no easy accomplishment considering her high visibility on the entertainment scene. With Reagan in the White House through 1988, the

Reagan children, and Jane Wyman, are guaranteed four more years of international media coverage.

As this book goes to press, *Falcon Crest* has completed its fourth successful season and Wyman is reported to be the highest paid actress on television. She is as famous and active today as she has ever been.

Former friends and associates of Wyman's (and, of course, Reagan's) are often circumspect in their recollections, and many are of the I'll-tell-you-but-don't-use-my-name school, for obvious reasons.

Jane Wyman and Ronald Reagan, along with everything else they have shared, share the fact that neither of them is, as are most of their contemporaries, a *former* star from a *former* era whose story has wound down to a quiet "in retirement" finish.

Wyman handles her newfound success with intelligence and humor. At the 1984 Golden Globe Awards, she defined herself and reminded people across the country to expect the unexpected from her. (*Two* generations of stars had come and gone since that day, more than thirty-five years earlier, when Jane had won her first Golden Globe Award.)

Top stars from all areas of show business were in the crowded room. Wyman was, of course, at the Lorimar table, seated with Cliff Robertson, Susan Sullivan, and other *Falcon Crest* regulars.

Louis Gossett, Jr., and Jill St. John were presenting the award for best performance by an actress in a television dramatic series. The nominees, in addition to Wyman, were Joan Collins and Linda Evans (for *Dynasty*), Tyne Daly (for *Cagney and Lacey*), and Stefanie Powers (for *Hart to Hart*). The envelope was opened and the winner announced: "Jane Wyman!"

Wyman, stunningly gowned in a high-necked, long-sleeved multicolored-sequin sheath, a diamond necklace glittering at her throat, seemed genuinely surprised. Amid loud applause she slowly made her way to the podium and received the award as the audience gave her a tumultuous ovation.

She faced the throng, beaming. "Well, my goodness, I was sitting there relaxing, having a perfectly marvelous time. . . ." The audience laughed. She continued, "I'm so grateful for this . . . we're having such a fine time . . . and I am such a bitch!"

There was a moment of stunned silence. Had this grande dame uttered such a word on national TV?

"I mean, you know," continued Jane, obviously referring to the character of Angela, "I don't know how you can be nice anymore and win anything. . . ."

The audience roared its approval.

"But I am really grateful for this," Wyman concluded, and she drew another round of heavy laughter and loud applause with her closing comments: "I'm having the best time of my life. . . . I'm a little too old to be happy, but just old enough to be grateful!"

Index

INDEX • • • • • • • • • • • • • • • • •

INDEX • • • • • • • • • • • • • • • • •